GYNESIS

GYNESIS

Configurations of Woman and Modernity

ALICE A. JARDINE

CORNELL UNIVERSITY PRESS

Ithaca and London

First published 1985 by Cornell University Press.
First printing, Cornell Paperbacks, 1986.
Second printing, 1987.

International Standard Book Number 0-8014-1768-6 (cloth)
International Standard Book Number 0-8014-9396-x (paper)
Library of Congress Catalog Card Number 84-45806
Printed in the United States of America
Librarians: Library of Congress cataloging information appears on the last page of the book.

The paper in this book is acid-free and meets the guidelines for permanence and durability of the Committee on Production Guidelines for Book Longevity of the Council on Library Resources.

for my mother(s)

CONTENTS

Contents

ACKNOWLEDGMENTS

Whatever the destiny of *Gynesis* is to be, none of its limitations and all of its strengths are due to the extraordinary women with whom I have worked. The contours of my questions were, in fact, mapped out during the meetings of two feminist study groups in Paris: to Rosi Braidotti, Anna Gibbs, and Jane Weinstock I dedicate the concept of gynesis; to Claire Duchen, Danielle Haase-Dubosc, Nancy Huston, and Naomi Schor I dedicate its writing. I owe thanks, in particular, to Rosi Braidotti, whose book forthcoming in France, *Itinéraires de la dissonance,* intertwines with my own, each echoing the other, in a way unique to collective feminist research and writing.

Julia Kristeva, in both personal and more intellectual ways, made this work possible. I am also grateful to my dissertation director, Leon S. Roudiez, Columbia University, who has never failed to provide me with the personal encouragement necessary to complete the task at hand. I have been particularly helped by those who read unselfishly and painstakingly all or parts of the manuscript in one or several of its versions: Rosi Braidotti, Jane Gallop, Nancy Miller, Naomi Schor, Peggy Waller.

I am also indebted to the Giles Whiting, Danforth, and Woodrow Wilson foundations for their generous contributions. My thanks go as well to my colleagues and the administrative staff of the Department of Romance Languages and Literatures at Harvard University for their support, and to the Columbia University Department of French, which made possible my stay at the Ecole Normale Supérieure (rue d'Ulm).

There are, of course, others—not the least of whom are the students of my spring 1983 seminar on feminist theory at Harvard. Also, I extend many

Acknowledgments

warm thanks to Anne Menke and Mary Gossy, my research assistants, and Susan Fuerst, my typist, for their generosity and care.

Finally, I give very special thanks to James, who stood by me through more than one season of solitude and discontent.

Acknowledgment is also due to those journals that allowed me to use all or part of the following articles in revised form: "Theories of the Feminine: Kristeva," *Enclitic* 4, 2 (Fall 1980); "Pre-Texts for the Transatlantic Feminist," *Yale French Studies* 62 (1981); "Gynesis," *Diacritics* (Summer 1982); and for Chapter 10, "Woman in Limbo: Deleuze and His Br(others)," *Substance* (December 1984).

The lines from "Diving into the Wreck" from *Diving into the Wreck: Poems 1971–1972,* by Adrienne Rich, are reprinted by permission of the author and the publisher, W. W. Norton & Company, Inc. Copyright © 1973 by W. W. Norton & Company, Inc. Lines from *Fragment,* by John Ashbery, are reprinted by permission of the author and the publisher, Georges Borchardt, Inc. Copyright © 1969 by Georges Borchardt, Inc.

ALICE JARDINE

New York City

Nothing can be said of woman.

Jacques Lacan

(A) woman does not represent something, she is not a distinct, defined personality.

Gilles Deleuze and Félix Guattari

However—it is woman who will be my subject. Still, one might wonder whether that doesn't really amount to the same thing—or is it to the other.

Jacques Derrida

Does not the combat against the phallic sign and against an entire monological culture finally sink into the substantial cult of woman?

Julia Kristeva

But in (a) woman's language, the concept as such would have no place.

Luce Irigaray

I do not think either that revolution can be brought about through language.

Hélène Cixous

"In which sense? In which sense?" Alice asks, vaguely perceiving that it is always in both senses at once, so much so that, for this one time, she remains equal to herself through optical effect.

Gilles Deleuze, Logique du sens

PRELIMINARIES

Texts and Contexts

In a discussion of the problems involved when "observing others," Paul de Man mentions in passing that, when we address two cultures, "the distressing question as to who should be exploiting whom is bound to arise."[1]

Most of this book was written in France to be read in the United States, and therefore one cannot be entirely certain either who it is "observing" or who its "others" are. Given that in-between state, I would like to begin by making explicit the book's and my own place of enunciation. This is an essential gesture (even if by now a somewhat common one) because of the specificity of the questions to be addressed, questions involving at least two national cultures (the United States and France), two sexes (male and female), and four discursive codes (most generally, fiction and theory; and more specifically, contemporary approaches to interpretation and feminism).

The questions I ask emerged from my concern with women as speaking and writing subjects, their relationship to language, and how sexual difference operates linguistically in a literary text. I have for the most part expressed this concern at the crossing of three investigations: first, the relationship between "theoretical" and "fictional" discourse and the constitution of particular ideological discursive fields; second, the specificity, if any, of texts written by men and women in Western culture; and, finally,

1. Paul de Man, *Blindness and Insight* (New York: Oxford University Press, 1971), p. 10. The context for this remark is provided by Claude Lévi-Strauss.

the differences among contemporary French and American literary practices. These investigations led me to ask the questions explored in this book, questions that need to be addressed by feminists who, while working in the United States, are or will eventually be in dialogue with what is now commonly called "modernity" in France or, more problematically in the United States, "postmodernism"—questions of special urgency for feminist literary and cultural critics.

Here, I shall briefly refer to a few of the most fundamental problems inherent in asking these questions, since such problems will come up time and again throughout this study. These are not in any way purely supplemental remarks, but rather larger questions about how to say "I" or "we" in the right tone of voice. They stem primarily from certain widespread assumptions about "comparativism" and "feminism."

Comparativism is, in itself, a nineteenth-century concept that, in recent years, has been much promoted in the United States and much criticized elsewhere. In the United States, the growth of interdisciplinary and comparative study has allowed us both to analyze the ideological function of isolated disciplines and to open up new areas for a critique of culture. When it also involves the importation and exportation of thought, however, it brings with it new problems: descriptivism, summary, anthologism—a certain analogical logic. Michel Foucault has analyzed this logic at its inception in the classical period: "From now on, every resemblance must be subjected to proof by comparison, that is, it will not be accepted until its identity and the series of its differences have been discovered by means of measurement with a common unit or, more radically, by its position in an order."[2] In order to posit an autonomous object, one compares A to B according to a model. This model can be an "idea," "principle," "politic," or "structure" over which the comparativist has complete control; he is, like God, "above it all." Jacques Derrida has pointed out that this assumption of an ideal that can be *applied* to two objects is also related to classical ideas of translation, where, again, for any text there is an ideal "text" (the text's meaning) that must simply be transported to another text.[3] A close analysis of the comparative spirit in general reveals that this logic of transportation, this separation of identities and differences, can operate not only abstractly, as intellectual, conceptual imperialism, but concretely as well—most notably in the forms of racism and colonialism.[4]

2. Michel Foucault, *The Order of Things* (New York: Random House, 1970), p. 55.

3. Theories of translation have been a major focus of much of Derrida's work, recently with special reference to Walter Benjamin.

4. See, for example, Edward Said, *Orientalism* (New York: Pantheon, 1978).

In the case of the American critic observing, reading, and writing another culture, this question of comparativism becomes particularly difficult. Whom are we writing to and for? Those working in contemporary French thought who ponder this problem are immediately immersed in not only a set of different spaces, but at least three different temporalities: the time of French thought (and its massive recent past), the time of importation and exportation of French thought to the United States (about ten years), and the time of America, "so far ahead of France" and yet assuming as fundamental truths certain ideas about the writing and speaking subject, language, and so on that many French writers and theorists have long since rejected.[5]

It must suffice here to remember that reading and writing across cultural boundaries very often produces a strange brand of text which rings totally false in the culture it is "translating." Inevitably? Perhaps. In any case, this problem of text and context—vibrating on the dangerous edge of a transparency theory of language—will be integral to the following dialogue.

This already complex question leads to the second general problem I encountered in beginning this study: the word feminism. As a generic term, "feminism" is semantically tortuous and conceptually hazardous. Generally understood as a "movement from the point of view of, by, and for women," it covers substantial ground and becomes particularly dangerous across borders. In the present case, involving principally France and the United States, any generic description of either French or American feminisms would immediately homogenize, colonialize, and neutralize the specificities of struggles that are often of quite epic proportions. Even the attempt to specify contexts and assumptions, as I am beginning to do here and will continue to do throughout this book, can take on the new, bizarre form of a "white, Western, intellectual woman's burden." Feminist criticism is, by definition, based in very precise political struggles and practices and remains inseparable from them. The "identities and differences" paradigm emphasized in comparative thought becomes even more troubling when we are considering feminist theory and praxis.

The specific intellectual and political stakes of the importation and exportation of feminist theory have come into sharp focus over the past few years with reference to France and the United States. American feminists have, on occasion, accused French women theorists of reverting to "essen-

---

5. This process is more, or perhaps differently, complicated today I think, at least for American graduate students, particularly those not in foreign language departments, who are thrown into an encyclopedic library on "contemporary thought" whose time of production and consumption is long past.

tialist" definitions of woman, of being hopelessly enamored of "male theoretical structures" (especially philosophical ones), natural definitions of woman, and so on. French women in turn often argue that American academic feminists are blind to the ways in which capitalist, patriarchal ideology governs their thinking; that they are more worried about tenure for their work *on* women than they are about working *with* women to change symbolic structures. The very violence of these mutual accusations not only is symptomatic of the larger political, economic, and intellectual climate in both countries, but also points to a lack of analysis of the relationship between feminist theory and dominant modes of production and exchange.

For example, it is not true that American feminists are insensitive to their relationship to the institution or to larger political problems, but rather that we are perhaps less willing than women theorists in France to open discussion of these problems by questioning certain ideological assumptions: assumptions about the values and practices of the transmission of knowledge, assumptions about efficacy, identity, difference, and representation within Western culture as a culture nourished by images produced and consumed within a capitalist economy. Perhaps one of the most difficult problems facing American feminists is, in fact, how to put into practice, with less political and intellectual naïveté than heretofore, the distinction between "political knowledge" and what we now know to be the mythology of "pure knowledge." One thing French women are reminding us of is that "pure knowledge" does not exist. Our very American tendency to analyze paradigms of possible substitutions through empirical when not ahistorical analysis of all that exists at a particular moment tends to evacuate history in a way incomprehensible to women theorists in Europe; they are, on the contrary, increasingly compelled by the necessity for diachronic analysis.[6] Our Anglo-American empiricist and humanist training, with its lack of emphasis on enunciation—its confusion of the third person (universal statements) with the first person (involving problems of subjectivity)—consistently distracts us from the *politics of enunciation*. Such a neglect can lead to the undesired effect of rendering every object produced—even theories—interchangeable with every other for the purpose of consumption. In fact, one of the major reasons for this

---

6. We will return quite often to these two basic axes of signification as presented by Saussure (especially in Chapter 3). It is, in fact, the relationships between these two axes, the axes of metaphor and metonymy, that still need to be rethought, and not only at the level of linguistics. For an introduction to their potentialities, see Ferdinand de Saussure, *Course in General Linguistics*, trans. Wade Baskin (New York: McGraw-Hill, 1966).

study was my feeling that women, who have historically filled in as trans-
lators of culture, are today, as "international feminists," running the danger of simply translating "woman as concept" from one culture to another.
There is, after all, a difference between really attempting to think differently and thinking the Same through the manipulation of difference.

While working in Paris with feminists, theorists, writers, and activists,
those of us who were not "French" discovered how precariously we were
balanced on the undecidable edge of differences among texts and contexts—experiencing the intensity of their written and spoken, theoretical
and political, limits. Those of us who, in addition, have since returned to
an English-speaking country to teach and write across the field of contemporary thought in France have become convinced that, beyond strict comparison, the confusions arising from that which is "far away" or "close,"
that which functions in culture as "image" or "belief," are still much in
need of further feminist analysis.

For example, the specific "Parisian atmosphere" in which I wrote this
study was one of intellectual crisis: where well-trodden topographies of
psychoanalysis, philosophy, and literature had been outworn; where
voices of the New Right had gained listeners (redescending into a fertile
underground with the victory of the Left); and where "feminism" was
going for below cost on the market while major cultural critics were calmly
announcing the "historicization" (death) of feminism as a movement.

Within these "contexts," I returned to text(s). Could the two be separated? And how does one situate texts in a context that can never be
saturated, whether it is "contemporary" or "historical"?

I am again referring to the very complex problems of *translation*—in the
most literal sense of the word as well as in the broader and more difficult
meaning of the intercultural exchange of ideas: as mentioned earlier, the
specificity of the problems inherent to the import and export of thought.[7]
One way to approach these problems is to provide necessary information
"about context," ranging from an analysis of cultural production (institu-
tions, the status of the intellectual, and so on) to reports on specific events.
To provide information is essential, but in the specific case of contemporary feminist thought, across national borders, this can often amount to
nothing more than introducing the category of "woman" into the dominant ideology of informational culture ("the more information, the better"), thereby erasing the most important things women have learned—

7. These are the notes of a "translator" as well—literal sense of the word.

the hard way—about the political. Rethinking a feminist approach to cultural translation involves finding new ways of sustaining what women have come to know through experience without reducing experience only to what we know.[8]

, I do not claim to have resolved these problems; but it does seem to me that one way to begin addressing them is to create problematics, not collect and consume them; to put texts into dialogue with each other, not to catalogue and explicate them.

This is what I have attempted to do in what follows. The structure of the questions addressed is almost wholly shaped by recent French theory. But, at the same time, the questions themselves are those of an American feminist hoping to contribute to American feminist theory. That is, neither my "comparativism" nor my feminism is co-relative, counterbalanced, with the same amount of "material" on both sides of a border—national or other. For example, the actual sequence of my original questions went something like this: (1) What are the qualities and qualifiers of this condition called modernity with and by which Western cultural artifacts are increasingly affected? (2) In what ways are contemporary encounters with modernity in France exemplary? (3) What are the implications of this modernity for feminism? (4) For Anglo-American feminism in particular? Hoping to avoid both the dangers of simple comparativism and the silence of non-position, I therefore see this study as an intervention, an inter-presentation, an inter-position of at least four discursive elements: modernity, contemporary French thought, feminism, and Anglo-American feminist theory. But of course, even an intervention, a gesture, runs certain risks, for in attempting this trans-position, I am neither "above it all" nor somewhere in the middle of the Atlantic. But then neither is my reader, no matter how I might have initially idealized her or him.

My guiding principle has been in some ways archaeological: I did not want to outline controversies and opinions, but rather to look at what makes them possible and at how they operate in what I will continue to call certain "contexts"—no matter how problematic the word. This kind of "comparativism" leads to no synthesis, no resolution of tension, no ultimate knowledge. In some ways, I have had to begin by asking some

---

8. Gayatri Spivak has pointed out well, I think, some of the dangers involved in translating feminism. See "French Feminism in an International Frame," *Yale French Studies* 62 (1981). In another mode, see Anna Gibbs et al., "Round and Round the Looking Glass: Responses to [. . .] *New French Feminisms*," *Hecate* 6:2 (1980).

very literal, "empirical" questions and then proceed, not to answer them, but, as we used to say, to think constantly against myself.

Finally, while I tend to privilege "fiction" and its rhetoric, this is not an essay in literary criticism per se. That is partly because "literary criticism" as defined institutionally in the United States has existed in France only sporadically as an autonomous field of inquiry (a certain form of structuralism being a primary example) and feminist literary criticism exists hardly at all.[9] A French essay or book on any given literary fiction, for example, demands from the reader a conceptual and lexical knowledge drawn from many disciplines, most particularly from philosophy. But second, and more important, I am just as concerned with modernity in other fields of knowledge (especially art and music) as in "fiction" and "theory." Here I focus on written texts, but am more concerned about the *process* of (reading and writing) woman than about examining the representation of women in literature. I am looking for the logical or not so logical operations that organize the fictions of "the real world," but am less interested, for the moment, in explicating why that world is represented in such a way, or in prescribing what might be done about it. One of the dangers of such a project is, of course, that one may end up simply psychoanalyzing the present political, critical situation through the use of texts as symptoms. I shall necessarily come back to this later. But if it is true that I tend to read symptomatically (metaphorically), my primary question has always remained metonymical: what can possibly come next?

Feminisms

After the almost unanimous theoretical enthusiasm and political energy of the late 1960s and early 1970s, the French *Mouvement de libération des femmes* (MLF) experienced a series of splits, rivalries, and disappointments that led them to stop, go back, think, read, and write again. In fact, the

9. "Feminist literary criticism can be reduced to the literary references in *The Second Sex* by Simone de Beauvoir, and to three recent books: *Surréalisme et sexualité* by Xavière Gautier (Gallimard, 1971), *La jeune née* by Catherine Clément and Hélène Cixous (10/18, 1975) which is more philosophical than literary, and finally *Les voleuses de langue* by Claudine Herrmann (des Femmes, 1976), the first strictly literary essay. [. . .] These aside, one can say that feminist literary criticism does not exist in France" (Christiane Makward, "La critique féministe . . .," *Revue des sciences humaines* 168 [1977]: 619). My translation. To this short list I would add Marcelle Marini, *Territoires du féminin avec Marguerite Duras* (Paris: Editions de Minuit, 1977), and Anne-Marie Dardigna, *Les châteaux d'éros* (Paris: Maspero, 1981).

term MLF now legally belongs to only one group in France—"Psychanalyse et Politique." And this group, according to its own literature and public stance, is most definitely opposed to feminism—as are many of the other women theorists, writing in France today, whose names are beginning to circulate in the United States. Who and what, then, do we mean by "feminist"? That word, as I mentioned earlier, poses some serious problems. Not that we would want to end up by demanding a definition of what feminism is and, therefore, of what one must do, say, and be, if one is to acquire that epithet; dictionary meanings are suffocating, to say the least. But if we were to take "feminism" for a moment as referring only to those in France who qualify themselves as feminists in their life and work, our task would be greatly simplified. For example, if I were to talk about feminist theorists in France, I would want to insist on including what might be called the "invisible feminists"—those younger women who are working quietly behind the scenes, in study groups and special seminars, trying to sort out and pick up the pieces left in the wake of the theoretical and practical disputes of the last few years. Or I might invoke the feminists who are attempting to map out some very new and long-awaited directions under Mitterand's administration; or the ones who have left France to work in the United States or at the Université des Femmes in Belgium. But, increasingly, when in the United States one refers to "feminist theories in France" or to "French feminisms," it is not those women one has in mind. The women theorists in France whose work has had or is beginning to have a major impact on *theories of writing and reading,* and who at one level or another are writing about women, at the very least do not call themselves feminists either privately or in their writing, and, at the most, posit themselves and their work as hostile to, or "beyond," feminism as a concept. These are the names we hear in the United States: Hélène Cixous, Sarah Kofman, Julia Kristeva, Eugénie Lemoine-Luccioni, Michèle Montrelay, among others. The sole exception is Luce Irigaray—a special and complex case, one I shall reserve for close attention at a later date in another place.

I would even go so far as to say that the major new directions in French theory over the past two decades—those articulated by both men and women—have, by and large, posited themselves as profoundly, that is to say conceptually and in *praxis,* anti- and/or post-feminist. Feminism, as a concept, as inherited from the humanist and rationalist eighteenth century, is traditionally about a group of human beings in history whose identity is defined by that history's representation of sexual decidability.

And every term of that definition has been put into question by contemporary French thought.

In this study, one of the things I have tried to accomplish is to clarify the "anti- and/or post-feminism" of contemporary French thinking as exemplary of modernity, without getting overly caught up in explicit value judgments or polemics.[10] And I have done this by concentrating on what I see as the major emphases of that French thought—as explored by the *male* theorists there.

Why focus on the men instead of the women? I do so artificially (with artifice). First, the women theorists in France whose names have been mentioned here are, to one degree or another, in the best French tradition and not unproblematically, direct disciples of those men. That is not meant as a criticism; but those women, like their male colleagues, must not be read as if they were working in isolation—especially in France, where, at least for the American, the tradition of the "school of thought" or the "literary salon" is still exorbitantly strong. Second, the work of these women is, of course, not at all absent from these pages: it is assumed as a primary source. Their work is this text's palimpsest to a very great extent. I took my cues from them, so to speak.[11] Finally, and most important, I have not included their work in any major way here because their rewritings of the men, their repetitions of and dissidence from those men, are exceedingly complex, meriting more attention than one or two chapters could provide. If most of these women reject "feminism" as a viable alternative for women today, or conceive of and practice a "feminism" unrecognizable to the Anglo-American feminist, it is because of the theoretical heritage from within which they are working. That is, although my readings of Hélène Cixous, Luce Irigaray, and Julia Kristeva, in particular, are evident throughout what follows, I felt it important to begin first with the

10. During the discussion following the presentation of an early version of "Gynesis" at an MLA conference in New York City, a lot of energy was expended over the words "feminist" and "antifeminist." It was almost as if the problems of translation foregrounded here could be resolved if everyone in the room could just come to an *agreement* about what feminism is or is not. The problems with that (primarily Anglo-American) approach to interpretation are, of course, made abundantly clear by many of the French theorists we will be concerned with here. What is important, they might say, is not to decide who is or is not a feminist, but rather to examine how and why feminism may itself be problematic; is itself connected to larger theoretical issues; is not a natural given but a construction like all others. This kind of questioning does not have to be undertaken from a conservative position; it can in fact provide feminism's most radical moments.

11. For example, Luce Irigaray's short discussion of "space" in *Ce sexe qui n'en est pas un* (Paris: Editions de Minuit, 1977), pp. 95–96, more or less generated Chapter 3. (See the translation by Catherine Porter, *This Sex Which Is Not One* [Ithaca: Cornell University Press, 1985].)

terms those women, writing in the 1960s and 1970s, also began with: feminism and modernity.

Feminism and/or Modernity?

The questions and problems raised in this book are grounded in a larger hypothesis: that the genuinely "new directions" in contemporary French thought in focus here are, in their "inspiration" and "conclusions," a radical attempt to delimit and think through what, once again, is called "modernity" in France or, more problematically in the United States, "post-modernism." My feeling is that any "detour" of feminism, whatever its place of origin, through contemporary French thought is a voyage into that (as yet still vague) territory of modernity so often avoided, in my opinion, by Anglo-American feminist thought. The generic term "contemporary French theory" designates for me the first group of Western writers after the Frankfurt School to try to come to terms with the threatened collapse of the dialectic and its representations which is modernity. Ultimately, the question I would want to put into circulation here is this: are feminism and modernity oxymoronic in their terms and terminology? If so, how and why? If not, what new ruse of reason has made them appear—especially in France—to be so?

Modernity

I am not certain that the way in which I am using the word "modernity" should or can be defined. But it might be helpful to briefly indicate what I do not mean. For example, while I do not primarily use the term modernity in the sense of the "modern"—as in "the Ancients versus the Moderns," or as used by Baudelaire, Mallarmé, Nietzsche—the history of the word cannot help but determine its use here.[12] While the term "avant-garde" is fraught with difficulties of definition, both politically and conceptually, in both the United States and Europe, many of those writers who have been qualified as avant-garde at one point or another since the turn of the century are of interest here as participants in the project of modernity.[13]

12. For a useful discussion, in this vein, of the term "modernity," see, for example, Paul de Man's "Literary History and Literary Modernity" in *Blindness and Insight*, pp. 142–65.
13. See, for example, Renato Poggioli, *Theory of the Avant-Garde* (Cambridge, Mass.: Belknap, 1968).

Finally, modernity should not be confused (as it most often is in the United States) with "modernism"—the generic label commonly attached to the general literary movement of the first half of the twentieth century. With "modernism," however, we are closest, at least in terms of the literary text, to what is of concern.

It is the word "postmodern," as commonly used in the United States, that perhaps most accurately applies to the specific set of writers important here: those writing, self-consciously, from within the (intellectual, scientific, philosophical, literary) *epistemological* crisis specific to the postwar period. To put it simply, they are those writers, whom we may call our "contemporaries," who, in John Barth's caustic formulation, do not try to pretend that the first half of the twentieth century did not happen.

He puts it this way: "It *did* happen: Freud and Einstein and two world wars and the Russian and sexual revolutions and automobiles and airplanes and telephones and radios and movies and urbanization, and now nuclear weaponry and television and microchip technology and the new feminism and the rest, and there's no going back to Tolstoy and Dickens & Co. except on nostalgia trips."[14] While Barth is speaking almost exclusively of "fiction writers," I extend his definition of "the ideal postmodern writer" to theorists as well—to those theorists who have understood the stakes involved in the intensified search for new modes of conceptuality able to account for, and perhaps change, the course of the twentieth century.

Not that all of these words, their various significations, the writers they designate, and so on "add up" to modernity as a problematic. But they do, in their collective emphasis, designate a particular attitude, a certain posture toward thinking about the human and speaking subject, signification, language, writing, etc. that is of direct interest in relationship to feminist thought.

As I have already more than implied, I think the condition of modernity has received the attention it deserves in France. For me, those discourses in France attuned to modernity, across several so-called disciplines (history, philosophy, science, literature, linguistics, psychoanalysis, etc.), are among the few European-American discourses struggling seriously enough either to account for the new texts and contexts of the world as it appears now or else to imagine other worlds whether possible or not. It is in France that intellectuals of two generations (many of them not French, a fact often forgotten in the United States) have rejected, each in her or his own ways,

14. John Barth, "The Literature of Replenishment," *Atlantic Monthly,* January 1980, p. 70.

parts or all of the conceptual apparatuses inherited from nineteenth-century Europe. This includes, necessarily, those that are based in movements of human liberation—including, of course, feminism. Why this rejection? The major reason has been cautiously and painstakingly laid out in texts written over the past twenty-five years: our ways of understanding in the West have been and continue to be complicitous with our ways of oppressing. These writers have laid bare the vicious circles of intellectual imperialism and of liberal and humanist ideology. They have elaborated at length how that ideology is based on reified and naturalized categories, or concepts like "experience" and the "natural"; or, in another mode, the Ethical, the Right, the Good, or the True. The clearest way, perhaps, to contain in one word the gesture they have performed on the texts and contexts of humanist ideology is to focus on the word *denaturalization:* they have denaturalized the world that humanism naturalized, a world whose anthro-pology and anthro-centrism no longer make sense. It is a strange new world they have invented, a world that is *unheimlich.* And such strangeness has necessitated speaking and writing in new and strange ways.

Gynesis

These new ways have not surfaced in a void. Over the past century, those master (European) narratives—history, philosophy, religion—which have determined our sense of legitimacy in the West have undergone a series of crises in legitimation. It is widely recognized that legitimacy is part of that judicial domain which, historically, has determined the right to govern, the succession of kings, the link between father and son, the necessary paternal fiction, the ability to decide who is the father—in patriarchal culture. The crises experienced by the major Western narratives have not, therefore, been gender-neutral. They are crises in the narratives invented by men.

Going back to analyze those narratives and their crises has meant going back to the Greek philosophies in which they are grounded and, most particularly, to the originary relationships posited between the *technē* and *physis, time* and *space,* and all the dualistic oppositions that determine our ways of thinking. And rethinking those oppositions has meant, among other things, putting their "obligatory connotations" into discursive circulation, making those connotations explicit in order, one would hope, to put them into question. For example, the *technē* and time have connoted the male; *physis* and space the female. To think new relationships between the *technē* and *physis,* time and space, and so on, within an atmosphere of crisis, has required backing away from all that has defined and immobilized the possibilities of their relationships in the history of Western philosophy, requestioning the major topics of that philosophy: Man, the Subject, Truth, History, Meaning. At the forefront of this rethinking has been a rejection by and within those narratives of what seem to have been the strongest pillars of their history: Anthropomorphism, Humanism, and Truth. And again, it is in France that, in my opinion, this rethinking has taken its strongest conceptual leaps, as "philosophy," "history," and "literature" have attempted to account for the crisis-in-narrative that is modernity.

In general, this has brought about, within the master narratives in the West, a vast self-exploration, a questioning and turning back upon their own discourse, in an attempt to create a new *space* or *spacing within themselves* for survivals (of different kinds). In France, such rethinking has involved, above all, a reincorporation and reconceptualization of that which has been the master narratives' own "nonknowledge," what has eluded them, what has engulfed them. This other-than-themselves is almost always a "space" of some kind (over which the narrative has lost control), and this space has been coded as *feminine,* as *woman.* It is upon this process that I am insisting in this study: the transformation of woman and the feminine into verbs at the interior of those narratives that are today experiencing a crisis in legitimation.

To designate that process, I have suggested what I hope will be a believable neologism: *gynesis*—the putting into discourse of "woman" as that *process* diagnosed in France as intrinsic to the condition of modernity; indeed, the valorization of the feminine, woman, and her obligatory, that is, historical connotations, as somehow intrinsic to new and necessary modes of thinking, writing, speaking. The object produced by this process is neither a person nor a thing, but a horizon, that toward which the process is tending: a *gynema.* This *gynema* is a reading effect, a woman-in-effect that is never stable and has no identity. Its appearance in a written text is perhaps noticed only by the feminist reader—either when it becomes insistently "feminine" or when women (as defined metaphysically, historically) seem magically to reappear within the discourse. This tear in the fabric produces in the (feminist) reader a state of uncertainty and sometimes of distrust—especially when the faltering narrative in which it is embedded has been articulated by a man from within a nonetheless still-existent discipline. When it appears in women theorists' discourse, it would seem to be less troubling. The still existent slippages in signification among feminine, woman, women, and what I am calling *gynesis* and *gynema* are dismissed (at least in the United States and increasingly by male feminist critics) as irrelevant *because* it is a woman speaking.

I have tried to introduce here briefly some of the reasons why feminists may not want to qualify, too rapidly, major texts of modernity in the West, especially in France, as necessarily feminist or antifeminist, most particularly when they are texts signed by women. I hope I have begun to convey, as well, how important I think it is for feminist theoreticians in France, England, the United States, and (especially) elsewhere to rethink the history, impact, place for, and possible future directions of contemporary interpretive modes with regard to feminist theory. For if, as I have only begun to suggest, modernity represents a perhaps unavoidable and, in any case, new kind of discursivity on, about, as woman, a valorization and speaking of woman, and if contemporary feminists are going to take modernity and its theorists seriously, then feminist theory must address some new and complex questions—questions that form the matrix of the pages to follow.

Are gynesis and feminism in contradiction, or do they overlap and interact with each other, perhaps even render each other inevitable, in some way? In what sense do certain of the texts of gynesis reintroduce very familiar representations of women in spite of themselves? To what extent is the process designated as feminine by those texts absolutely dependent on those representations? When we posit that process as one incarnated by *women*, are we not falling back into the anthropomorphic (or gynomorphic?) images thinkers of modernity have been trying to disintegrate?

On the other hand, in what ways do some of the major texts in question exceed those familiar representations of women? How do women theorists' texts of gynesis differ from those of male theorists; or French texts of gynesis from American ones? If the gynesis seemingly intrinsic to modernity is but the product of male fantasy, does that necessarily mean it offers no radical tools for women? How might these texts offer new ways of connecting the most radical insights of feminism to the larger questions facing the West as it moves toward a new century?

Most important, if modernity and feminism are not to become mutually exclusive and, at the same time, if feminism is not to compromise the quality of its attention to female stereotyping of whatever kind, what could be new strategies for asking new kinds of questions?

In the first part of this book, "Intersections," I discuss generally the problematization of woman in contemporary thought, and most particularly in contemporary French thought—a problematization directly related to that thought's explorations in modernity. Why, at the end of the twentieth century, has "the feminine" become a wide-ranging area of concern? Why is it used as a metaphor of reading by some of the most influential writers working in France today? How and why this "problematization of woman" poses particular problems for contemporary feminist theory in the United States is the focus of Chapter 2, while Chapters 3 and 4 trace the ways in which the crises associated with modernity have led to this expansive putting into discourse of woman. How do French theorists situate those crises historically, politically, and conceptually? How does what has been diagnosed as the breakdown of the paternal metaphor in Western culture lead these theorists to valorize other metaphors—new metaphors that pose difficult problems for "feminism" as a concept?

In the second section, "Interfacings," I examine in detail three of the major topologies of contemporary French thought and its recent history. I emphasize, in particular, the breakdown of the conscious, Cartesian Subject, the default of Representation, and the demise of Man's Truth.

The third section, "Intertexts," includes close readings of selected texts by Jacques Lacan, Jacques Derrida, and Gilles Deleuze—three of the best-known participants in the process of gynesis in France, and writers who have had the most direct influence on both feminist and antifeminist thinking there. I also read *with* these writers several "fictions" they have selected as somehow exemplary of their "theories": Marguerite Duras with Lacan, Maurice Blanchot with Derrida, and Michel Tournier with Deleuze.

In the fourth and final section, "Interferences," I return to the question of "comparativism"—no longer in terms of American feminist questions and French explorations of modernity, but, rather, in terms of how both my questions and those explorations may be grounded in cross-currents of cultural specificity. I do this by looking at several American and French fictional texts written by men—within the context of the questions raised to that point. The writers chosen are exemplary to the extent that their particular imaginative strategies for exploring the "feminine" seem both indicative and representative of the theoretical problem being examined. It was also my concern to select writers who fall somewhere within the "mainstream" of their respective cultural traditions—not because they are widely read, although they may be, but because their writing is self-consciously determined by the conceptual frameworks previously examined.

In some afterwords, I return briefly to the women theorists with whom I began.

One Last Note

Hegel, in the first volume of *The Aesthetics,* tells an anecdote about a fish who reproached his painter for not having given him a soul.[15] The problem is, who was speaking? Was it the *real* fish or the *painted* fish or something in-between? My interventions at the crossroads of modernity and feminism could leave me open to the same kind of reproach on both sides of the Atlantic. This is especially likely since I am not principally interested in painting contexts or texts, representing modernity or feminism, or defining women or woman. Rather, I am foregrounding a new kind of interpretant which has surfaced from the interactions among all of these—a "woman-effect" for which I have offered another name: *gynesis.*

Whatever the risks of this project, I hope that by pointing out the limits, contradictions, and promises of such an interpretant it will open new spaces for women to write in.

15. G. W. F. Hegel, *The Aesthetics,* vol. 1, trans. T. M. Knox (Oxford: Oxford University Press, 1975), p. 42.

GYNESIS I

INTERSECTIONS

The set of points which two configurations have in common.

I

The Woman-in-Effect

Woman is the only vase left in which to pour our ideality.
                                                    Goethe

Faced with the abundantly heterogeneous theoretical production in France over the past twenty years, those who remain nonetheless
fascinated by "the literary substance"[1] cannot help but find it difficult to
determine a place from which to speak. That is, of course, unless they
choose to remain faithful to a "Belief" or a "School," or—an increasingly
common resort—to practice a kind of breathless journalism, documenting
the rise and fall of the latest Truth. A vertigo of reading strategies can
easily set in, ironically rendering the literary artifact untouchable, solitary.
Avoiding this vertigo can lead to repetition and isolation within one particular ideology of the text. Considering its sources out of context (as in
"imported"), or from a purely polemical stance, can produce a conservative brand of eclecticism, or political naïveté.

The vertiginous critical condition to which I refer is certainly not foreign to feminist theoreticians. While proceeding from a "belief" (in wom-
en's oppression), we are nevertheless, necessarily, caught up in a perma-
nent whirlwind of reading practices within a universe of fiction and theory
written, but for a few official exceptions, by men. Not believing in
"Truth," we continue to be fascinated by (elaborate) fictions. This is the
profound paradox of the feminist speaking in our contemporary culture:
she proceeds from a *belief* in a world from which—even the philosophers
admit—*Truth* has disappeared. This paradox, it seems to me, can lead to

---

1. "La chose littéraire" is a term used by Shoshana Felman for that which resists interpretation, whether or not coded as literature. See *La folie et la chose littéraire* (Paris:
Editions du Seuil, 1978).

(at least) three possible scenarios: a renewed silence, a form of religion (from mysticism to political orthodoxy), or a continual attention—historical, ideological, and affective—to the place from which we speak.[2]

If this is not a uniquely modern set of choices, it is, at least, one of particular urgency as the sense grows that we are rapidly moving into another as yet unclear network of epistemological and textual constraints.

Among the numerous French writers emphasizing the neurotic borders of "Western Thinking" and exploring the possible frontiers of modernity is Jean-Joseph Goux. He has mapped out what he terms "a history of symbolization": the adventures of a certain conception of conception.[3] Let us briefly follow his logic through the historical labyrinth he constructs so that we may arrive more quickly at the "woman" in question here.

Goux's version of history begins with Moses' anger at the worship of the golden calf, a female deity—*mater*—and the Jews' ensuing departure from Egypt with its female icons and hieroglyphic imagination. This literal and figurative departure from Egypt has been transcribed throughout the entire Platonic and Judeo-Christian tradition, according to Goux, and what has emerged from this transcription is *the* founding fantasy: the active negation of the Mother. Since the beginning of Western patriarchal history, "woman" has been but the passive matter to which "Man" could give form through the ever-increasing spiral of abstract universals: God, Money, Phallus—the infinity of substitution. Goux very carefully delineates the symbolic history of this Idealism: a certain relationship to death and desire, a fear of fusion, prohibition of incest with the Mother, the horror of "nothing to see" (castration), the anxiety of presence and absence, the separation of form and content, spirit and matter, value and exchange. Woman—whether incarnated, banned from the Temple, or incarcerated in the Oedipal family—has occupied the space of substitution on the paradigmatic axis of the metaphor.[4]

---

2. The dominant media in Europe and the United States have predicted (are, in fact, producing) renewed silence on the part of radical feminists, not only in function of current reactionary politics or recuperation, but in terms of the passing of a certain necessity; charges of turning woman into a religion are made regularly against both feminists in the United States and such groups as "Psychoanalysis and Politics" in France. The third alternative, while perhaps idealistic in itself, is both Marxist and a contemporary *topos*.

3. Jean-Joseph Goux, *Economie et symbolique* (Paris: Editions du Seuil, 1973), and *Les iconoclastes* (Paris: Editions du Seuil, 1978).

4. This long history of idealism also includes the birth of the novel, what Lukàcs has described as the literary form of the transcendent homelessness of the idea. See Georg Lukàcs, *The Theory of the Novel* (Cambridge, Mass.: MIT Press, 1971), esp. pp. 40–41, 122. See also Peter Brooks, "Freud's Masterplot," *Yale French Studies* 55/56 (1977): 298.

At the end of the nineteenth century, something clearly happened. The temples and statues began to shake and, in particular, two new sciences were born: dialectical materialism and psychoanalysis.[5] According to Goux, it is no accident that each of these sciences posits three parallel phases. In the case of Marxism: 1) the separation of Man from Nature; 2) Man versus Nature; 3) the interaction of Man with *another* Nature (historical materialism). In the case of Freudianism: 1) separation from the Mother; 2) Man versus Woman; 3) reunion with *another* Woman.[6] Goux then emphasizes the fact that the end points in these systems are remarkably similar; they involve, respectively, a reuniting of form with matter—*mate-rialism* (but only after a long period of *paterialism*) and a new relationship to the feminine[7] (but only after castration). For Goux, history has been the history of Man and men, but now we are entering a new historicity. The End of History, the Death of Man: a true *jouissance*[8] as we move beyond the fear of falling back into the original maternal abyss and move toward a "new access to the feminine." This (re)union with the feminine is the end point of History—u-topia—where all images have been banned, God and his correlate the Subject are dead, money no longer circulates, and the Phallus, as the ultimate metaphor in patriarchal culture, collapses into metonymic indifferentiation.[9] In any case, it would seem to be the beginning of the end of patriarchal history and its result, a situation characterized by Philippe Sollers as that of "Puppet-men, women struck with terror, with respect to the virtual one-woman who reaches toward the loneman seen as god who does not exist."[10]

As with all utopias, this one may—or may not—help us to live now. We might say that what is generally referred to as modernity is precisely

5. The almost simultaneous appearance on the historical scene of the human sciences in general (especially linguistics), cinema and photography, feminism, and so on, raises questions needing special attention.

6. See "Différence des sexes et périple de l'histoire" in *Les iconoclastes*, pp. 191–232. This set of Hegelian structural analogies is, of course, of the most classical kind. But how to separate the dancer from the dance?

7. As most readers of recent French theory in translation know by now, the word "feminine" in French does not have the same pejorative connotations it has come to have in English. It is a generic term used to speak about women in general, and approaches our word "female" when valorized in a contemporary context. This said, because of that context and its history, the word is not always as innocent as it appears.

8. For a discussion of this word, see "Notes on the Translation" in Julia Kristeva's *Desire in Language: A Semiotic Approach to Literature and Art*, ed. Leon S. Roudiez (New York: Columbia University Press, 1980), pp. 15–16.

9. Goux shows that this is also, in part, the logical end point of Judaic conceptual systems—the inside of the Temple. See, especially, *Les iconoclastes*.

10. Philippe Sollers, "Freud's Hand," *Yale French Studies* 55/56 (1977): 336.

the acutely interior, unabashedly incestuous exploration of these new female spaces: the perhaps historically unprecedented exploration of the female, differently maternal body.[11] In France, this exploration has settled on the concept of "woman" or "the feminine" as both a metaphor of reading and topography of writing for confronting the breakdown of the paternal metaphor—a tool for declaring war on the Image within the more general twentieth-century iconoclastic imagination. Goux is not alone in his insistence on the necessity to *name* and *rename* what has remained impossible for Man to think, through and beginning with a series of analogies whose common element is "woman."

In fact, it has become increasingly difficult to find a major theoretician in France today who is not concerned in one way or another with "woman," the "feminine," or variations thereof. When the ear and eye first become attuned to this semantic network, it seems that one is not only wandering through an extended isomorphic system but perhaps confronting a gnostic illusion. The "feminine" has become—to use an old expression of Roland Barthes—"a metaphor without brakes."

At the price of selecting here a single exemplum, I propose the following.

In 1978, Jacques Derrida presented a paper in the Columbia University Theory of Literature Seminar.[12] At one point during his presentation, he spoke of Maurice Blanchot's *La folie du jour* as an "invaginated text." There was a barely noticeable ripple of glances among the women present; notes were passed: "Who would speak? From what position? After all, why say anything?" One brave person (a woman) finally asked why Derrida had used the word "invaginated." The response? "I was expecting that question, but *not* from you" (the woman—in real life—is an American feminist working in French theory). That is, the philosopher expected this question from an American feminist, but not from someone familiar with contemporary theories of reading in France. The awaited question did receive an elaborate response: primarily, the neutral etymological origins of the word (from botany). I might add that this question allowed the philosopher to speak for another twenty minutes.

---

11. I should say *ideological* and *symbolic* exploration, since this exploration has also increased *literally* (in, for example, gynecology, obstetrics, genetics, and psychiatry).

12. The paper has since been published in different form as "Living On" in *Deconstruction and Criticism* (New York: Seabury, 1979), pp. 75–176. See also his further discussion of the term "invagination" in Jacques Derrida and Christie V. McDonald, "Choreographies," *Diacritics* 12 (Summer 1982), esp. pp. 70–75. We will come back to "invagination" in Gynesis III.

What are the implications of the fact that the philosopher who has most radically clarified in order to denounce the economy of the symbolic function in Western reason, as well as the analogy of metaphor, can only do so through using this "metaphor of reading"? Is not the use of such "neutral terms" as "hymen" or "invaginated" strangely suggestive of Diderot's "indiscreet jewels," where the "truth" can never come from a woman's mouth but only from her genitals?[13] Is Derrida speaking of the "invaginated text" with a different intention from that of V. S. Pritchett, who has used the same term in a much more traditional way while trying to prove that a certain kind of novel is a "female thing"?[14] How can we talk about intention? And why can the philosophers not resist speaking of "woman"? Would the woman in the audience have had the same reaction if it had been a female proponent of "feminine writing" (*écriture féminine*) speaking of "the invaginated text"? Is it necessary to be a woman in order to speak as a woman? What does it mean to speak *for* woman? As Shoshana Felman has pointed out, isn't that what men have always done?[15]

These are just some of the questions that can lead to an aporia for those women critics attempting to take modernity and its new spaces seriously—especially for those walking the tightropes between French and American theoretical discourse. In France, the rapid putting into discourse of "woman," indeed, the movement toward a "semiosis" of woman, over the past several decades has become problematic in retrospect. It is always a bit of a shock to the feminist theorist when she recognizes that the repeated and infinitely expanded "feminine" in these theoretical systems often has very little, if anything, to do with women. If everyone and everything becomes Woman—as a culture obsessively turns itself inside out—where does that leave women, especially if, in the same atmosphere, feminism is dismissed as anachronistic along with Man and History? In the United States, we continue to import the arguments *pro* and *contra* but rarely attempt to address the terms of the exchange itself. It has thus become a truism to say that the resultant intellectual short-circuits, when not dead ends, are due to irreconcilably different philosophical, psychoanalytic, and literary traditions. But does that mean that, as American feminists, we have to leave the room?

13. On Diderot's jewels, see Jane Gallop, "Snatches of Conversation," in *Women and Language in Literature and Society,* ed. Sally McConnell-Ginet, Ruth Borker, and Nelly Furman (New York: Praeger, 1980).
14. V. S. Pritchett is quoted by Michael Danahy in "Le roman est-il chose femelle?" *Poétique* 25 (1976): 89.
15. Shoshana Felman, "Women and Madness: The Critical Phallacy," *Diacritics* 5 (Winter 1975).

Gynesis I: Intersections

In considering this new semiosis of woman, one is drawn to what would seem to be a—I hesitate to say *common*—concern among the theoreticians of modernity: a search for that which has been "left out," de-emphasized, hidden, or denied articulation within Western systems of knowledge. Gynesis has taken its place in France within a movement away from a concern with identity to a concern with difference, from wholeness to that which is incomplete, from representation to modes of presentation, meta-discourse to fiction, production to operation, and from Universal Truth to a search for new forms of legitimation through para-scientific (when not mathematical) models.[16]

This overall philosophical fascination with what (who) has been left out of Western thinking and writing, as well as with possibilities for a new discursive and social contract, indeed, a new historicity,[17] has been accompanied by an increase in fictional and theoretical writing by women, about women. These parallel and more than interlaced movements inevitably overlap and conflict: work by women theorists (re)joins the overall concern with what and who has been left out of Western thinking; in turn, the larger concern (re)joins "woman" or at least that which has been historically connoted by the word woman. The result has been that "woman" (as well as that which has connoted the female) has been *problematized* in new ways as both concept and identity.[18] In the search for new kinds of legitimation, in the absence of Truth, in anxiety over the decline of paternal authority, and in the midst of spiraling diagnoses of Paranoia, the End of Man and History, "woman" has been set in motion both rhetorically and ideologically.

At the most fundamental level, this interrogation operates: first, metonymically in discourse *about* women; and second, metaphorically in discourse *by, through, as* woman.[19] The problem is that within this ever-

16. The word "legitimation" (which I prefer to its awkward English translation, "legitimatization") is from the Latin *legitimatio*. As mentioned in "Preliminaries" (above), it refers to the *process* of justifying an inheritance (human or otherwise) according to "law," "right," or "common sense." It is most often opposed in French to "natural." Its closest semantic counterpart in current Anglo-American debates might be "authority"—but, in any case, it always involves the question of how to recognize power.

17. See especially, Jean-François Lyotard, *La condition postmoderne* (Paris: Editions de Minuit, 1979).

18. "Woman" is and has always been, of course, the original problematic object. "The heroine of the masculine imagination is essentially a double figure: the incarnation of contradiction" (Nancy Miller, *The Heroine's Text* [New York: Columbia University Press, 1980], p. 74). This contradiction, however, and its intrinsic polysemia at the level of the signified and referent, seem to have metamorphosed into an undecidable at the level of the signifier itself.

19. See Shoshana Felman's discussion of Foucault and Derrida with regard to Logos and Pathos in *La folie*.

increasing inflation of quotation marks around the word "woman," women as thinking, writing subjects are placed in the position of constantly wondering whether it is a question of women or woman, their written *bodies* or their *written* bodies. To refuse "woman" or the "feminine" as cultural and libidinal constructions (as in "men's femininity") is, ironically, to return to metaphysical—anatomical—definitions of sexual identity. To accept a metaphorization, a semiosis of woman, on the other hand, means risking once again the absence of women as subjects in the struggles of modernity. The attempt to analyze, to separate ideological and cultural determinations of the "feminine" from the "real woman"—seemingly the most logical path for a feminist to follow—may also be the most interminable process, one in which women become not only figuratively but also literally impossible.

It might be objected by those not actively engaged in current debates surrounding feminism and modernity that to consider the problematics of gynesis in this way is simply to fail to distinguish the literal from the figurative;[20] that it is to misunderstand how metaphor and metonymy must inevitably operate;[21] or that it is to imply, once again, some new kind of male conspiracy theory about—that is, against—women.

To the extent that the problematization of woman at the core of gynesis intimately involves rhetoric (metaphor, metonymy, connotation, etc.); given that the sign is always more powerful than the message; and taking into consideration that the majority of writers in question here are men— all of the above objections are to some extent accurate. I am implying that the literal and the figurative are henceforth joined in entirely new ways; that metaphor and metonymy are no longer adequate for describing that union; and that the new fictions and theories of modernity may, in fact, be satisfying a repressed desire in men (and women?) for what may turn out to be a very old and, in any case, very readable plot.[22]

---

20. As Claudine Herrmann has pointed out, this would not be a new argument to discourage women from speculating on the world. See Claudine Herrmann, *Les voleuses de langue* (Paris: Editions des Femmes, 1976), esp. pp. 13–14.

21. Much has been urgently written about metaphor and metonymy in the last few years. For an introduction to some of the problems involved, see Michel Le Guern, *Sémantique de la métaphore et de la métonymie* (Paris: Larousse, 1973); or, in another vein, Jonathan Culler's helpful article, "The Turns of Metaphor," in *The Pursuit of Signs* (Ithaca: Cornell University Press, 1981). Harold Bloom thinks that metaphor and metonymy have become the "shibboleth for weak interpreters" (see Harold Bloom, "The Breaking of Form," in *Deconstruction and Criticism*, p. 11).

22. I am thinking here, in particular, of Roland Barthes's definition of a kind of text that is beyond the univocal and yet not quite "integrally plural" in *S/Z*, trans. Richard Miller (New York: Hill & Wang, 1974).

But I am also implying something more than that: that the deeply rhetorical and therefore political adventure of gynesis does not need to return, and may in fact not allow a return, to that plot. The writers in question are women's *compagnons de route,* our intellectual fellow travelers into the twenty-first century. They actually represent only a very small corner of the contemporary theoretical stage, in spite of what the majority would have us believe. The distance between their work and the dominant cultural text we live is immeasurable; in that sense, their work is perhaps comparable only to that of radical feminist theory.

"Woman," as a new rhetorical space, is inseparable from the most radical moments of most contemporary disciplines. To limit ourselves to the general set of writers in focus here, "she" may be found in Lacan's pronouncements on desire; Derrida's internal explorations of writing; Deleuze's work on becoming woman; Jean-François Lyotard's calls for a feminine analytic relation; Jean Baudrillard's work on seduction; Foucault's on madness; Goux's on the new femininity; Barthes's in general; Michel Serres's desire to become Penelope or Ariadne . . . "She" is created from the close explorations of semantic chains whose elements have changed textual as well as conceptual positions, at least in terms of valorization: from time to space, the same to other, paranoia to hysteria, city to labyrinth, mastery to nonmastery, truth to fiction.

As Stephen Heath has put it in his essay on difference, today that which is designated unrepresentable is what is finally the most strongly represented.[23] I would add that, through gynesis, what has always been the most represented—women—while at the same time declared the most unrepresentable (woman) have changed places, have changed spaces in an attempt to move beyond the representations of History towards the utopias of modernity.

> Women have learned to see women through the eyes of men in literature and through the eyes of women in life.
>
> Claudine Herrmann

We have already begun and will continue to explore how the problematization of woman in contemporary French theory poses particularly vexing problems for the American feminist exploring the new territories of modernity. More attuned than many of her French sisters to the devious history of the "eternal feminine" and "the Images of Women in Fiction,"

23. Stephen Heath, "Difference," *Screen* 19 (Fall 1978): 51–113.

and to the fact that "Woman" is the poet's most constant creation, these American feminists face new versions of the anxiety of influence. Caught between the predominantly American feminist's "know thyself" (your *true* self versus "false images") and the modern discovery that there is no more self to know, she may even feel obliged to opt for one camp over the other. For example, those of us attempting to move away from psychological readings grounded in a transparency theory of language without succumbing to the neutrality of pure formalism may sometimes proceed in a schizophrenic manner reading American Feminist Criticism as background and French Theory as foreground, adopting a kind of "yes, I know characters are not real but . . ." approach to the literary text.

Woman, valorized under the banner of demystification, has become the site of inquiry within a period of profound binary crisis. The tropologies of the feminine presented through gynesis, this new presentation of the irrepresentable, are certainly important elements within the larger critique of classical reasoning. But for those American feminists still sensitive to gender-determined reading, these demystifications and tropologies can prove troubling, particularly when accompanied by violent attacks on "feminism" via critiques of its roots in classical logic.[24] What may be the most widely shared and solid ground for the multiple manifestations of feminist theory—not assuming that the speaker is male—somehow gets lost in the fray; somehow seems undeserving of the wholesale critique feminist theory has received from those supposedly most sympathetic to it, especially in France.

While struggling to find new configurations of desire outside of the logic of substitution, do we not run the danger of (belatedly) developing nothing but the negative of the Great Western Photograph? What philosophical discourse today explores, it has also produced. While women are busy refusing the metaphors trapped in the chains of masculine desire, have the philosophers of modernity found a differently same "woman" for producing new images in what is henceforth "a modern society no longer nourishing itself with beliefs (as before) but with images"?[25] When a man says, "I too am woman," he is sure of himself.[26] Perhaps the inflationary

24. Baudrillard, Deleuze, Derrida, Lacan, Lyotard and Cixous, Kofman, Kristeva, Lemoine-Luccioni, and Macciocchi are among the theorists in France who have adopted the most explicitly negative attitudes toward classical feminism.

25. Roland Barthes, *Sollers écrivain* (Paris: Editions du Seuil, 1979), p. 89. All quotations from original French titles are my translation unless otherwise indicated.

26. See, for example, the discussion of Gerard Manley Hopkins in Sandra M. Gilbert and Susan Gubar, *Madwoman in the Attic* (New Haven: Yale University Press, 1979), p. 10.

feminocentrism of gynesis—not, historically, the first such symptom of paranoia—has been confronting the breakdown of the paternal metaphor with nothing less than *catachresis*—sometimes metaphor, sometimes metonymy, the only name for that which is unnamable—God—or, perhaps . . . Woman. When we read those who would assert that in order to have a body, one must be female;[27] or, more precisely, "It is impossible to dissociate the questions of art, style, and truth from the question of the woman"[28]—shall we welcome voices announcing a new historicity or must we be careful that, like Helen, we are not left in Egypt with only an image of ourselves transported to Troy as a pretext for war?

How then might the feminist theorist proceed? One of the primary assumptions of this study is that we cannot continue to pursue our investigation of what constitutes sexual difference from within our epistemological legacy. We cannot go back, but the path in front of us is riddled with potentially dangerous detours. Is there a way to avoid taking an exit from signification, the kind of exit reserved only for a funeral procession, a *theôria* back into a u-topian desert, without being forced to pursue a feminism whose teleology is more than compatible with the patriarchal text? What is the potential for articulating new feminist fictions, both theoretical and other, formed by the necessity for women as subjects to remain active in and attentive to the signifying practices of our times?

A feminist critic very concerned with these questions, Elaine Showalter, has, for example, distinguished between those feminists concerned with woman as reader—*feminist critique*—and those concerned with woman as writer—*gynocritique*.[29] According to Showalter, the first continues to analyze the male imagination while the second develops new models based on the female experience.[30] She argues, convincingly I think, that feminists have perhaps tried too long to adapt male critical systems to women's texts. This may be true. But to say this is to assume that the two sexes and their imaginations can somehow be separated—an assumption incompati-

27. Michel Leiris, for example, anticipates well neo-feminist slogans.

28. Jacques Derrida, *Spurs/Eperons,* trans. Barbara Harlow (Chicago: University of Chicago Press, 1979), p. 71. (Derrida repeating the feminist sentence.)

29. Elaine Showalter, "Towards a Feminist Poetics," in *Women Writing and Writing about Women,* ed. Mary Jacobus (London: Croom Helm, 1979), pp. 22–41.

30. This emphasis on *female* experience has elsewhere been presented in counterpart to feminine and feminist writing in England by Elaine Showalter, *A Literature of Their Own* (Princeton: Princeton University Press, 1977) and discussed, if very differently, by Julia Kristeva (in "Women's Time," *Signs* 7:1 [Autumn 1981]) as the sign of a qualitative change in the intonation of the women's movement in France over the past decade. It is perhaps the second term—experience—which is the most problematic, especially in attempts to unravel the differences between Anglo-American and French philosophical traditions.

ble, I think, with the major challenges of modernity's fictions. If we all remain divided between the two, it is because they cannot be separated in any culture; this, at the very least, has been reaffirmed by the inevitably mystical when not reactionary nature of some neo-feminist thinking.[31] The complexities of the intrinsically erotic choice of an "object of study" aside, the attempt to posit a new form of catharsis—to purify (women's) writing of male topoi—is a return to the worst extremes of our metaphysical tradition. The elaboration of a feminist strategy of reading and writing reaching through to the other side of and perhaps even beyond that tradition while in dialogue with it is what is most difficult.

It is, I think, at the sensitive point of contact between the American and French theoretical stances evoked thus far that some progress might be made or, at least, new kinds of questions asked. This involves thinking through the apparent contradictions between that French and American thinking characterized by the conflict between *woman as process* and *woman as sexual identity*. This is not to imply a one-to-one cultural correspondence. The work being done by theorists, male and female, feminist or not, in both countries is far too rich and multiple to be reduced to the number two and, politically, one often perceives only the most visible (or audible).[32] There are, nevertheless, two very different sets of reading effects being produced in the two countries, each with its own set of debates and limitations.[33] For example, Christiane Makward has written of neo-feminist thought in France, "The theory of femininity is dangerously close to repeating in 'deconstructive' language the traditional assumptions on femininity and female creativity"; while Carolyn Burke has noted that American feminists have perhaps "analyzed the constraints of the social context more avidly than the contradictions within ourselves."[34] Thinking

31. In France, women involved in the group Questions Féministes have used the term "neo-feminism" to designate, specifically, the theories of the group "Psychoanalysis and Politics" (*Psych. et Po.*). Since then, this term has come to mean something close to what Julia Kristeva calls "the second generation" of feminists (in "Women's Time"), although many who would place themselves in that generation are diametrically opposed to *Psych. et Po.* In general, "neo-feminism" refers to thought in which emphasis is placed on isolating the "specifically and uniquely female."

32. We will be returning to the problem of "cultural specificity" explicitly, if briefly, in Gynesis IV.

33. Elaine Marks, in her article "Women and Literature in France," *Signs* 3:4 (Summer 1978) has characterized the American feminist gesture as performing on the *oppression* of *women* and the French gesture on the *repression* of *woman*. This has been a very helpful formulation, but, like all such culturally specific formulations (including my own), it does do injustice; implied here is that oppression in France and repression in the United States are not at issue.

34. See Christiane Makward, "To Be or Not to Be . . . A Feminist Speaker," in *The Future of Difference,* ed. Hester Eisenstein and Alice Jardine (Boston: G. K. Hall, 1980), and Carolyn Burke, "Rethinking the Maternal," in the same collection (forthcoming in paperback, Rutgers University Press, 1985).

through, cross-culturally, two versions of what we might call "the-woman-in-effect" must necessarily include the process of going back to the postulates in which they are grounded. Some French feminists, for example, continue to criticize the cultural assumptions underlying neo-feminist thought in France, thus bringing them closer to (even if they remain distant from) their American counterparts—and vice versa. But to think both reading effects at the same time has perhaps become possible only recently. The necessary encounter between the two reading effects will not take place here, in the following brief considerations, but it is certain that the encounter cannot take place anywhere else without these considerations.

For the American feminist, there is first the leap of faith into a *post-Freudian*, post-Hegelian, and post-Saussurian movement away from representation and the sign as transcendence; that is, whatever their attitudes toward one another, theorists in France continue to emphasize the effects of the human subject's inscription in culture through language—the recognition, for example, that the signifier "woman" does not necessarily *mean* the biological female in history. "Woman," "the feminine," and so on have come to signify those *processes* that disrupt symbolic structures in the West. On the other hand, there is what critics in France have not ceased to call the American feminist pre-Freudian (pre-Nietzchean, pre-Saussurian, etc.) misreading of description as prescription and our valorization of "natural reality" over "psychic life"—the famous American "refusal of the unconscious," insistence on the "self" and emphasis on language only as a natural, communicative function. For these critics, American feminists are anti-theory and apolitical, anchoring their critical undertakings only in naturalized experience. Some have attempted to mediate these contradictions, for example, by simply bringing the "French Freud" to the attention of American feminists. But, as Jane Gallop has shown, this cannot be done without first embracing "a psychoanalysis that has been returned to its original audacity through an exchange with linguistic theory."[35]

The work before us, then, must address itself to some additional and difficult questions: What exactly is the metaphorization process surrounding the term "woman" in contemporary French theory? While avoiding a certain (primarily American) biologistic psychology, one-to-one corre-

---

35. See Jane Gallop's discussion of Juliet Mitchell in "The Ghost of Lacan," *Diacritics* 5:4 (Winter 1975): 24; reprinted in *The Daughter's Seduction* (Ithaca: Cornell University Press, 1982).

spondence of the sign, as well as the notion of a woman's world as separate cultural space or identity, to what extent can we speak of "woman" *without* referring to the biological female? To what extent has the attempt in France over the past twenty years to bypass the human subject and dialectics led to the return of traditional notions of the "feminine"? That is, given that "woman"—as real or imagined—has always been that which allowed for (male) "contemplation," how can we avoid once again the *absence* of women while we are attempting to think difference differently? Finally, how are the "theories of the feminine" in France useful to those of us working in American feminist theory and in what ways must we go beyond this work in order to mediate and rethink the "Franco-American theoretical gap"?

Jean-François Lyotard, a self-confessed male philosopher, has admitted that what is truly at stake in the contemporary women's movement is the status of metadiscourse itself[36] (echoing women theorists in Europe who have been saying that for years). Lyotard speaks of metadiscourse as a truth-functional discourse—that is, as a discourse which authorizes itself to say what it says as a *truth* that must be understood—and, ultimately, which suggests that there is a lack of truth in the statements of our daily lives. As he has stated, "When a 'feminist' is reproached for confusing the phallus, symbolic operator of meaning, with the penis, empirical sign of sexual difference, it is admitted without discussion that the meta-linguistic order (the symbolic) is distinct from its domain of reference (realities)."[37] What *is* the relationship between metadiscourse—even that which refuses to call itself meta- while remaining truth-functional—as it has developed in France and what we are calling here a primarily American feminist emphasis on the "truth-value" of our everyday experience (which that metadiscourse in France is constantly denying or deferring)?

It is perhaps through a putting into practice of the contra-dictions between (American) feminist thought—a primarily ethical discourse as prescription for action—and a certain (French) discourse—emphasizing linguistic and, therefore, symbolic process—that a neutralization of the question of sexual difference can be avoided. Lyotard points out that this neutralization is the ultimate goal of capitalism: the erasing of differences to increase exchange value. Luce Irigaray speaks of the *"sexual indifference sustaining the truth of all science, the logic of all discourse."*[38]

36. See his article, "One of the Things at Stake in Women's Struggles," *Substance* 20 (1978).
37. Ibid., p. 15.
38. Luce Irigaray, *Ce sexe qui n'en est pas un* (Paris: Editions de Minuit, 1977), p. 67.

The avoidance of the neutralization of sexual difference through a new kind of attention to language involves, above all and first of all, the elaboration of a new theory and practice of the speaking subject. This search for a new speaking subject should not be thought of as a search for new synthesis or transcendence, but as a *strategy*—in the strongest sense of the term, even if that sense has been coded as "male." Only by participating in this elaboration may women remain aware of our position in the signifying chain. We know that we must avoid homologation—the inscription of "woman" into the discursive truth of the dominant order is not subversive to that order. As Lyotard has suggested, however, some women theoreticians may therefore attempt to remain outside of magisterial discourse, rejecting it as phallocentric: but such a position, through its very exteriority, can only reinforce the central position of the discourse of power. The Masters do not care at all about what the slaves *believe* as long as the slaves remain on the exterior of the empire. It is perhaps through what we might call a new French-American Connection, a different conjunction of *ethical* concerns with *process,* that what Marguerite Duras has called "the last theoretical imbecile" may begin to perceive that the question of woman and language is not one of fashion; it involves rather a profound rethinking of both the male and female speaking subjects' relationship to the real, imaginary and symbolic, as well as of the status of metadiscourse itself.

Work by women in France on new theories of the speaking subject and language has assumed the contours of the larger emphasis on language in France over the past few decades, but has provided those emphases with added weight: the recognition that the status of women is determined not only at social and political levels, but by the very logical processes through which meaning is produced. This recognition is very different from those of a certain kind of American feminist attention to "women's language"— based on empirical studies of women's "speech-acts."[39] We might clarify this contrast, even if the clarification is ultimately inaccurate, by saying that these latter, empirical, studies examine language "externally" while the effort in France is to explore signification "internally." For women theorists in France, however else they may disagree, the "human subject," "reality," "identity," and "meaning" are not natural givens that can be enumerated and analyzed, but are rather *logics* produced through language as it constructs and deconstructs representations. For them, the investiga-

39. See, for example, Robin Lakoff, *Language and Women's Place* (New York: Harper Colophon, 1975), and Mary Ritchie Key, *Male/Female Language* (New York: Scarecrow, 1975).

tion of how biological difference introduces the speaking subject into the play of language reveals sexuality as intrinsic to any theorization of any practice, especially literary practice. Amid much disagreement about how it should be done, there is nevertheless total agreement that there must be a thorough requestioning of our concept of language, of the role of the unconscious, of various conceptions of the speaking subject, and of the symbolic, ideological, and political assumptions underlying the theorization process itself. They see these questions as having the highest priority for feminists, especially for those working in modern theory but who remain wary of its heritage, of even its most radical presuppositions.

One of the most important and primary theoretical relationships being explored in France is, then, that of the relationship between language and the speaking subject. Without the preliminary understanding that this relationship as classically defined is no longer adequate, modernity remains but an abstract idea. We will pursue in detail this problem of the subject in the next section, but it is essential here to remember that any theory of language is based on a conception of the subject which that theory either posits, implies, or denies.[40] Despite the multiple variations in Western theories of language, a common conception of the subject has united them: it has always been a question of some kind of organic identity, a *homo loquens* in history, a subject acquiring its position through cognition. From the Stoics to Descartes and on through even the greater part of the twentieth century, the logic of the subject has based itself upon the practice of the sign, on language as transparence, the neutral agent of representation and communication. This subject has never questioned itself, has never truly doubted itself—it never had an unconscious in any case. It has been master of its discourse, a Man.

As already mentioned, many feminist cultural critics have finally come to see that we cannot pursue our investigation of what constitutes difference (by which I mean, tentatively, sexual difference) within this epistemological legacy of representation and its comfortable conception of the speaking subject and language. Once traditional conceptions of the speaking subject and language have been rejected, however, the real problems begin. One may retreat from those problems: accept on faith that there are male and female subjects, defined existentially; ignore the problem; or replace the human subject by abstract entities. For example, one may emphasize various forms of "involuntarism" where, as Edward Said has put it, the subject has no control, meaning is erased, and only those

---

40. See works by Julia Kristeva, esp. *Polylogue* (Paris: Editions du Seuil, 1977).

processes anterior to signification are explored.[41] In that way, any consideration of the subject's functioning as social practice may be avoided. There may be, in fact, a complete silence as to the potential for changing symbolic and social structures—an observation that has to disturb any feminist not yet ready to throw out promising (if fledgling) work on the female subject along with the finally dethroned universal (male) Subject. Julia Kristeva has written that this kind of emphasis on involuntarism can lead to a nonproductive redundancy in the interior of the symbolic chamber: the sound of the philosopher's own voice—contemplation adrift.[42] Other new theories of the subject originally seen as promising by many women theorists come to rely on a principle of "anonymity": one posits a society of anonymous, sexually indistinct beings who could, ultimately, only be organized according to a male economy in patriarchal culture. Finally, there is the strategy of simply gendering the traditional cognitive subject as female. This process of "adding" to the subject the attributes of "woman" as produced by Western culture—woman as the involuntary (the unconscious, the unthought, the unsaid) or women as anonymous (non-subjects, without a name)—reminds us, once again, that any theory that does not thoroughly rethink the speaking subject takes the risk of precipitously denying sexual difference altogether.

Edward Said has suggested, in the same article mentioned above, that perhaps the single most important question we must ask ourselves today is: What has kept the Western contract together?[43] Has not one essential component of that contract been a certain conception of "woman"? The demise of the dominant systems of meaning in the West cannot be radically thought through by another added discourse, but only by another kind of speaking and writing. In the meantime, feminists must be careful not to speak *for* women, to become theologians of woman. And this involves neither avoiding theory nor embracing it, but playing it off against itself; placing a violent new thought where the old thought falters and creating new fictions. These fictions must not, on the other hand, be the already overdetermined products of an exclusion model, fictions based only upon that which has been excluded from the empire. We cannot simply turn the Emperor's coat inside out, for in fact he wears no clothes.

41. For a discussion of this notion in reference to the work of Jacques Derrida, see Edward Said, "The Problem of Textuality: Two Exemplary Positions," *Critical Inquiry* 4:4 (Summer 1978).

42. See Julia Kristeva, *La révolution du langage poétique* (Paris: Editions du Seuil, 1974), pp. 128–34.

43. Said, "The Problem of Textuality," p. 700.

Or, if you prefer, for a culture busy unraveling itself from within an imaginary labyrinth, Ariadne remains just around the corner. But Ariadne, like Truth, was never really there in the first place. To recognize the ways in which we surround ourselves with our fictions is a step toward finding new ways for thinking the organization of sexual difference as grounded in cultural and political reality without positing that reality—man or woman, for example—as somehow preexisting our thought and fictions.

That is, a radical reconceptualization of the speaking subject and language is, in particular, essential to the rethinking of feminism as concept and practice in the late twentieth century. At the same time, the explorations of "woman," with reference to both, in contemporary French thought, are not enough to do so because of the ways in which reality and its fictions have been deemphasized. The (American) feminist in dialogue with (French) contemporary theory may be in a special position to approach this problem by remediating and rethinking the feminist insistence on personal experience as practice with the movement of these theoretical fictions as experience and practice—thus working, potentially, toward a new disposition of the ethical grounded in symbolic process.

A certain definition of feminism may be prey once again to the silence of anachronism. The problem is how to avoid this without losing sight of original feminist priorities: understanding how the feminine operates in culture (as what Meaghan Morris would call "a condition of possibility");[44] the relationship of women writers and theorists as subjects to cultural production; the real political implications bound to the interrelationships among these conceptions, language, and sexual difference. This involves, in particular, a continual attention to how the speaking and writing subject is sexually coded in the writers, critics, and philosophers we turn to for our critical habits. In the case of feminist literary criticism, this might be approached, first, by continuing to explore fictions (whether coded as literature or theory) so as to establish a topology of textual strategies used against the symbolic by both men and women, modalities of foreclosure, particularly today within a culture experiencing a violent ambivalence toward the father; that is, a tropological exploration of the movement and transformation of rhetorical and thematic spaces rather than a topical list of definitions and identities. Then, within the topology, there can be an examination of the promises and limitations of the woman-in-effect as radical strategy of reading and writing for any thought focused

44. Meaghan Morris, "French Feminist Criticism," *Hecate* 5:2 (1979): 64.

on modernity as the exploration of the woman's body. Finally, and only then, we can begin to isolate the marked differences between *men's* and *women's* textual experimentation—as well as to imagine what feminist criticism might be in an era that has been diagnosed as one of "post-representation."

An extremely problematic notion, this "era of post-representation," intrinsically linked to modernity, is, ideally, neither utopian nor apocalyptic. It designates, in fact, for better and worse, an operational, informational, cybernetic culture seen by some as an inevitability (due to modern technology) or, in fact, is dreamt of as a potentially positive rather than destructive force for cultural renovation. In either case, how the process of representation as it has been known is being and will continue to be displaced (and not, as often predicted, disappear) in postmodern culture presents a major problem for feminist theoreticians. More simply put, what might be a "feminist criticism" when it is no longer, strictly speaking, the "representation of women" that is at stake?

The only way we can begin even imagining an answer to that question is to start with the simple recognition that if man and woman exist, they do so only within the symbolic. How individuals, both male and female, exist in the symbolic as well as in sexual difference is determined by language, and by the political; for example, in the form of artistic and theoretical, economic and power, class and sexual systems at any given moment. The denegation of the symbolic function also varies in tone, intensity, and effect according to the total disposition of those systems. In our contemporary culture, oscillating between hysteria (confusion of sexual difference) and paranoia (its reinforcement), all of these systems must be thought together, especially if *women* hope to invent new configurations within which women may act as subjects. The choices we make about that invention are not isolated, but reverberate throughout our definitions of ethics, morality, politics, and feminism. Women cannot be thought of as somehow having been excluded from the symbolic; "woman" cannot be given priority as panacea; nor can the articulation between women and woman go unthought. Any specificity of men's or women's writing remains a question for the present—and the future. In the meantime, the "woman-in-effect" can only be thought beginning with how the monological structures we have inherited are constantly reimposed and rearranged, and (particularly) with how women both mime and reject those structures and even become their most adamant support systems. It is especially urgent today to look at how those systems are being once again rearranged, as we move toward a new economic crisis, a growth of micro-

fascist movements, and a reawakening of the sacred, of old religious teleologies as well as new ones from other worlds we have chosen to ignore.
Our deepest feminist beliefs may be swept away by new grids of writing
and desire—within which, no doubt, the feminine will remain a metaphor
and the maternal a secret, but differently. An understanding of how that
metaphor and that secret are currently being displaced or reaffirmed within theocentric structures—by men and women—will enable us, perhaps,
to envision a feminist strategy more attentive to the rational violence of an
ever-spiraling technocracy.

Women must not become (to displace Michel Foucault's image) that
profoundly archaic silhouette—poet and madwoman—who finally took a
peek at modernity and then quickly closed the door.

2

Feminist Tracks

> The words sung in the next room are unavoidable.
> But their passionate intelligence will be studied in you.
> John Ashbery, Fragment

In Walter Abish's short story "Crossing the Great Void,"[1] Zachary—a deaf young man who, rather predictably, hates his uncle for having an affair with the mother he loves—feels compelled to search for his father, who was declared as missing, many years before, somewhere in the Great North African Desert. That Desert is described as empty and blank, as blank as a white sheet of paper—punctured only by the rhythm of Zachary's mother's high heel shoes clicking across the floor, "[framing] in his mind a succession of shots that puncture his eardrums, that puncture the blank piece of paper in his hand, that puncture the blankness, the vast blankness of all the deserts in the world" (p. 99). Zachary is fascinated by all those deserts—voided of any *image* (except that of his father, which exists only in his mind's eye) and heralding a *silence* to match only that of deafness (in his own ears), a deafness brought about, says the narrator, by "hearing his mother recount the same story over and over again" (p. 103). It is only upon meeting Track—a modern young woman who knows the Dark Continent intimately—that his dream of searching for his lost father becomes "real," is named:

> Since you appear to be so intrigued by North Africa, you'll be interested to know that the map of Blitlu, an oasis in the center of the Great Desert, is tatooed on my back, Track said the next time she came by to pick up her car.

1. Walter Abish, "Crossing the Great Void," in *In the Future Perfect* (New York: New Directions, 1977), pp. 98–113. All further page references in text.

Your back?

She had taken him by complete surprise. He was dumbfounded. He was also unprepared for what was to follow that evening at her place. He had no prior experience, no knowledge upon which he could base an appropriate response when hours later, at her house, she unbuttoned her blouse and proceeded to take it off. With the lights off, it was too dark in her bedroom for him to see the map of Blitlu. In addition to your hearing aid you also seem to need glasses, she said matter-of-factly. He was convinced that her remark was devoid of malice. It was not an accusation, but merely a statement of fact. (p. 105)

Zachary proceeds to kill his uncle and set off for (the) Blitlu (on Track's back) to find his father—and to claim his uncle's property, which, he has just learned, is to be found in a place named "Blitlu." He leaves representation, mimesis, maps, and memory behind: "For the first time he could peer into himself and see, so to speak, nothing that might make him feel uneasy [. . .] and, above all, no faces, absolutely no faces, except one that came and went without any prior warning—although he attempted to expunge it from his mind, eliminate all traces of it from his brain, but Track in all her nakedness kept embracing him" (pp. 109–110).

All that Zachary has upon which to base his quest for his missing father is an old book: a book on "deserts," written by a major general in the army, a book entitled *Crossing the Great Void*. But that is not quite all. There is also a small scrap of paper, slipped carefully between the pages of the book, on which Track had always written "up until now correct" directions to Blitlu. There is no way of knowing how correct they are now. Nonetheless, from the last town on the outskirts of the desert, Zachary sets off for the emptiness of the oasis at the center of the desert. An old doorman with a whistle remains behind at the front of the hotel—a man and a whistle, a picture-soundtrack, frozen in the reader's memory as the only existent image of Zachary's father. It is, after all, Zachary's mother who has always possessed his father's image in the photograph, by her bed, of an old man with a whistle. Zachary's father has been framed.

Among all the pathways, roads, tracks, and spaces in Abish's short story, all crisscrossing their ways through false images, illusions, and misconnections, which direction might or should the feminist critic take? At the level of the narrative, she will recognize immediately the guilty mother and the woman introduced into the narrative only to provide an enigma, to keep the hermeneutic machine turning. She might also document a rather obviously acute case of Oedipal anxiety.

But rather than pursue an interpretation at this point, let this almost plot-summary stand simply as an allegory, a surface from which to re-depart. But let us now sharpen our focus, concentrate more specifically on literary criticism, rephrase some of the questions raised thus far with regard to possible new intersections for modernity and feminism through explorations in gynesis. *Gynesis:* a new kind of writing on the woman's body, a map of new spaces yet to be explored, with "woman" supplying the only directions, the only images, upon which Postmodern Man feels he can rely.

Annette Kolodny wrote not too long ago that "as yet, no one has formulated any exacting definition of the term 'feminist criticism.'"[2] Like Elaine Showalter (see Chapter 1), she distinguishes between those women who write about "men's books" and those women who write about "women's books."[3] Feminist criticism, within those parameters, is as multiple and heterogeneous as are the "methodologies" available for use. She adds: "[These investigations] have allowed us to better define the portrayal of and attitudes toward female characters in a variety of authors and, where appropriate, helped us to expose the ways in which sexual bias and/or stereotyped formulations of women's roles in society become codified in literary texts."[4] This short statement by Kolodny summarizes well, I think, feminist criticism in its most fundamental gesture: an analysis (and critique) of fictional representations of women (characters) in men's and women's writing.

If the "author" is male, one finds that the female destiny (at least in the novel) rarely deviates from one or two seemingly irreversible, dualistic teleologies: monster and/or angel, she is condemned to death (or sexual mutilation or disappearance) or to happy-ever-after marriage. Her plot is not her own, and the classical feminist critic is at her best when drawing the painful analogies between those written plots and their mimetic counterparts in "real life."[5]

2. Annette Kolodny, "Some Notes on Defining a 'Feminist Literary Criticism,'" *Critical Inquiry* 2:1 (Fall 1975): 75.
3. She also mentions a third category: "any criticism written by a woman, no matter what the subject" (Kolodny, p. 75), but does not pursue it, implying its inadmissibility to any feminist.
4. Kolodny, "Some Notes," p. 75.
5. Now classical feminist readings of the repetition seemingly inherent to male fictions are those of Simone de Beauvoir and Kate Millett. Recent books in the United States (e.g., Nancy Miller, *The Heroine's Text*) and in France (e.g., Anne-Marie Dardigna, *Les châteaux d'éros,* and Claudine Herrmann, *Les voleuses de langue*), while based in this gesture, go beyond it through their use of structuralist and poststructuralist reading strategies.

Increasingly, women feminist readers reach the point where they can no longer read "the men." That is, they begin to find the repetition unbearable. This is true of both kinds of male "fictions"—"fiction" and "criticism." This limit, when reached, is particularly relevant in the case of criticism, however, when one realizes that the majority of male critics (in all of their incarnations) seem not to have read (or taken seriously) what feminist criticism has produced. They continue either to ignore gender or else to incorporate it into an untransformed reading system, with an ironic wink of the eye, a guilty humanistic benevolence, or a bold stroke of "male feminism."[6]

This is perhaps one of the reasons why the focus on women writers (and critics) has given such fresh energy to feminist criticism. The analysis of female literary traditions, of the intersections between texts by women and prevailing literary conventions, and of female revisions of literary movements has changed the face of American literary criticism. Focusing on women writers, feminist critics can leave repetition behind, feel that they are charting an unknown territory which, at the same time, is strangely familiar. This mixture of unfamiliarity and intimate, identificatory reading seems, indeed, to be the key to a new creative feminist reading and writing style.

There is no doubt that this change in focus has produced some of the most important Anglo-American feminist criticism to date.[7] The movement toward defining a female tradition (as a female subculture, counterculture), and elaborating a feminist poetics (as hermeneutic) based on writing by women, has been a steady one. In fact, it may be the only way for feminist criticism per se to advance. For example, Kolodny, in the same article, first—*briefly*—refers to certain precautions that must be taken by the feminist critic looking for a uniquely "feminine mode": the avoidance of the nature/culture aporia (as an "unanswerable question"), the necessity

---

6. See, for example, Annette Kolodny's response to William Morgan's "feminist" objections to her "separatism": "The Feminist as Literary Critic," *Critical Inquiry* 2:4 (Summer 1976): 821–32.

7. Three of the perhaps best known book-length studies on the possibilities of a female literary tradition include: Ellen Moers, *Literary Women* (London: Women's Press, 1963); Elaine Showalter, *A Literature of Their Own;* and Gilbert and Gubar, *The Madwoman in the Attic.* Other widely read studies include: Susan Koppelman Cornillon, *Images of Women in Fiction* (Bowling Green: Bowling Green State University Press, 1972); Judith Fetterley, *The Resisting Reader* (Bloomington: Indiana University Press, 1978); Jacobus, ed., *Women Writing and Writing about Women;* Patricia M. Spacks, *The Female Imagination* (New York: Avon, 1972). There are, of course, many others, as well as countless important article-length studies; as a parallel gesture, anthologies, biographies, and histories of more and lesser-known women writers are increasing.

of asking, first, whether women's writing *is* different from men's before asking *how,* and so on. She then, nevertheless, continues *at length:* "All of these precautions notwithstanding [. . .] I would be less than honest if I suggested that I had not already begun to be able to catalogue clearly demonstrable repetitions of particular thematic concerns, image patterns, and stylistic devices among these authors."[8] The core and interest of the article is a survey of those concerns and of how we might begin to document them in women's texts.[9]

There are, however, at least two important questions that have been elided by this dual option on how to proceed—questions at the heart of what interests us here. Within the framework of these two options (produced by retaining the distinction between "male" and "female" authors), one question concerns what might be called the feminist posture toward our cultural canon. This is not a new question by any means, but it has not been adequately posed and its uncertain status seems to be at the center of some of the most radical disagreements—personal, political, professional—among feminist critical schools. Shulamith Firestone once wrote, "It would take a denial of all cultural tradition for women to produce even a true 'female' art."[10] Is this not so as well of feminist criticism, at least at its foundations? The feminist critic's "material" is all of "Man's History" or, at least, that of Western civilization. When working on "the men," feminists are involved, whether they like it or not, in an anti-culture project. From within this position, it is extremely difficult to avoid extremes: either that of methodically and completely rejecting what we may loosely call our patriarchal heritage (an endless and, sometimes, apolitical position) or that of deciding who are the "good guys" and the "bad guys." When working on "the women," one must ultimately decide either that there is some mysterious transhistorical thread linking them all, or that "some are okay" and "others are not." On the other hand, when the criteria are more largely political or ideological and the sex of the author is ignored (or bracketed), one can rarely avoid the dangers of what one critic

---

8. Kolodny, "Some Notes," p. 79.

9. Another helpful article, first published in Germany, addresses many of the same questions: Silvia Bovenschen, "Is There a Feminine Aesthetic?" *New German Critique,* no. 10 (Winter 1977): 111–37.

I should also mention here, early on, that it is this side of Anglo-American feminist criticism that has been most fervently attacked in France as being humanistic rather than political. *Humanistic* in that it looks for an unknown "specificity of the woman writer" to be given *expression;* whereas it would be *political* to look at the words "specificity," "woman," "writer," each in the structure of its definition, and work to change that structure. See Stephen Heath's "Difference."

10. Shulamith Firestone, *The Dialectic of Sex* (New York: Bantam, 1970), p. 159.

has called "the obligatory chapter on the 'woman novelist.'"[11] This approach assumes that a woman writer is not writing as a woman but as a "neuter" within a particular political and historical configuration, but that s(he) is just not ultimately as "important" as the men. She remains in her separate chapter with subcategory status—where she has always been.

Further, to the extent that feminist criticism is confined for the most part to the academy, these variations, while certainly not mutually exclusive, do tend to generate a split between the "radical" critic and the "recuperative" critic. The former attempts to remain radically anti-cultural (a difficult posture to maintain in a literature department), while the latter (most often self-consciously) serves an integrative function, supplementing the "core curriculum" with courses on women writers. One might argue that this split exists to the same extent between any politically radical critical stance and the academic norm. Feminist criticism's relationship to the dominant tradition is certainly not unlike that of, say, Marxist criticism. But it also resides strangely elsewhere in that it is unclear, *when gender is accounted for,* what part of that cultural tradition (including Marxism) one should attempt to use as a "positive pole." Only texts by women? Texts by the "okay men"? Those lending themselves to a certain political reading whether written by men or women?

This conflict between feminist reading and the constantly renewed cultural canon operates most acutely, for the feminist critic, at a personal level. First, there is the woman who has chosen to assume a feminist discourse within the academy after having chosen her "field of knowledge." She would not be working in "literature," "art," etc. if it were not positively valorized in her life and, most often, in her class or social milieu. Her "work" comes into conflict with her "life." Second, although clearly not a separate category, there are an increasing number of women, often younger women, who have developed their interest in "literature" and "feminist theory" coextensively. If they continue in their career, their work ("anti-canon") at some point comes into contradiction with their "job" (teaching the canon). They find themselves in the position of the "naughty daughter": tolerated if they can manage to separate their "work" from their "job" (or teach one course "for women"); dismissed if they refuse to rescue patriarchal culture on a daily basis.

The implications of the feminist critic's relationship to men's writing, women's writings, the canon, the academy, etc.—problems deserving much more attention—become even more complex when the focus of

11. Miller, *The Heroine's Text,* p. 154.

one's energies is modernity or, more precisely, contemporary thought reflecting on the postmodern gesture. For a modernity presenting a new kind of discursivity on woman and women, a valorization and speaking of woman through gynesis, the feminist postures so briefly surveyed here become even more highly problematized.

The second question needing attention with regard to the dominant modes of Anglo-American feminist criticism is that of *address*. If it is more than annoying that men's question, addressed to each other, is still primarily "But what do women want?" it sometimes appears that feminist literary critics have still not asked "What do *we* want?"—and the answers to that question depend a great deal upon those with whom we are in dialogue. The question itself is already overdetermined culturally (woman as the supplicant); but the question remains alive, nonetheless, for the public feminist critic.

This question is related to the polemical or prescriptive problem that Kolodny speaks of in the article with which we began. While I strongly agree that one must not prescribe how or what someone should write, I cannot see how or why a feminist critic would want to or be able to "separate political ideologies from aesthetic judgments" while "[continuing] for some time, to be avowedly 'political'" (nor how she could evaluate Norman Mailer's *The Naked and the Dead* as "probably the finest novel to come out of World War II").[12] However one feels about Mailer, what is troubling here is the separation of "ideology" not only from "politics," but from something called "aesthetic judgment" as well. If Kolodny is saying that feminist criticism must have a strategy of evaluation rooted in its own time and history in order to avoid idealization, I agree. But if she is implying that the kind of future answers feminists want can be separated from the kind of questions they ask now, I do not. And the answers will in part depend upon whom we address the questions to. That is, to and for whom are feminist critics writing? Is there a desire for men to start writing "about" woman in a "feminist style"?[13] For them to stop writing about women altogether? Do feminist critics want the male critics to read them? Or do they want just women to do so? It is essential to ask these banal and yet surprisingly unanswerable questions because feminist scholarship has reached something of a double bind, raising numerous

12. Kolodny, "Some Notes," pp. 89–90. I continue to use Kolodny's article here only in an exemplary mode—one that is inevitably unfair to one of our finest feminist critics.

13. The expression "feminist style" is that of Josephine Donovan, "Feminist Style Criticism," in *Images of Women in Fiction: Feminist Perspectives*, ed. Susan Koppelman Cornillon. If this is a goal of feminist criticism, it has been reached.

strategical and political problems as well as contributing to the "disagreements" mentioned earlier. The style of any feminist criticism is radically determined by its addressee. The radical feminist today tends to write only to women; the so-called recuperative feminist may write to women, but wants the male critics to overhear; and she needs for them to like what they overhear. Not only does this raise several "spectres of separatism," as Kolodny puts it,[14] but not thinking about whom one is writing to—as men have always done while writing to themselves—is to assume that one's reader is, once again, neuter or the same. One feminist in France, sensitive to this problematic, has developed an interesting strategy: explicitly writing to, addressing men, knowing that women will overhear the men thinking they understand when they do not. Her letter both does and does not reach its destination.[15] This strategy recognizes, at the very least, that the one writing or reading is always more than just one, writing or reading several texts which are not simply pieces of an autonomous whole. And that brings us back to modernity—and to France.

My reader will no doubt have noticed that the questions raised thus far, within a labyrinth of "men," "women," and "neuters" difficult to sort out, have been based for the most part on Anglo-American feminist concerns. While the translation of French theory into English has begun to produce a promising, hybrid mode of feminist inquiry, especially in film criticism, the distinctions between Anglo-American and French critical modes remain remarkably tenacious. The sex of the author, narrative destinies, images of women, and gender stereotypes continue to be the touchstones of feminist literary criticism as it has developed, most particularly, in the United States. When the feminist critic turns to France, she learns that this bedrock of feminist inquiry has been increasingly and rapidly dislodged: there, in step with what are seen as the most important fictional texts of modernity, the "author" (and his or her intentionalities) has disappeared; the "narrative" has no teleology; "characters" are little more than proper name functions; the "image" as icon must be rendered unrecognizable; and the framework of sexual identity, recognized as intrinsic to all of those structures, is to be dismantled.

We will be looking here at this new kind of inquiry where it intersects with what we are calling the fundamental feminist gesture. Of these intersections, three are particularly relevant.

14. Annette Kolodny, "The Feminist as Literary Critic," p. 821.
15. I refer here to Luce Irigaray.

The first concerns the word "author," and more generally the complex question of the speaking subject as evoked in Chapter 1. Lacanian psycho-analysis and Nietzschean and neo-Heideggerian philosophies in France have torn this concept apart. As Michel Foucault reminds us: "None of this is recent; criticism and philosophy took note of the disappearance—or death—of the author some time ago. But the consequences of their discovery of it have not been sufficiently examined, nor has its impact been accurately measured."[16] First, the "I" and the "we" have been utterly confused; the "I" is several, psychoanalysis has shown; and, further, one of the major ruses of Western metaphysics' violence has been the appropriation of a "we" by an imperialistic if imaginary "I" (a whole individual with an interior and exterior, etc.). The notion of the "self"—so intrinsic to Anglo-American thought—becomes absurd. It is not something called the self that speaks, but language, the unconscious, the textuality of the text. If nothing else, there is only a "splendid unanimity," or a plural and neuter "they." Contemporary fiction is cited as that which enacts this anonymity within a lottery of constantly shifting pronouns.

The assurance of an author's sex within this whirlpool of decentering is problematized beyond recognition. The policing of sexual identity is henceforth seen as complicitous with the appropriations of representation; gender (masculine, feminine) is separate from identity (male, female). The question of whether a "man" or a "woman" wrote a text (a game feminists know well at the level of literary history) becomes nonsensical. A man becomes a woman (*devient femme*) when he writes, or, if not, he does not "write" (in the radical sense of *écriture*) what he writes, or, at least, does not *know* what he's writing. It is only a question of signature—of the name of the father—appropriating and reifying an unlocalizable process that is feminine in its essence . . . "And behind all these questions, we would hear hardly anything but the stirring of an *indifference:* 'What difference does it make who is speaking?'"[17] The feminist's initial incredulity faced with this complex "beyonding" of sexual identity is largely based on common sense (after all, *someone* wrote it). But is it not that very sense (sense "common to all," that is, humanism) that the feminist is attempting to undermine? On the other hand, when you problematize "Man" (as being at the foundations of Western notions of the self) to the extent that French thought has, you are bound to find "woman"—no matter who is speaking—and that most definitely concerns feminist criticism.

16. Michel Foucault, "What Is an Author?" trans. Josué N. Harari, in *Textual Strategies,* ed. Josué Harari (London: Methuen, 1980), p. 143.
17. Ibid., p. 160; my emphasis.

The second major intersection of importance is the status and stakes of representation, where the tools of representation (and of feminist criticism)—narrative, characters—are recognized as existing only at the level of the fantasies that have entrapped us. To analyze endlessly those fantasies is to ask for repetition. It is that process which moves beyond, behind, through these fantasies—the enunciation and disposition of *phantasies*[18]—which must be examined. That "process" is attached to no self, no stable psychological entity, no content. And here again, "theory" is presented in step with a certain kind of contemporary "fiction": "Classical narration camouflages the phantasy by the convention of characters, or by multiple logical justifications, which studies of actantial and narrative functions have examined. [Vladimir Propp, A. J. Greimas, etc.] By liberating itself from these conventions, the modern text lays bare the phantasy as produced by the conflictual state at the interior of the subject of the enunciation; the modern text is even specifically destined to present this conflict as such."[19]

This process, rendered tangible in modern works of art and music as well as in writing, in counterpart to form, melody, identity, has always existed, but has been localized (controlled and effaced) to a high degree in the West, within acceptably "feminized" domains, especially "religion" and "literature." Philosophy, as the traditional guardian of reason, has relegated it, most often pejoratively, to that which is "oriental" or "mystical" as opposed to the "theological." To focus exclusively on that process in the West may be only to valorize a kind of primary narcissism as it is located by modern psychoanalysis within the mother-infant dyad; hence the traditional link, for example, between modernist fiction and conservative politics. But to radically *rethink* that process and liberate it beyond fantasy and its static, predictable forms means rethinking and liberating that which has been relegated to Greek *physis*—allowing it to speak, perhaps even making it speak differently, in new spaces, within entirely new structural configurations. As suggested previously, this project has everything to do with woman and thus with women.

The third intersection, perhaps the most problematic of the three, is the radical requestioning of the status of *fiction* and (intrinsically) of *truth* in contemporary thought. One of the oldest of metaphysical problems, this is the newest and most fundamental problem for modernity. First, in what we have literally called fiction:

18. Here I follow Juliet Mitchell and others in maintaining the distinction in English between "fantasies" (conscious) and "phantasies" (unconscious).
19. Julia Kristeva, *La révolution du langage poétique*, p. 318.

The end of Beckett's *Molloy* is often given as an example of the status of truth in fiction: "Then I went back into the house and wrote, It is midnight. The rain is beating on the windows. It was not midnight. It was not raining." [(London: John Calder, 1959), p. 176]. These utterances are interpreted as typical examples of the unreality of fiction: *writing* would be the positive form ("It is midnight . . . etc."), *reality,* the negative form ("It was not midnight . . ."). However, the negative form is neither more real nor more true than the positive form; both are discourses that mutually presuppose each other, and their reciprocal negation constitutes a single and same mode of language, that is, a *fiction* that is precisely this nonsynthetic reunion of "is" and "is not," opposing and formulating each other all at the same time, and in this way adding to their dichotomy a third "term," undefined, where the subject in process searches for itself.[20]

Contemporary fiction, watching its own writing, has rendered this "third term" particularly visible.

Of course, this heightened awareness of the fictional process is not limited to what is commonly called fiction; as process, it has infiltrated our daily lives in the West, provoking new kinds of crises in legitimation between discourse and reality. For example, through mass media, the fictions of others are lived as never before, and as the fictional process becomes more pervasive, the temptation to rescue written fiction from the immediately depressing multiple fictions of the modern world becomes stronger. While this represents an overall problem for the contemporary critic, I think it touches upon a particularly personal dilemma for feminists: the need felt to protect our written fictional heritage, now in danger of disappearance within a technological society, while at the same time laying bare the logical, ideological, and historical links between that heritage and patriarchal culture.

What does the foregrounding of the fictional process, the radical re-questioning of the status of truth and fiction in theory (and fiction), imply for feminist criticism? As mentioned before, the feminist critic is traditionally concerned with the relationship between "fiction" and "reality" (the latter perceived, ultimately, as the truth)—with how the two intersect, mime each other, and reinforce cultural patterns. The "theories" of that reality as written by men do not seem to conform to our own—so they must be fictions? And what then is feminist theory's difference? For example, to treat both the so-called theory and fiction under consideration in this study as fictions is to make a gesture assumed by contemporary thought and is also to conform to the feminist impulse.

20. Ibid., pp. 352–53.

What are the implications for feminist criticism—a criticism that points out the fictions of the male imagination as not conforming, or as conforming too painfully, to the *reality* of women's lives in the world—if "truth" and "reality" are, henceforth, radically and irrevocably problematized? Even more pointedly, we might ask: is all of this another male fiction, or is it a larger process that can begin to free women—and men—from Man's Truth?

More important, perhaps, what is it that so disarms (when it does not anger) traditional feminist criticism faced with these new directions in contemporary thought—beyond the Self, Representation, and Man's Truth? Why do these two modes of inquiry, feminism and postmodernism, prove so resistant to each other at these intersections when their projects are so irresistibly linked? If, as suggested in the last chapter, this contemporary thought finds its equal only in the most radical moments of feminist theory, why are these intersections so difficult to negotiate?

In terms of the work privileged in this study, principally that of Lacan, Derrida, and Deleuze, some possible reasons surface.[21] First, just at the historical moment when feminist criticism has found a clear and increasingly acceptable voice, it must confront and is confronted by a group of writers who, again, are thinking and writing in strange new ways. Radical changes in theoretical understanding have required radical changes in vocabulary and style as well as in conceptualization. Feminist theorists tend to see what is actually that understanding's most radical force—its emphasis on language—as mere rhetorical acrobatics, as a new ruse on the part of Reason.

Second, in the writings of those theorists participating in gynesis, woman may become intrinsic to entire conceptual systems without being "about" women—much less "about" feminism. First, this is the case literally, inasmuch as the texts in question are based almost entirely on *men's* writing and, most important, on fiction written by men. For example, a survey of such disparate but logically related writers as Lacan, Derrida, and Deleuze—or Cixous, Irigaray, and Kristeva—yields remarkably few references to women writers. (To women, yes; one even finds passing

---

21. Why these particular writers? They all three deal with woman and women explicitly and therefore openly lend themselves to our questions. Other writers, such as Roland Barthes and Michel Foucault, for example, might have done as well; but in their texts, the signifiers woman and women are a very present absence—much more difficult to excavate. In general, the questions posed here are relevant to any modern text in which there is 1) a desire to increase the signifiable; 2) an explicit problematization of gender; and 3) a pronounced ambivalence toward the mother's body.

remarks on women theorists—Lou Andreas-Salomé, Marie Bonaparte, Melanie Klein—but to women writers, no.) Lacan has much advice for women analysts, but only focuses once on a woman writer (Marguerite Duras)—as having understood his theory (without him).[22] Derrida, to my knowledge, never explicitly mentions a woman writer.[23] Deleuze and Guattari refer to Virginia Woolf as having incorporated the process of what they call "becoming woman" (*le devenir femme*) in her writing—but "not to the same extent" as Henry James, D. H. Lawrence, or Henry Miller.[24]

Women writers are even more implausibly absent from the women theorists' texts. While the specificity of the female subject (and even that of a vague, never-named female *writing subject*) is a major question in many of their texts, women writers are not. Cixous, the leading figure of "Psychanalyse et Politique" and its women's bookstore Des Femmes, is perhaps the foremost theoretician in France on the specificity of "feminine writing" (which does not mean writing by a woman). Yet it is not women writers who are the focus of her work. Her focus is on the male poets (Genet, Hölderlin, Kafka, Kleist, Shakespeare) and on the male theoreticians (Derrida, Heidegger, Kierkegaard, Lacan, Nietzsche). Because in the past women have always written "as men," Cixous hardly ever alludes to women writers; one recent exception is her reading and public praise of Clarice Lispector (whose narrative is more "traditional" than one might have expected).[25] Irigaray and Kristeva are uniquely concerned with analyzing the male tradition: from Freud to the philosophers to the avant-garde. The women disciples of all of these theorists do sometimes mention contemporary women writers (Michèle Montrelay mentions Chantal

22. "[Elle] s'avère savoir sans moi ce que j'enseigne." Jacques Lacan, "Hommage à Marguerite Duras," in *Marguerite Duras* (Paris: Albatros, 1979).
23. Excluding Marie Bonaparte—essential to Derrida's critique of Lacan in "The Purveyor of Truth," *Yale French Studies* 52 (1975)—I can find only three oblique exceptions to this observation. The exceptions are especially oblique in that *a particular woman* is never named in them. They are: a footnote to "Violence and Metaphysics": "On this subject, let us note in passing that *Totality and Infinity* pushes the respect for dissymmetry so far that it seems to us impossible, essentially impossible, that it could have been written by a woman." (*Writing and Difference*, trans. Alan Bass [Chicago: University of Chicago Press, 1978], pp. 320–21); his references to an article by Barbara Johnson in "Envois" (*La carte postale* [Paris: Flammarion, 1980], pp. 162–64); and his dialogue with Barbara Johnson apropos her paper on Mary Shelley's *Frankenstein* in *Les fins de l'homme*, ed. Philippe Lacoue-Labarthe and Jean-Luc Nancy (Paris: Galilée, 1981), pp. 75–88.
24. Gilles Deleuze and Claire Parnet, *Dialogues* (Paris: Flammarion, 1977), esp. pp. 55–60.
25. Cf. Hélène Cixous, "L'approche de Clarice Lispector," *Poétique* 40 (November 1979). The reader might also want to refer to her discussion with Michel Foucault on Marguerite Duras: "A propos de M. D.," *Cahiers Renaud-Barrault*, no. 89.

Chawaf, Marguerite Duras, and Jeanne Hyvrard),[26] but such references are not in any way central to their theses.

The (very American) kind of empirical categorizing of texts in which I have just indulged is perhaps ultimately not very useful. But this lack of textual reference to women should at least be pointed out, given our "intersections." For the second reason that gynesis is not necessarily about women is more abstract: within traditional categories of thought, women can (have) exist(ed) only as opposed to men. Indeed, women, especially feminists, who continue to think within those categories are, henceforth, seen as being men by many of the theorists mentioned thus far. It is perhaps this particular conclusion that renders the work in question the most suspect for feminist theoreticians, for it explicitly negates their own status as readers.

But there is one final reason for the absence of an alliance between traditional feminism and modernity: the theoretical writing in question does not enjoy a valorized position in the vast majority of French and American critical circles, while feminism, especially as linked to women's studies in the United States, is one of the few viable critical discourses around. Ironically, this situation would seem to be due in part to the "feminine status" of the texts of modernity themselves. These intensive explorations of gynesis, especially by male theorists, have themselves been genderized as feminine and treated accordingly; the connotative threads that make up the actual fabric of gynesis have problematized the gender and hence critical handling of these writers' own texts.

All of the questions presented here hover at the very limits of representability. Can or should feminism be something other than an attention to the *representation* of women (in several senses of the word)? If gynesis as process has most certainly always been marginally at work in the West, especially in religious and literary texts, in what ways are its more visible links to modernity subject to feminist analysis? Is feminist theory as a search for the female self (most characteristic of Anglo-American criticism) in complete contradiction with the, strictly speaking, antifeminist insistence in France on the liberating potentiality of losing the self? Might there be a way to imagine a new kind of feminist hermeneutics able to give up its quest for truth; capable of self-reflection on its own complicity with

26. Michèle Montrelay, *L'ombre et le nom* (Paris: Editions de Minuit, 1977). One feminist critic has devoted a major study to a woman writer: Marini, *Territoires du féminin avec Marguerite Duras*.

inherited systems of representation? If feminism is to remain radical and not become but patchwork for a patriarchal fabric ripped apart by the twentieth century, what kinds of alliances will it be able to form with the most radical modes of thought produced by that century? These are indeed a set of historical intersections.

For Modern Man does seem to be crossing some kind of Great Void. There is a Track to be followed and he has been told that the map to the Oasis is inscribed on her Body. Is it a question, as with the Biblical Zachary, of reconstructing the Empty Temple evoked by Goux[27] as but a prelude to a new Messianic Era? Or does Zachary know that, deaf and blind, his Quest is already historically amiss, and that, always already Oedipalized, he would not recognize the Image of his Father at *any* crossroads? Most important, is Track to accompany him in his quest? If yes, in what way? And if no, where is it that she would like to go instead? What will she ultimately make of this unexpected twist in the patriarchal story? Perhaps . . .

> It was to be the last time he saw her.
> Are you thinking of going back to Blitlu, he asked?
> Can I drop you here . . . I don't want to run into your Uncle, she said.
> My uncle . . . How do you know my uncle?
> He's everybody's uncle, she said, condescendingly.[28]

27. See Chapter I, above.
28. Abish, "Crossing the Great Void," p. 107.

3

Crises in Legitimation:
Crossing the Great Voids

> The legitimate renunciation of a certain style of causality per-
> haps does not give one the right to renounce all etiological
> demands.
>
> Jacques Derrida

In *The Postmodern Condition,* Jean-François Lyotard defines
the postmodern as "incredulity with regard to the master narratives."[1] He
goes on to say that this lack of belief, this suspicion in the West, is no
doubt due to scientific progress, but that—on the other hand—our accelerating scientific progress has already presupposed a lack of belief. According to Lyotard, we cannot possibly know the origin or the historical why
of this incredulity, we can only *describe* its present manifestations, the
places where it appears most consistently: "to the obsolescence of the
master narrative device of legitimation corresponds notably the crisis of
metaphysical philosophy, and that of the institution of the university
which depends upon it. The narrative function loses its foundations, the
great hero, the great perils, the great quests, and the great goal."[2] Lyotard
here emphasizes two such places, one literal, the other figurative, each
dependent upon the other: the university and the narratives of a certain
philosophy. The crisis in legitimation in the West is necessarily a crisis in
the status of *knowledge*—traditionally, the ability to decide what is true and
just—functions that have remained inseparable up to the present. According to Lyotard, any attempt to attribute this crisis in legitimation to

1. Lyotard, *La condition postmoderne,* p. 7.
2. Ibid., pp. 7–8.

specific causes (Technology? Capitalism?) would be caught in the same impossibility of knowing. We can only talk about the seeds of this crisis. They were buried, for example, in two of the major kinds of narratives of the nineteenth century: those of speculation (for example, Freud) and emancipation (Marx).

Lyotard emphasizes that this crisis in legitimation is, first and foremost, a crisis in governing, in the validity of the social contract itself, rather than in that of any one particular ideology, within patriarchal culture. Although paternity per se is not a major topic in Lyotard's text, he makes it clear that the crisis is not sexually neutral. He does this primarily through his descriptions of the only viable source and place he sees for legitimacy in postmodern culture: "para-logic." This kind of logic is dependent upon and valorizes the kinds of incomplete "short stories" historically embedded, hidden, within so-called "scientific" or "objective" discourse: the kinds of short narratives that this discourse attempts to evacuate in order to shore up its "Truths."[3] These short narratives are described as anti-systematic, antimethodical; their proponents would be in favor of "temporary pacts" rather than "universal social contracts."[4] They are the components of what Lyotard will call, in a later article, a new kind of "pseudo-theory": "a feminine relation of ductility and ductibility, polymorphism."[5] Lyotard argues in favor of establishing a "philosophy of fairies [*sic*] and women" whose primary characteristics would be anonymity, passivity, and a theatrics of faceless masks. But his rather timid insights into how the crises in question are crises in the fables, systems, and theories imagined by men become bolder and more explicit elsewhere; for example, in his "One of the Things at Stake in Women's Struggles": "Deceitful like Eubulides and like realities, women are discovering something that could cause the greatest revolution in the West, something that (masculine) domination has never ceased to stifle: there is no signifier; or else, the class above all classes is just one among many; or again, we Westerners must rework our space-time and all our logic on the basis of non-centricism, non-finality, non-truth."[6]

The slippage in male theoretical discourse from the *feminine* (anonymity, passivity, and so on) to women (as metaphysically opposed to men) and, finally, to "we" ("we Westerners") will be of concern through-

---

3. On scientific discourse and gender, see Evelyn Fox Keller, "Feminism and Science," *Signs* 7 (Spring 1982).
4. Lyotard, *La condition*, p. 98.
5. Jean-François Lyotard, "For a Pseudo-Theory," *Yale French Studies* 52 (1975): 126.
6. Lyotard, "One of the Things at Stake in Women's Struggles," p. 16.

out this study. What is important here is simply the recognition that delegitimation, experienced as crisis, is the loss of the paternal fiction, the West's heritage and guarantee, and that *one* of the responses to that loss on the part of those engaged by modernity has been to look to the future, to *affirm* and *assume* that loss.

Other reactions to this disinheritance are most often tainted by nostalgia. This nostalgia tends to take the form of a critique of what is called conformity or mass culture: of "the society without a father" where (male) authority is no longer internalized and (female) "primary instinctual wishes" are no longer controlled.[7] From the critical theory of the Frankfurt School to the pop-critique of Christopher Lasch, the discussion of loss of authority inevitably comes around to women, who return, empirically, as among those principally to blame for this loss.[8] Other forms of sociological nostalgia are more complex and sophisticated; for example, nostalgia is itself considered as a topic, as an inevitable symptom of something being "wrong": "the nostalgia for a sociality of more uncertain pacts and rituals, the nostalgia for freedom from the social contract and its relationships, the nostalgia for a more cruel but more fascinating destiny of exchange, is more profound than the rational demands of the social with which we have been rocked to sleep."[9] The only recognition that can help us return to this ritual state, according to Baudrillard, is that of "femininity as the principle of uncertainty"—femininity as *seduction*. And, according to him, it is women who are blindest to this fact; it is women who are working against the possibilities for true cultural renewal. For women to demand autonomy or recognition of sexual difference is for them to desire power, to act as men, to lose the female power of seduction regarded by Baudrillard as the best way to master the symbolic universe.[10]

It may be true that social hysteria on a large scale—signaled by both men's and women's confusion about their own gender—entails a loss of seduction. But once again, only *women* are seen as responsible for, indeed guilty of, blocking the flow of desire. Curiously, Baudrillard's modern code of conduct for young ladies echoes a form of traditional maternal discourse, the "secret wisdom" mothers have historically shared with their

---

7. See Jessica Benjamin, "Authority and the Family Revisited," *New German Critique* 13 (1977).

8. See, for example, Alexander Mitscherlich, *Society without the Father: A Contribution to Social Psychology,* trans. Eric Mosbacher (London: Tavistock, 1969); and Christopher Lasch, *The Culture of Narcissism: American Life in an Age of Diminishing Expectations* (New York: Warner, 1980).

9. Jean Baudrillard, *De la séduction* (Paris: Galilée, 1979), p.208.

10. Ibid., pp. 19–22.

daughters: how they must awaken the desire of men, but never respond to or initiate it, for that is the secret of women's power.

Another variant of nostalgia, in another mode and, here, from another culture, is that for "inner speech," for that which is "secret," "quiet" and "private." As George Steiner puts it, "at the present juncture it would appear that 'total emancipation' has in fact brought a new servitude." The rendering explicit of sexuality has brought about a "drastic reapportionment," according to Steiner. And once again, as we might expect: "This would be most dramatically so in the case of middle class women, many of whom will have passed within a generation from zones of near-silence or total inwardness in respect of sexual language to a milieu of permissiveness and, indeed, of competitive display." Women who speak are men and, therefore, threaten the very *humanity* of Man: "Because it lies at the heart of consciousness, sexual experience offers both a denial and challenge to the genius of language . . . and it is through this genius that *men* have, *at least until now,* principally defined their humanity."[11]

Loss of legitimation, loss of authority, loss of seduction, loss of genius—*loss.* I thread my way quickly through the narratives of these few somewhat randomly chosen theoretical fictions to emphasize only a small corner of the contemporary network that articulates this loss by speaking of woman—and women. It extends, of course, beyond theory, from politics to journalism to fiction. It may be that men always feel as if they have "lost something" whenever they speak of woman or women. In any case, within the network of the Cartesian orphans of the twentieth century, those who are nostalgic are certainly the least interesting: faced with this loss, we can only return to the family (Adorno, Horkheimer, Lasch), to the sacred (Baudrillard), or to the "aesthetic" (Steiner). If I have emphasized that nostalgia here, it is because my interest from this point forward will not be with that melancholic search for a recognizable solution, but, rather, with those discourses of modernity which have *assumed, internalized,* and *affirmed* the loss—that is, the difference—of modernity, even if only temporarily, even if all they can ultimately suggest for the future is that everyone have access to his or her own computer terminal (Lyotard).

The state of crisis endemic to modernity is experienced primarily as a loss, or at least a breakdown, of *narrative.* The two figures placed, at least conceptually, at the inceptions of narrative—metaphor and metonymy—

---

11. George Steiner, "The Distribution of Discourse" and "Eros and Idiom," in *On Difficulty* (Oxford: Oxford University Press, 1978), pp. 80, 135–36 (my emphases).

have thus become the obsession of those human sciences in-formed by modernity.[12] The intensive analysis of their forms and functions, across so-called disciplinary boundaries, attests to a wide-ranging reorganization of figurability; one that began to take shape at the end of the nineteenth century, but that has only today touched enough fields of knowledge to be recognized as entailing a major repositioning of conceptual boundaries in the West, a reimagining of the status of the image itself. The analogical link and mimesis of metaphor—the possibilities for difference and re-semblance—and the contiguity and syntax of metonymy—the possibilities for continuity and desire—have themselves become primary objects of modernity's passionate rethinking.

Now, if "what created humanity is narration,"[13] then it may be that Humanity itself has been a myth that has outlived its time; or perhaps the West's momentarily delinquent narratives will soon fall back into their legitimate places; or perhaps we are talking here about something else, about another kind of question altogether:

> Here there is a kind of question, let us still call it historical, whose *conception, formation, gestation,* and *labor* we are only catching a glimpse of today. I employ these words, I admit, with a glance toward the operations of child-bearing—but also with a glance toward those who, in a society from which I do not exclude myself, turn their eyes away when faced by the as yet un-nameable which is proclaiming itself and which can do so, as is necessary whenever a birth is in the offing, only under the species of the nonspecies, in the formless, mute, infant, and terrifying form of monstrosity.[14]

In any case, those writing modernity as a crisis-in-narrative, and thus in legitimation, are exploring newly contoured fictional spaces, hypothetical and unmeasurable, spaces freely coded as *feminine*. Gynesis, designating the process of internalizing these feminine spaces while accounting for those crises, is either static or dynamic depending upon the narrative in which it is embedded. Let us now look briefly at three of those narratives, traditionally called "disciplines," or "fields of knowledge": philosophy,

---

12. On these two figures and narrative, see, for example: Brooks, "Freud's Masterplot," p. 280. Cf., in particular, Roman Jakobson's famous essay, "Two Types of Language and Two Types of Aphasic Disturbances," in Jakobson and Halle, *Fundamentals of Language* (The Hague: Mouton, 1956); Jacques Lacan's "The Agency of the Letter in the Unconscious," in *Ecrits: A Selection,* trans. Alan Sheridan (New York: Norton, 1977); as well as Le Guern, *Sémantique de la métaphore et de la métonymie.* On metaphor, see especially Derrida's "White Mythology: Metaphor in the Text of Philosophy" in *Margins of Philosophy,* trans. Alan Bass (Brighton, Sussex: Harvester, 1982), pp. 207–73.

13. Pierre Janet, *L'évolution de la mémoire et la notion du temps* (Paris: F. Alcan, 1928), p. 261.

14. Derrida, *Writing and Difference,* p. 293.

religion, history. We shall look there for threads of gynesis while exploring the fabric of several discourses in France that are *in the process of* describing themselves as experiencing a crisis in legitimation: a set of theoretical fictions presented here without privilege and without hierarchy—a kind of story with little or no history. (I shall come back to that problem later.)

Philosophy, Religion, History: Boundaries, Spaces, Connotations

> I was unable to avoid expressing my thinking in a philosophical mode. But I am not addressing philosophers.
>
> Georges Bataille, *Méthode de méditation*

In describing what she sees as a typical fantasy of the adult male, Michèle Montrelay focuses on the following image:

> First, a central tube which cannot be the closed and satisfying container of an interior. It's not that the plan of the container is non-existent. Intestine, pipe, image of cavern, of dark, deep, inner spaces, all that exists, but submitted to forces of suction that empty them in the most painful fashion. Or else, the void is already established . . . Or else, the fullness is such a tremendous threat it must be parried at all costs . . . Inside, either it's the void, or else a superfluidity that must be jettisoned as soon as possible. A kind of vague and terrifying suction. A permanent state of blurring. On the surface—and isn't that characteristic of male sexuality—there's an eye.[15]

As Montrelay goes on to say, we do not need to wonder about this fantasy: "You have all read Sade, Bataille, Klossowski, Lacan" . . . It would not be difficult to add numerous other names to her list. This orifice, penis, mouth, anus, egg, eye, vagina seems to incorporate that which has fascinated male philosophers and male artists in dialogue with philosophy from the beginning of Western time: boundaries and spaces. The suction, the breath, of space is a movement which must be *contained* . . . or *thought* . . . for we are talking about the very definition of the world.[16]

In fact, one is tempted to see the exploration of boundaries and spaces as the very essence of philosophy.[17] This becomes clear when one examines

---

15. Michèle Montrelay, "Toward the Other Body" (unpublished paper).

16. One of the most audacious of contemporary philosophers in this realm is Gilles Deleuze. We will come back to him in detail later.

17. See especially Michelle Le Doeuff, *L'imaginaire philosophique* (Paris: Payot, 1980). See also Luce Irigaray's *Speculum de l'autre femme* (Paris: Editions de Minuit, 1974).

the "exemplary images" used by philosophers since antiquity to define the world: for example, Plato's "cavern," Descartes' "closed room," Kant's "island," or, in another register, Kierkegaard's "finger in the mud." One of the most familiar examples, very close to our own time, is Alexandre Kojève's illustration of his ontology through the use of *the* Sartrean image: the gold ring whose hole is as essential to its existence as is its gold.[18] The mutual interdependency of the parts of any such structure has had infinite variations, but those variations, now historicized, are no longer sufficient for modernity, according to the philosophers: the crisis in the discursive itineraries of Western philosophy and the human sciences isomorphic to it involves first and foremost a problematization of the boundaries and spaces necessary to their existence, and this, in turn, involves a disruption of the male and female connotations upon which the latter depend.

In his early essay, "Structure, Sign, and Play in the Discourse of the Human Sciences,"[19] Jacques Derrida shows that both the concept and the word *structure* are as old as the West and that that structure has always assumed a center, a presence, an origin—one with different names according to the historical moment. At some point, however, there was an event, a disruption, and as Derrida puts it, one began to suspect there was no center; the center was decentered; the structure began to collapse.[20] Like Lyotard, he insists that trying to name the event or time that brought about this decentering would be naïve. We can only name the work that opened the way to this decentering: the Nietzschean critique of metaphysics, the Freudian critique of self-presence, and the Heideggerian destruction of metaphysics, of onto-theology, of the determination of being as presence.[21]

What was disrupted, decentered, put into question, particularly by these writers, was the "Big Dichotomies,"[22] those that had allowed Western philosophers to think about boundaries and spaces, about structures—most especially about Culture and Nature—up until the nineteenth century. Since then, the major concern of philosophy, the human sciences, and the natural sciences seems to have been the same: as Lévi-Strauss says in reference to anthropology, "It would not be enough to reabsorb partic-

18. Alexandre Kojève, *Introduction to the Reading of Hegel*, trans. James H. Nichols, Jr. (New York: Basic Books, 1969), p. 214.
19. Jacques Derrida, "Structure, Sign, and Play in the Discourse of the Human Sciences," in *Writing and Difference*, p. 278.
20. Ibid., p. 280.
21. Ibid.
22. I borrow this expression from Meaghan Morris. See "French Feminist Criticism."

ular humanities into a general one. This first enterprise opens the way for others . . . which are incumbent on the exact natural sciences: the reintegration of culture in nature and finally of life within the whole of its physico-chemical conditions."[23]

This collapsing of both human and natural structures back into their so-called sources involves an exceedingly complex destructuring, disintegration, of the founding structures in the West through the exploration of the spaces that have defined them. From biology to nuclear physics, from the plastic arts to telecommunications and computer sciences, from architecture to mathematics, from modern theatre and music to contemporary fiction, the collapsing of certain structures into, within, and through new spaces is what is at stake: modernity as a *re*definition of the world.

The dichotomies defining boundaries and spaces up until "the event" that is evidently so difficult to define are the dichotomies of metaphysics: the possibility of Man giving form to content, a certain conception of conception, how to create something different from the same, how to build a structure. As Hélène Cixous and others have abundantly shown, the dichotomies necessary to those structures have never been sexually neuter; they are the classically heterosexual couples of Western philosophy. For example:[24]

Male		*Female*
Mind	vs.	Body
Culture	vs.	Nature
Techne	vs.	Physis
Intelligible	vs.	Sensible
Activity	vs.	Passivity
Sun	vs.	Moon
Day	vs.	Night
Father	vs.	Mother
Intellect	vs.	Sentiment
Logos	vs.	Pathos
Form	vs.	Matter
Same	vs.	Other

The list is endless. But when the structures based in these dichotomies began to vacillate, there also began, necessarily, an intensive exploration of those terms not attributable to *Man:* the spaces of the *en-soi,* Other, with-

23. Claude Lévi-Strauss, *The Savage Mind* (London: Weidenfeld & Nicolson, 1972), p. 247.
24. See, for example, Hélène Cixous, "Sorties," in *La jeune née* (Paris: 10/18, 1975), pp. 115–246.

out history—the feminine. Most important, through those explorations, the male philosophers found that those spaces have a certain force that *might be useful to Man if they were to be given a new language.*

Here we are at the heart of gynesis. To give a new language to these other spaces is a project filled with both promise and fear, however, for these spaces have hitherto remained unknown, terrifying, monstrous: they are mad, unconscious, improper, unclean, non-sensical, oriental, profane. If philosophy is truly to question those spaces, it must move away from all that has defined them, held them in place: Man, the Subject, History, Meaning. It must offer itself over to them, embrace them. But this is also a dangerous and frightening task, for, as Walter Benjamin put it: "It is a metaphysical truth [which we cannot lose sight of] that all of nature would begin to lament if it were endowed with language. (Though to 'endow with language' is more than to 'make able to speak.')"[25]

Throughout the history of metaphysics, the only way to give a language to Nature, to Space, has been through the *technē*—through technique.[26] The technē has been seen as the active, masculine aspect of "creation"; it either accomplishes what female, passive *physis* is incapable of doing, or else it imitates her. In either case, it is active, transitive, programmatic, and operative, giving a narrative to physis through the art(s) of mimesis; its origin and telos is to make nature speak, to give her a narrative.[27]

Modern definitions of technique and technology demonstrate their semantic and ontological origins in the Greek and Roman *technē*.[28] Scientific and technological knowledge may have replaced more traditional ways of knowing, but the process has remained the same—as well as the *subject* of that process. The subject of technique and its technologies is the *ego cogito*—Man in history, Man of progress. This process, closer to our own time, becomes *praxis,* but the subject does not change: "What Marx calls *praxis* is the meaning which works itself out spontaneously in the intercrossing of those activities by which man organizes his relations with nature and with other men."[29] It is important to point out here that technique and its derivations should not be confused with experience as

25. Walter Benjamin, "On Language as Such and on the Language of Man," in *One Way Street,* trans. Edmund Jephcott and Kingsley Shorter (London: NLB, 1979), p. 121.

26. For a thorough discussion of the *technē* in the context of the history of rhetoric, see Roland Barthes, "L'ancienne rhétorique," *Communications* 16 (1970): 173. The present schematic overview cannot, of course, substitute for close analysis of "sources"—but that is another project.

27. See, especially, Barthes on *inventio* in "L'ancienne rhétorique," p. 197.

28. Cf. Martin Heidegger, *"The Question concerning Technology" and Other Essays,* trans. William Lovitt (New York: Garland, 1977); and Lyotard, *La condition,* esp. p. 73.

29. Merleau-Ponty, *In Praise of Philosophy,* trans. John Wild and James M. Edie (Evanston, Ill.: Northwestern University Press, 1963), p. 50.

productive of meaning. According to the philosophers and founders of rhetoric, experience is as mute and passive as are the fragments of the real that remain *beyond the technē,* outside of the creative process. Experience can be brought to *expression* (idealism) or turned into a *practice* (dialectical thought), but in and of itself, without mediation, it remains passive.

The space or *Topic* acted upon by the technē, the one from which Man may extract his arguments or within which he is forced to base his actions—most especially when this space becomes internalized as his soul or his thoughts—has undergone astounding semantic transformations throughout Western history. But it is always some kind of place, space, reserve, or region. Most often, before the nineteenth century, it was called Nature or Matter—to which Man could give form and from which he could then produce culture. Even in the nineteenth and twentieth centuries, the names for this space have continued to multiply: among its modern equivalents are *force* (Hegel), *hylē* (Husserl), and *pratico-inerte* (Sartre). These spaces remain, as in the past, nothing more than material multiplicities, purely sensorial and without intentionality.

At the end of the nineteenth century the possible relationships between technique and its spaces began to change radically, however, at the same time as the radical upheavals in familial, religious, and political structures seemed to accelerate. Suddenly, technique was engulfed by the very spaces that until that time had remained its passive sources, its objects. Technique itself became an object of both fear and wonder; space and matter were beginning to speak a language that Man did not want to hear. Although technique had always been an ambiguous instrument, one of both death and civilization, by the early twentieth century, its potentials for destruction as well as new forms of life began to overwhelm Man.

For instance, the invention of photography was an event of exemplary importance for philosophers thinking about these new relationships, these new kinds of spaces with new potentials. This particular technique actually turned Man into an object, it "froze" him, and, as Walter Benjamin would say many years later, destroyed the "aura" of the work of art. In the photograph, there is no more physis, but only a new kind of space, what Benjamin called a new nature: "another nature speaks to the camera in as much as it speaks to the eye; and, especially, it speaks in another mode because a space consciously elaborated by man is replaced by one where he operates unconsciously."[30] A new space, which was suddenly larger (or smaller) than Man, found a language, began to objectify Man, to turn him into an image.

30. Walter Benjamin, "La photographie," in *Poésie et révolution* (Paris: Denoël, 1971), p. 19.

The anguish of Man—faced with this particular technique—has not diminished; it was, for example, described with passion by Roland Barthes just before his death: "In front of the lens, I am at the same time: he who I believe myself to be, he who I hope to be seen as; he who the photographer believes me to be; and he whom he uses to exhibit his art . . ."[31] Barthes evokes the violent experience of becoming and then being an object ("a micro-experience of death"), of being turned into an Image, nothing but a source for others' use.[32] And beyond a solely existential anguish, the instantaneous slippage between subject and object—the oscillation between the two—as he describes it, sounds remarkably similar to how *women* have described the process they undergo in patriarchal systems of representation.[33] It is almost as if technique, as concept and practice, has turned Man into an Object-Woman.[34]

In the twentieth century, these new spaces for and of technology, these new "natures with a language," capable of, at least potentially, objectifying Man—from the Freudian unconscious to atomic physics—forced themselves upon the philosophers. But how to think this new energy, this new force, this thought, this language, organized in space, in matter?

Jean-Paul Sartre once glimpsed the possibility of a "speaking matter,"

---

31. R. Barthes, *La chambre claire* (Paris: Editions du Seuil, 1980), p. 29.

32. Ibid., esp. pp. 30–31.

33. The experience of becoming and being an object has been central to feminist theory since Simone de Beauvoir's *The Second Sex*. On woman as specular object, see especially Irigaray's *Speculum*.

34. Full discussion of this highly self-conscious speculative leap cannot be undertaken here, but a note sketching the grounds for it is certainly in order.

One of the most promising and fertile areas of feminist criticism is that of photographic and cinematic theory—where male scopophilia, fetishism, and voyeurism are analyzed, often in relation to the Lacanian pre-mirror stage and its attendant lack of sexual differentiation. (See, for example, Laura Mulvey, "Visual Pleasure and Narrative Cinema," *Screen* 16:3 [Fall 1975]. Other journals devoting extensive space to the image and sexual difference include *Camera Obscura* and *M/F*. Parallel developments may be found in psychoanalytically oriented feminist analyses of pornography: e.g., Claire Pajaczkowska, "Imagistic Representation and the Status of the Image in Pornography," paper presented at the International Film Conference, University of Wisconsin, March 1980.)

Julia Kristeva, among others, has analyzed the specificities of specular pleasure within contemporary culture. Of particular relevance here is the following remark in reference to the dream as cinema deprived of a public: "Let us note the lack of dissociation between the object as waste, itself not yet separated from the body proper, and the paternal eye [the Subject], which represents the first instance of visual and/or symbolic representation. The indistinction object-waste/eye-symbolic instance is inevitably accompanied by another: the hesitation around sexual difference: active or passive, seeing or seen, my eye or his eye, 'man' or the erotic object of the Father's sadism ('woman')." (Julia Kristeva, "Ellipse sur la frayeur et la séduction spéculaire," in *Polylogue*, p. 378.) Other articles of immediate interest include: Roland Barthes, "The Rhetoric of the Image," in *Image-Music-Text* (London: Hill & Wang, 1977); Janet Bergstrom, "Alternation, Segmentation, Hypnosis: Interview with Raymond Bellour," *Camera Obscura* 3/4 (Summer 1979); and Umberto Eco, "L'analyse des images," *Communications* 15 (1970).

but, as Vincent Descombes has pointed out, he rapidly withdrew his suggestion. The notion that the female connoted (natural) *en-soi* could ever *modify itself* with the male connoted (human) *pour-soi*[35] in order to attain the dignity of a being created in, of, by, and for itself is rejected by Sartre because this Being-conscious-of-itself would be the *ens causa sui,* that is, God . . . and "[with Sartre] the passage from *human* subjectivity ('I speak of the world.') to absolute subjectivity ('The world speaks of itself.') is prohibited."[36] Sartre's conclusion is that all Man can do in the twentieth century is proceed "as if": "Everything happens as if the world, man, and man-in-the-world succeeded in realizing only a missing God [*un Dieu manqué*]."[37]

Almost but not quite a God . . . Could it be that the end result of the history of technique, here incarnated by Man's *pour-soi,* is the creation of an *automaton,* a kind of "spirit-in-matter"? Could this be the phantasmatic, utopian end point not only of all technical progress but of philosophy itself? A kind of sacred materiality that can communicate nothing detached from itself? A kind of "pregnant matter," as Derrida might put it? So closely associated with Western notions of God, this "spirit-in-matter" is terrifying, *unnameable;* it can engender itself; it has no need of a mother or father. It is beyond the representation that Man has always presented himself with and controlled. It is, in its essence, an indistinctness between the inside and the outside, between original boundaries and spaces. To think this indistinctness in the twentieth century has been to think a crisis of indescribable proportions, to throw all of the Big Dichotomies into question: for if the exterior is interior, then the interior is also exterior; Man's soul is outside of him-self; history is but the exterior of his own no longer interior imagination.

An exploration of this crisis, as an exploration of the figural, has been experienced as a necessity by those philosophers attuned to the violence of technique and its technologies in the twentieth century. Either Nature, for modern Man, can become nothing more than a complex "data bank," a source from which he will extract what he needs until it is empty, or she can become more plastic, she can be assumed and affirmed—saved from

35. These connotations are now widely recognized in feminist criticism; for an introduction, see, for example, Dorothy Kaufmann McCall, "Simone de Beauvoir, *The Second Sex,* and Jean-Paul Sartre," *Signs* 5:2 (Winter 1979).

36. Vincent Descombes, *Modern French Philosophy* (translation of *Le même et l'autre: Quarante-cinq ans de philosophie française*), trans. L. Scott-Fox and J. M. Harding (Cambridge: Cambridge University Press, 1980), pp. 52–53.

37. Jean-Paul Sartre, *Being and Nothingness,* trans. Hazel E. Barnes (New York: Philosophical Library, 1956), p. 623.

her own violence? Instead of *making* physis speak, perhaps Man should let her speak. But to do this, to conceptualize this confusion of borderlines, the Philosopher-Man cannot remain at the center as in the past. He has modeled himself, rather, after Orpheus, "[who] did not descend into night in order to put himself in the position of being able to produce a harmonious song, to bring about the reconciliation between night and day and to have himself crowned for his art. He went to seek the figural instance, the other of his *very work,* to see the invisible, to see death."[38] Like the "artist," the Philosopher-Man in the late twentieth century must descend, then find and embrace that *figure,* figurative device, which has no *visage,* no recognizable traits. And that figure, Eurydice, is *woman.*[39]

It is no accident that Lyotard has here chosen the Orpheus myth to exemplify the problem of the figural, of the imagistic, for modern Man. Already a central myth for many philosophers, especially since the nineteenth century, this myth has taken on special significance in contemporary French thought (most notably, in echo to the work of Maurice Blanchot).[40] Orpheus is the poet who descends into Hades to search for Eurydice; but if he wants to rescue her and bring her out into the daylight, he must not, above all, turn and look at her. But, of course, he does look (in French, *il la dévisage*) and thus *loses* her and, at the same time, *finds* his poetry and his song. That is, in order to find the poetic *figure,* the *visage* must not be seen: "La figure est ce qui n'a pas de visage" (the figure is that which has no face).[41] Like literature, philosophy will have to put aside its fear of moving beyond what is merely human and male (the *visage*); it must accelerate its search for Eurydice, for what is female, for the *figure,* if it wishes to invent new songs.

In fact, modernity has increasingly been qualified as what Gilles Deleuze calls the process of *dévisagification,* a kind of de-individualization.[42] For him, the visage, the identifiable face, is "black holes on a white wall," an abstract, European, white male machine that has a definite social function:

38. Jean-François Lyotard, *Dérive à partir de Marx et Freud* (Paris: Editions de Minuit, 1973), pp. 59–60.

39. *Figure,* in French, is both a generic term for the face and a rhetorical term (as in English). *Visage* refers to that aspect of the human face which renders it recognizable, representable.

40. E.g., Maurice Blanchot, *The Space of Literature: A Translation of L'espace littéraire,* trans. Ann Smock (Lincoln: University of Nebraska Press, 1982).

41. Lyotard, *Dérive,* p. 59.

42. For an extended discussion of the *visage* versus *figure* problematic in the context of modernity, see Gilles Deleuze and Félix Guattari, "Année zéro: Visagéité," in *Mille plateaux* (Paris: Editions de Minuit, 1980), pp. 205–34.

"to be identified, catalogued, recognized."[43] For Jacques Derrida (reading Emmanuel Levinas), the visage is: "expression and [. . .] speech. Not only as glance, but as the original unity of glance and speech, eyes and mouth [. . .]."[44] Citing Aristotle, Ludwig Feuerbach, Hegel, Kierkegaard, and Levinas (among others), Derrida shows that the visage—(Man's) identity and (Man's) humanity—is that which has always commanded: "The face is presence, *ousia*. The face is not a metaphor, not a figure."[45]

Following the directions of Derrida's own footnote at this point, we find the following statement, still in reference to Levinas: "It would be useless to attempt, here, to enter into the descriptions devoted to interiority, economy, enjoyment, habitation, femininity, Eros, to everything suggested under the title *Beyond the Face,* matters that would doubtless deserve many questions."[46] I would respond "Most certainly," but would argue that the ways in which those questions are tied to gender deserve more attention: why is it Eurydice who must incarnate the almost monstrously duplicitous role of visage/figure? Or else, when not Eurydice, why is it Christ (as pointed out in different ways by other writers like Eugénie Lemoine-Luccioni and Deleuze)?[47] Or God, as written by Edmond Jabès?[48]

These questions remain open, but the genderization of the visage as male (hence to be rejected) and of the figure as female (hence to be embraced) is one of contemporary philosophy's own peculiar modes for gynesis. It is not a terribly original one. First of all, the indistinctness and distortion of the visage, the descent into the uncharted space of night, has everything to do with the infantile exploration of the *mother's face*—the first point of reference mapped by the infant in search of the breast.[49] But second and most important, it has always been the woman's figure, her lack of visage, of individual traits, of identity and humanity, that has saved the male artist.

> I no longer look into the eyes of the woman I hold in my arms but I swim through, head and arms and legs, and I see that behind the sockets of the eyes there is a region unexplored, the world of futurity, and here there is no logic whatever.

43. Deleuze and Parnet, *Dialogues,* p. 25.
44. Jacques Derrida, "Violence and Metaphysics," in *Writing and Difference,* p. 100.
45. Ibid., p. 101.
46. Ibid., note 40, p. 315.
47. See: Eugénie Lemoine-Luccioni, "Beauté," in *Partage des femmes* (Paris: Editions du Seuil, 1976), pp. 160, 162, 170; and Deleuze and Guattari, "Visagéité," esp. pp. 216–23.
48. "Tous les visages sont le Sien; c'est pourquoi Il n'a pas de visage." ("All faces are His; this is why HE has no face.") Quoted by Derrida in "Violence and Metaphysics," p. 109.
49. See, for example, René Spitz, *De la naissance à la parole* (Paris: PUF, 1968), pp. 57–63.

This passage from Henry Miller's *Tropic of Capricorn* is cited by Deleuze and Félix Guattari as a perfect example of the road to be taken by modern thought: "Yes, the *visage* has a great future, provided it is destroyed, undone. En route toward the asignifiant, toward the asubjective. But we still have explained nothing about what we feel."[50]

But then neither has the feminist critic.

The philosophers thinking about the status of the image in modernity have increasingly devoted a large portion of their attention to the history of religion in Western culture. For the history of the West has not only been that of metaphysics, of its structures and dichotomies. It has also been that of Judeo-Christianity: the strange dialogue between the Greek and the Jew—and their sons.[51] What has been diagnosed by philosophy as a crisis of indistinctness between the inside and the outside, between a certain space and a certain boundary, between metaphor and metonymy, is seen to be a crisis, as well, of a confrontation with the Judeo-Christian God and the denial, displacement, or resurrection of the possibilities of His *image(s),* of the figurability of the sacred.

For example, if the Greek father was there to confer authority on his son, either through his *presence* (Pure Life) or his *absence* (Death), the Judaic father turned his back on the son and disappeared from the Temple. The Judaic father cannot be represented any more than could the maternal idols over which the Judaic Temple was built. If Oedipus was able to accomplish his primordial desire through a confrontation with the Father, Abraham was not led by desire, but closed his eyes in order to *listen* to rather than to see God the Father. In Judaic thought, there is only the Father's voice warning against all representations, all images—an empty space whose boundaries are the ear. The Christian father—as grounded in Catholicism—is, on the other hand, abundantly represented through triangular mediation: the concept of the trinity. With Christianity, the curiously maternal Holy Ghost and Son will unite with the Judaic father's voice and representationally unite in Celestial Love. Protestantism is seen

50. Deleuze and Guattari, "Visagéité," pp. 209–10. Also see Henry Miller, *Tropic of Capricorn* (New York: Grove, 1961), p. 121.

51. See, for example, Matthew Arnold, *Culture and Anarchy* (Cambridge: Cambridge University Press, 1950); Sigmund Freud, *Totem and Taboo,* vol. 13 of *The Complete Psychological Works of Sigmund Freud,* trans. James Strachey (London: Hogarth, 1955); Friedrich Nietzsche, *The Anti-Christ,* trans. H. L. Mencken (New York: Alfred A. Knopf, 1918). This problematic has been most thoroughly explored in France by J. F. Lyotard, J. Derrida, J. J. Goux, and J. Kristeva. For a detailed discussion in English of the emergence of rabbinic interpretation in modern literary theory—the theory engaged in a life-and-death reading war with our dominant Greco-Christian tradition—see Susan Handelman, *The Slayers of Moses* (Albany: State University of New York Press, 1982).

as having suppressed once again the material imagistics of Catholicism (witness the short history of Protestant art), thus rejoining the Judaic gesture; but, at the same time, Protestantism transferred the absent presence of the Judaic father's voice into the real. The Father became a terrifying, *Human* presence—veiling his frailty—where no mediation is possible.

The links between the history of the sacred image and the crises in figurability intrinsic to modernity are numerous and complex. For whatever the status of the Father throughout his history, he has served as the ultimate judge, the self-sufficient Idea that has given the Western world its contours. Recent analyses of the demise of the paternal function in the West have therefore not failed to link the presence or absence of his image to the crises in figurability at the roots of modernity. For example, Jean-Joseph Goux and others have linked those crises once again directly to the techne and its primary configurations: metonymy and metaphor.[52] According to Goux, Judaic thought has been historically figured as linear and horizontal: it is law, history, and at the foundation of desire—even if that desire can never be fulfilled in the *real* because of the undeniable presence-absence of the Other. The history of Judaism would be that of terrestrial displacement. While Judaism and Christianity can no more be separated than can metonymy and metaphor, Christianity is seen primarily as substitutive and vertical: it is faith, passion, and, like Platonism, between heaven and earth. What has surpassed or overflowed this double-axed conceptual frame in the West has either been rendered taboo or else sacrificed accordingly. For example, in a different register and from another point of view, Julia Kristeva has traced, at length, how the crisis in figurability which surfaced in nineteenth-century Europe is rooted in the fundamental, Biblical structures of taboo (as metonymic) and sacrifice (as metaphoric).[53]

That is, modernity is a rethinking not only of secular boundaries, but of sacred boundaries as well—in an attempt to both reconceptualize and control the archaic spaces that, hidden in the shade of the Big Dichotomies, finally emerged in all of their force in the nineteenth century. The automaton speaks, but it is as yet unclear whether it is an angel or Satan. Dialectics was a tentative response to this aporia, an iconoclastic gesture rejoining the taboo structure of Judaism. Psychoanalysis was another. We shall certainly come back to these later.

52. See Goux, *Les iconoclastes,* and, especially, Handelman's *The Slayers of Moses:* "We have maintained that metonymy is a characteristic mode of rabbinic hermeneutics and metaphor of Christian thought" (p. 137).

53. Julia Kristeva, *Powers of Horror: An Essay on Abjection,* trans. Leon S. Roudiez (New York: Columbia University Press, 1982), p. 95.

But what was and still is this space so suddenly out of control, this loss of purity and terrifying force? Another God? The aftershock of God's Death? New figures must be found beyond theocentric representation. The *technē* has been threatened from the interior and exterior by a language it may have produced but which, in any case, it cannot seem to control. Freud heard that language, as did Nietzsche; and they both could only, if in different ways, *represent* it as the unmediated violence of Mitra, the Great Mother. The language threatening the end of the world is seen by the philosophers at the threshold of modernity as emerging from an unrecognizable, anonymous space formerly hidden in the shadows: the face filled with light of the young "Persian God" who, today, still remains incomprehensible, unknowable, unnameable, and impossible to control. Modernity's task will be to name this unnameable. Philosophy will have to unite with religion to think this space by turning back on itself, by finding a new definition of sovereignty (beyond God), and, most important, by rethinking in its entirety what in the West has been called History: "And mankind reckons *time* . . . from the *first* day of Christianity! *Why not rather from its last?—From today?*—The transvaluation of all values! . . ."[54]

There is, then, on the part of some of the most important historians and philosophers of modernity, at least one generally accepted consensus from within this continuing figurative crisis: the West is approaching or has already traversed the *ending* of a certain strictly delimited history: that of metaphysics and Judeo-Christianity. But to speak of an end is already to adhere to a certain logic—*the* logic of that history. And so even history— that most encompassing of master narratives, the one to which we in the West have always been able to turn as a last resort—becomes problematic in and of itself (it becomes historicizable) and turns back upon itself.

It would be impractical to try even to sum up the major revolutions the word "history" has been through in France over the past quarter of a century. Suffice it to say that "history" as a concept has been questioned, as we might expect, from within the context of an entire "new (re)genera-tion" of French philosophy. This (re)generation has taken place within what Vincent Descombes (rather unhistorically but at least clearly) has termed the passage from the generation of the three H's (Heidegger, Hegel, and Husserl) to the generation of the three "Masters of Suspicion" (Marx, Nietzsche, and Freud) and, most important, beyond.[55] The overall interrogation in France of all systems of historical thinking has emphasized most strongly their mutual dependence on certain fundamental concep-

---

54. Nietzsche, *The Anti-Christ*, pp. 181–82.
55. See Descombes, *Modern French Philosophy*.

tions of the speaking subject, language, and religious structures. "History" as teleology and project, whether elaborated within a "Marxist" or "Idealist" framework, is presented as another collapsing structure that must be thought in and of itself. This has led to a kind of acceleration in the historicization of Western history and its limits, leading, ultimately, to a set of accelerating, interdisciplinary extrapolations: history is linked to the *cogito,* to the paternal function, representation, meaning, denotation, sign, syntax, narration, and so forth. At the same time, that which has been "left out" of history and the fields of its extrapolated concepts has been revalorized as their (feminine) "foils."

If the seeming isomorphism among philosophical, religious, and figurative crises is increasingly welcomed by feminist theoreticians, the breakdown of historical modalities of thought, and the above-mentioned genderizations, pose a series of difficult questions. For, once again, feminism is necessarily about women—a group of human beings *in history* whose identity is defined by that history's representation of sexuality. It is hardly necessary to point out that the ways of thinking about feminism in the West are already overdetermined; that they are based on systems of inherited thought: in most cases, on empiricism or on existential, concrete thinking. There is, after all, an insistence by feminists on what is simply called *reality:* a pragmatic definition of truth, or, as Descombes writes in reference to Sartrean humanism: "the true is the result." This has led to the rejection of the word "feminism" by some women in France as simply a complex play of humanist ideology; or else, it has culminated in an attempt to live in two times: historical time ("reality") and written time ("elsewhere"). An increasing majority, however, retain the word "feminism"—admitting there are problems with it but insisting on using it now, concretely (that is, existentially). As they might say: If humanism was about putting the word "Man" where "God" had been used before, and if therefore feminism is nothing but another humanist gesture in that it replaces "Man" with "Woman," so be it—for now. Some have suggested that "feminism" is nothing more than a historical moment itself—having arisen, flourished, and died within a historical trajectory beyond which the West is moving rapidly. From this point of view, Feminism is just as anachronistic as is History.

History as anachronistic? This conceptual oxymoron is in fact what is being examined in France. A new conception of history means a new conception of time—a *retreat* from time and emphasis on space. Some of those examining new spaces—whether transversal, interior, or hidden behind what we used to call Time—have remained within schemes of causality. Others have rejected causality completely and, through an emphasis on language, have shown the part played in history by chance, discourse, or writing. What is most striking about all of these destructurings, however, is their common emphasis on the fact that 1) we seem to have traversed *three precise epochs* in the West and 2) we are now rapidly moving into a *fourth* as yet unknown. This is not an uncommon modern periodization of "History"—from Erich Auerbach to Deleuze, male theorists have consistently posited a tripartite configuration of Man's life.[56] But what is striking about this configuration in contemporary France is its relative autonomy in relationship to "empirical facts." In contemporary French thought, it is not the "event" that assumes importance as a historical mark, but the epistemological *configurations* surrounding that event, especially with regard to language.

For example, as outlined in Chapter 1, Jean-Joseph Goux has emphasized that these three epochs correspond to the three stages in Marxist and Freudian thought; in fact, Goux himself has constructed a four-layered historical telescope capable of taking that thought into account. Michel Foucault, while rejecting both Freudianism and Marxism, has also emphasized three epochs (and a new fourth one) in history—but he adds that we cannot in any fashion dialecticize them or discuss the links between them. For him (and others), the suggestion that there is an end to History, analogous to the end of an individual's life, is an anthropomorphic assumption already inherent in schemes of causality.

What are the three epochs presented as essential to Western Time? The first would seem to run up to and, in some cases, through the Renaissance. The second expands through the seventeenth and eighteenth centuries; and the third begins somewhere in the late eighteenth or early nineteenth century and continues—until when? Although Foucault once suggested 1950 as the end point of the third epoch, we are at present unable to say whether we are actually still enclosed in it or already beyond it. Many theorists would agree, I think, that we are both within and without it at the same time; here again, boundaries become problematic—or else act as veils to hinder us from knowing.

Let us briefly explore the attributes of these three clearly outlined stages before exploring the unclear horizons of the fourth. And although this

56. For two dissimilar discussions of the same phenomenon, see, for example, the Epilogue to Erich Auerbach's *Mimesis,* trans. Willard R. Trask (Princeton: Princeton University Press, 1953) and "Deleuze," *L'arc* 49 (1972; reissued 1980): 57–58. I insist upon *male* writers here because it is becoming increasingly clear that *women's* periodization of history might be completely different. For an introduction to the problem, see *L'histoire sans qualités* (Paris: Galilée, 1979); the bibliography is especially useful.

three-tiered model is accepted by many others, let us allow Foucault and Goux—intellectual opponents in many other ways—to guide us through this accelerating historicization of history.

The first epoch is presented as having lasted until the sixteenth century. For Goux, as for Freud, this was the space of the Mother; or, according to Marx, Nature. In any case, Man as concept certainly did not yet exist. This first stage was history's *unconscious*, the space of primitive production, primitive language, animism, magic, and mythology. Even at a more developed stage (that of Asiatic production for Goux), words were not yet separated from things and there was not yet one God. This "preconscious" state was, more specifically, that of hieroglyphics and polytheism. According to Baudrillard, this cosmology was also that of ritual and duality, where language operated as symbol according to certain rules of playful figurability.

With the movement into the productive mode of Greek and Roman antiquity, the relativity among values, figurative language and the numerous Gods began to be centralized into general values: the sign, monotheism, and philosophy were born; the tribunal was erected, and the Father made his appearance within a culture oscillating between monarchy and democracy. René Girard has qualified this time (fifth century B.C.) as one of sacrificial crisis: a crisis of differences which, according to him, continued to echo right up to the time of Elizabethan England.[57] In fact, the period extending from fifth-century Athens until about the fourteenth or fifteenth century is seen by many of these theorists as a continuum in which an ultimate value, as a form, as a Father, was simply caught up in the process of consolidation.

Foucault, looking at this world finally stabilized in the Renaissance, describes its methods of knowing as based in resemblance.[58] Nevertheless, the world was not completely transparent, and there did appear "a somber space" that was to be progressively clarified: that space was nature, and it was there to be "known."

The next major epoch discerned by these writers would seem to be the seventeenth and eighteenth centuries. The end boundaries of this epoch are more difficult to locate than the earlier ones, but, in general, they were somewhere in the nineteenth century. For Goux, the classical period was one of advanced "metaphysical thirst." The systems established in late

57. René Girard, *Violence and the Sacred*, trans. Patrick Gregory (Baltimore: Johns Hopkins University Press, 1977), p. 49. ["Crise des différences" was translated as "crisis of distinctions." I prefer "crisis of differences" and have retained it here.]

58. Foucault, *The Order of Things*, esp. pp. 25–30. All further page references in text.

antiquity were completely consolidated; the classical period was the West's conscious: superphallic, superparanoid, totally phonetic. Its attributes were the law, the social contract, the polarity of the sign (dialectics), aesthetics, meaning—the expanse of Oedipus. For Foucault, it was the age of representation analyzed in *The Order of Things,* where only identities and differences were of import. The space of Nature had retreated and, in fact, all that survived of the earlier epoch of resemblances were those processes relegated to and confined within the carefully defined borders of the Western imagination: games—and literature.

Finally, after a comparatively brief time, the third epoch of "History" was upon the West—an epoch that would slowly merge into the fourth and ultimate vision of the world. This third epoch, begun in the nineteenth century, is similar to the first (as Communism is to Nature for Marx, or the Woman to the Mother for Freud) but also, ultimately, unpredictable. According to Foucault, the threshold from classicism to modernity was crossed when "words ceased to intersect with representations and to provide a spontaneous grid for the knowledge of things" (p. 304). The nineteenth century brought with it, according to him, the two most significant forces of modernity: the return of language as no longer naturally linked to the world; and the appearance of Man—along with his unthought.

The closest Foucault comes to naming this "unthought" is in his discussion of its manifestations as the "unconscious" of Man: "in the existence— mute, yet ready to speak, and secretly impregnated with a potential discourse—of that *not-known* from which man is perpetually summoned towards self-knowledge" (p. 323). It is between the lines of that discussion that the analogies between the unthought and the other spaces of modernity already mentioned become apparent. It is also where the female connotations of that unthought become clear: this silent but potentially talkative unthought is both internal and external to Man; it is not lodged in Man as a "shrivelled-up nature" but is, rather, Man's Other, next to him. It is an indispensable but "obscure space," an "insistent double," same but different (pp. 326–27).

According to Foucault, Man's project thus far has been to lift "the veil of the Unconscious" by giving it a language, by reanimating the inert (pp. 327–28). But it would seem that this project—that of Man allowing this Other to become the same as himself—has failed. According to Foucault, Man and the spaces of modernity are not to last, together, for long. For those spaces, that unconscious, that unthought, that Other, are larger than Man or his History. What comes after Man is, however, as yet unclear, and

Foucault feels free to evoke it only in a language that, in its evocation of birth, is strangely reminiscent of Derrida's monstrosity yet to come (pp. 306–307). The fourth epoch, after Man and History, can as yet be barely glimpsed; only in madness—or in a certain fictionality—can we begin to perceive this new era, without Man, where language shows itself in the nude (p. 374); where "Death dominates every psychological function" (p. 375); where there remains only "the explosion of man's face [*visage*] in laughter, and the return of masks" (p. 385).

Foucault is not alone with his apocalyptic vision. For Goux, every aspect of life in modernity has become a simulacrum and mask; differences have become the Same. In his vision of the world, it is no longer a question of ritual, law, or contract but of norms and models; no longer symbols or signs, but operations and signals; no longer Oedipus but Narcissus. Metonymy and metaphor no longer lend legitimacy to our perceptions; they themselves are lost within total figurative confusion. Contemporary writers in France react to this new age with horror and, increasingly, nihilistic cynicism. The West is experiencing another sacrificial crisis, according to some (Girard)—the inevitable result of democratization, rendering the Other the Same. It is, however, even more violent than those experienced before—in Athens or the Renaissance; it has become an essential violence.[59]

In terms of gynesis, Goux is the most explicit about this new era. Instead of using words like the Other, the unthought, the shadow, or the abyss, he ultimately takes an optimistic turn and heralds this new age as "the genital stage"—the last stage of both Man and History. The new social grid after Man will be "hyper-natural"—because the ends of Man and his History are the ends of Nature. The opposition between History and Nature will no longer hold, in fact, for this new era: hyper-nature will call for a thought that is "nonphallocentric, noncentralized, a way of thinking still not conceived of, based in networks, a polynodal and non-representational organization."[60] For Goux, the end of history is "the crossing-over into the place of the Other, the *return* to the place of signifying productivity, then its conscious extension" (p. 243). Man will disappear into the space of the Other, explore it, and, ultimately, *become* it—that is, *her*. For Goux, the space engendering meaning, beyond History, beyond Man, "locates at the same time the coming into symbolic existence of *woman* as such—that is, *beyond* the phallic symbolism which represented

---

59. Girard, *Violence and the Sacred*, p. 318.
60. J. J. Goux, *Economie et symbolique*, p. 93. All further page references in text.

her" (p. 257). A new genital culture will rejoin Mother-Nature transformed into a Hyper-Nature (p. 274), and *"it is the feminine sex that inherits the legacy of the maternal breast"* (p. 274). It is when this transformation is fully accomplished that the West will enter its *superconscious:* science will allow the suppression of the Human Subject—and, ultimately, an engendering without Mother and Father will become the hyper-natural norm.

Without Images, without the Father and without the Mother, without Man or History. The discourses of philosophy, religion, and history all rejoin, and each echoes the other two when contemplating the ends of Man. And it is Woman and her "obligatory connotations"; Woman as other than the Mother, who represents for the male theorists of modernity the *space* at the end point of Man's symbolization—utopia—or the Empty Temple of the Judaic thought at our foundations: "the access, by man, to the female sex as different from the maternal abyss; a 'utopian' ending where the void which was the source of anguish becomes the source of jouissance."[61]

One of the questions throughout this study must remain: a jouissance for whom?

61. J. J. Goux, *Les iconoclastes,* p. 232.

4

Spaces for Further Research: Male Paranoia

> But what if the object began to speak?
> Luce Irigaray, *Speculum of the Other Woman*

The key master discourses in the West—philosophy, religion, history—have thus had to confront, since the nineteenth century, a new space which refuses to stay silent within its frame of representation. This nature—this space, object, and Other—is, in a sense, no longer natural. It is described as the motor of a world without a God.[1] What is henceforth necessary for any human subject who desires to describe the modern world will be to walk through the mirror, dismantle the frame held together by the Big Dichotomies and operate a trans-position of the boundaries and spaces now tangled in a figurative confusion. The inside and outside seem to turn inside-out like a glove. Even history cannot name the resultant re-lining, for this Master of the Masters has itself turned capricious.

That all of the words used to designate this space (now unbound)—nature, Other, matter, unconscious, madness, hylē, force—have throughout the tenure of Western philosophy carried feminine connotations (whatever their grammatical gender) is not something we need to dwell on here. Those connotations go back, at the very least, to Plato's *chora*.[2] Julia Kristeva has pointed out that space in general has always connoted the

---

1. Could this be the same "motion in matter," needing no God, fleetingly glimpsed by the Marquis de Sade in 1795? See "Philosophy in the Bedroom," in *The Marquis de Sade*, trans. Richard Seaver and Austryn Wainhouse (New York: Grove, 1965), esp. p. 300.

2. On the *chora*, see Kristeva, *La révolution du langage poétique*, pp. 22–30. On these connotations in general see Cixous, "Sorties," in *La jeune née*.

female: "'Father's time, mother's species,' as Joyce put it; and, indeed, when evoking the name and destiny of women, one thinks more of the *space* generating and forming the human species than of *time,* becoming, or history. The modern sciences of subjectivity, of its genealogy and accidents, confirm in their own way this intuition, which is perhaps itself the result of a sociohistorical conjuncture."[3]

The questioning of this space, its dis-integration, will not leave these connotations behind: if thinkers from Plato ("cavern") through Hegel ("integral emptiness") retained them (for one side of the equation), so too will Jacques Lacan ("Other"), Jacques Derrida ("text"), and Gilles Deleuze ("body-without-organs")—if differently. This new space, new place, is tenaciously feminine. Moreover, the woman-subject usually becomes a kind of "filter" for questioning this space ("a place of passage, a threshold where 'nature' confronts 'culture' ").[4] But that is another problem; in fact, the mystification produced by imagining "that there is *someone* in that filter" *is* the problem.[5]

The new kinds of questions being asked about this space from within the master-discourses-in-crisis have led to gynesis; at the same time, they have inevitably guided those discourses' approaches to what is commonly called "literature"—that mass of fictional spaces we have not here, all appearances to the contrary, left behind. For to question figurability, the symbolic status of the image, the paths and impasses of narrative, and so on—to work at the edges of the unnameable—*is* to deal with literature, with the literary substance itself.

The newborn discourses of the nineteenth century, what the French habitually call the "human sciences," moving into the place formerly occupied by other master discourses, were born, precisely, within and in response to the crisis in figurability briefly outlined here. For example, one of the most important children of the nineteenth century was psychoanalysis: a new human science that unabashedly questioned this space and its uncontrollable languages, the relationship of boundaries to spaces, of subjects to objects. It thus necessarily became a rival of its former masters—philosophy, religion, and history: it has been accused of their shortcomings, exalted as their savior. The fact that psychoanalysis was born from women's "hystericality"; that its most consistent emphasis has been

---

3. Julia Kristeva, "Le temps des femmes," *34/44: Cahiers de recherche de sciences des textes et documents,* no. 5 (Winter 1979); trans. Alice Jardine and Harry Blake, "Women's Time," *Signs* 7:1 (Autumn 1981): 15.
4. Julia Kristeva, "Motherhood According to Bellini," in *Desire in Language,* p. 238.
5. Ibid.

on localizing, defining, and confining the linguistic space of the Other; that it has had to protect so rigidly its own borders and bridges from surrounding fictions, while at the same time going to fiction to find its own spaces, have been some of my points of departure into the specificities of gynesis. The web of female connotations surrounding the exploration of contemporary spaces finds its most insistent denotations in psycho-analytic fictions.

Before we turn more explicitly to the spaces of specific texts, however, we cannot simply dismiss the problem of "causality"—that *bête-noire* of twentieth-century thought. For it is certain that the feminist reader of these explorations cannot help but wonder 1) what *happened* in the nineteenth century to bring about this desperate search, on the part of the masters, for a new definition of the world; and 2) why the process has accelerated at the end of the twentieth. Of course, it is causality itself that is in question here: a disbelief in origins, heredity, legitimations, intentionality, progress. To mention causality is to step outside of all that is most interesting in contemporary thought. But, on the other hand, might not the notion of an "epistemological break" or "ending" be a fiction itself? Has the West not traversed several mythologies of the "end"—from heaven to the Apocalypse?[6] Sidestepping both of these questions for the moment, I shall only touch here upon some of the more important aspects of what might be called the "causality paradigm"—topics for further research, ideally by feminist philosophers and historians.

The specific manifestations of gynesis with which I am primarily concerned in this book are not as "abstract" as they might at first appear. They do constitute, after all, a reading effect, a reading process, based in a textuality which, as outlined in "Preliminaries," seems to have attained its apogee in *France*. Indeed, the contours of the questions being asked here have been, admittedly, almost completely formed by contemporary thought in that country. When thinking about the problem in this way, some may come to feel that if it is, in fact, in France that the process of reading and writing has been most radically affected by confrontations with the larger symbolic explorations of modernity, then we can and must talk about the "causality paradigm" only in terms of France. More specifically, and as Geoffrey Hartman has put it, "I myself am inclined to argue that every literary theory is based on the experience of a limited canon or generalized strongly from a particular text/milieu."[7] In the case of France,

6. See, for example, Frank Kermode, *The Sense of an Ending: Studies in the Theory of Fiction* (New York: Oxford University Press, 1967).

7. Geoffrey Hartman, "A Short History of Practical Criticism," *New Literary History* 10 (1978–79): 507.

it would certainly not be difficult to point to the names of those writers and their texts that have nourished the problematics of the last twenty-five years. Such a bibliography would include, as its very lowest common denominators: Antonin Artaud, Bataille, Blanchot, Klossowski, Mallarmé, and Sade, as well as Kafka and the English modernists, especially Joyce. A study of the particularities and timing of the importation of Germanic thought into France in the twentieth century would necessitate adding to that list, for example, Freud, Hegel, Heidegger, Husserl, Marx. It is also important to remember that the explosion of critical languages in France over the past two decades has been intrinsically and explicitly linked to: 1) very precise political battles (especially the events surrounding the general strike of May 1968), and 2) the increasing perception of a "crisis in literature."

That is, might we not be talking here about a very provincial battle? As Tzvetan Todorov, in still another context, has said in reference to Blanchot: "What if his prophecy of doom applied not to literature in general but only to that of the West? Even more modestly, could it not be said that what is at stake is only the literature of France?"[8] Some would answer yes to this question—it is purely a question of local politics.[9]

But the struggles with the structures relegated to us by Western history extend far beyond France. The very concept of *Europe* as a whole was already deeply problematized by the end of the nineteenth century, particularly with the advent of ethnology. As Derrida has put it: "In fact one can assume that ethnology could have been born as a science only at the moment when a decentering had come about: at the moment when European culture—and, in consequence, the history of metaphysics and of its concepts—had been *dislocated,* driven from its locus, and forced to stop considering itself as the culture of reference."[10] Derrida reminds us that this dislocation was discursive, political, economic, and technical—all levels inseparably linked to the downfall of metaphysics and its modes of

8. Tzvetan Todorov, "Reflections on Literature in Contemporary France," *New Literary History* 10:3 (Spring 1979): 518.

9. This kind of insistence on "comparative contexts" can lead to important political insights. For example, in another vein and on another topic, it has been pointed out by Fredric Jameson that the differences between American New Criticism and Russian Formalism, so often compared, can be traced directly to their respective "canons." The former's contemporaries were Eliot and Pound, and they tended to privilege Elizabethan verse drama and Dante. The Russian Formalists, on the other hand, came out of the Russian Revolution and were influenced primarily by Mayakovsky and Khlebnikov. The split between avant-garde art and left-wing politics in America is shown by Jameson to have been largely a local phenomenon. See Jameson, *The Prison-House of Language* (Princeton: Princeton University Press, 1972), pp. 45–46.

10. Jacques Derrida, "Structure, Sign, and Play," in *Writing and Difference,* p. 282.

thought. As other cultures began knocking on the empire's door, that empire began to fear for its boundaries, and in the twentieth century this process could only accelerate. As Kristeva has pointed out in a different context, by 1929, those pillars which had traditionally supported the concept of a "nation" or "ensemble" of related nations—economic homogeneity, historical tradition, linguistic unity—were irreversibly weakened. Both the identities and loss of identities of "Europe" were being rapidly, endlessly rearranged, nation by nation.[11]

The European *ensemble*, confronted with systems of production and belief foreign to its own, has always either colonized and imperialized or else retreated into its own boundaries, refusing to question those boundaries or acknowledge the differences of the spaces beyond them. But in the twentieth century, European *thought* has been forced to explore that *unknown*, the unthought—that Other than themselves, intimately, in different ways from before, for otherwise it could not continue to exist, at all.

Many other systems of causality have been suggested to account for the beginning of the end of the European master discourses in the nineteenth century. Some see it as the inevitable result of the growth of capitalism—especially to the extent that Capital, amoeba-like, always rapidly ingests all that is foreign to it; it can make any process its own. Others have suggested that the movement away from those discourses toward imagining a new space was absolutely integral to scientific developments. From the steam engine to the discovery of DNA and beyond, Western Man has increasingly dreamed of joining his visions of the "world" to scientific discourse in one large formula. Others, more pessimistic and always more conservative, simply qualify the late nineteenth century (and again the late twentieth) as "decadent," as refusing to recognize the objective, timeless, and transcendent values of Western culture.

Feminists studying this epistemological knot might, however, find other notes of emphasis. Let us return to post-1968 France. It has been pointed out by several feminist theorists that the putting into discourse and valorization of "woman" in French thought since 1968 can be directly linked to the rise of the feminist movement there: "feminism is the fashion of the day and the men on the left who have gone through Marxism, Maoism and the other 'isms' naturally stop at feminism at present as the only 'valid' movement which is left (to them.)"[12] In fact, one feminist philosopher has extensively analyzed the historical "coincidence" between

11. Kristeva, "Women's Time," pp. 13–15.
12. Danielle Haase-Dubosc and Nancy Huston, "L'un s'autorise et l'autre pas" (unpublished paper), p. 1.

the rise of the women's movement and the crisis in Western systems of knowledge as well as of those systems' turning toward an interest in "the feminine"—the "feminization of philosophy": "If women are presented in philosophy, *for* philosophy, it is to the extent that philosophy has no other way out; at this point it feminizes itself."[13] She also points out a contemporary paradox adjacent to this "coincidence": "it so happens that women enjoy in the media [as 'liberated women'] the same success as a certain philosophical thought [the 'new philosophers'], all the while being menaced [like 'philosophy'] with effective disappearance."[14]

But this observation on contemporary France could be extended far beyond its national and temporal borders. It is certainly no accident that the very existence of "Europe" as a symbolic and economic entity, as defined by its dominant mode of thinking (metaphysics), became such an issue at the same time as the women's movement resurfaced after 1968. But what about the time before that?

The more carefully the feminist critic considers the two major "epistemological breaks" in Western history as seen by contemporary male philosophers in France, the more she is tempted to return to so-called empirical versions of history to see what links there might be between *women's history* and these major conceptual revolutions for which it would seem to be so "impossible to establish any causality." While the relation between women's voices and dominant culture is far too complex to be confined within the perameters of male periodization, the temptation to see some such striking links is strong. Hypothesis: might it not be that a series of if not causal at least etiological links could be established between those periods in the West when women were most vocally polemical and those so called "epistemological breaks"? To my knowledge, this question has not been adequately examined, but is certainly worthy of serious consideration by feminist historians.

For example, the first transition period—between the Middle Ages and the Renaissance—was a period when "woman" was at the height of discursive circulation: a circulation in which women came to play a decisive part. Feminist historians generally agree that the rise and consolidation of Christianity had combined with the classical tradition during the Middle Ages to produce a thoroughly misogynist culture throughout Europe.[15]

13. Rosi Braidotti, "Féminisme et philosophie" (diss., University of Paris I, 1981), p. 44.
14. Ibid., pp. 46–47.
15. For a summary of this misogynist tradition with special reference to Britain, see in particular Katherine M. Rogers, *The Troublesome Helpmate: A History of Misogyny in Liter-*

The famous "Querelle des femmes" began in the tenth and eleventh centuries (extending to the sixteenth and, according to some, beyond), producing such texts as Roger de Caen's *Carmen de mundi contemptu* and a series of Church Councils devoted to keeping woman in her place (for example, the Council of Paris in 1023). The literature of courtly love throughout the twelfth and thirteenth centuries, in its ambivalent and simultaneous hatred and idealization of "woman," would do nothing to subvert, in any significant way, the fundamental attributes of woman by then firmly established: "stupidity, irritability, inconstancy, loquacity, frivolity, drunkenness, gluttony, perversity, hypocrisy, selfishness. [. . .]"[16]

Toward the end of the Middle Ages, the representation of woman became one of drastic extremes. *Le roman de la rose* and the subsequent tide of literature it generated could serve here as a symbol of the change in question. Begun in 1220 by Guillaume de Lorris and completed in 1265 by Jean de Meun, *Le roman de la rose* incorporated in one volume a radical change from courtly inspiration and its ambivalence to an extreme, solid hatred of women: "Also it is really the thinking of Jean de Meun and not that of Guillaume de Lorris that was a problem at the end of the Middle Ages. With him, antifeminism had arrived at a veritable crystallization: it was no longer possible to allow the development of a duty of response. From the midst of the quarrel that broke out around him appeared the first concerted adventure of feminism."[17]

The *querelle de la Rose*, the *querelle des femmes* was at its height;[18] and the atmosphere thus created divided the Church and the humanist movement alike.[19] But, most important, the querelle also produced the first woman in France to live by her pen: Christine de Pisan, who produced a response to de Meun in her *La cité des dames*.[20] The ensuing angry, rhetorical battles

---

ature (Seattle: University of Washington Press, 1966); and with regard to France, Maïté Albistur and Daniel Armogathe, *Histoire du féminisme français* (Paris: des Femmes, 1977), esp. pp. 19–174. Joan Kelly's "Early Feminist Theory and the Querelle des Femmes, 1400–1789," *Signs* 8:1 (Autumn 1982): 4–28, is a veritable gold mine of bibliographical references to important feminist work on the medieval and Renaissance periods. Also see Régine Pernoud, *La femme au temps des cathédrales* (Paris: Stock, 1980). My thanks to Nancy Jones for her guidance through the labyrinths of what can and cannot be said with any certainty about this complex period of transition with regard to women's voices.

16. Théodore Lee Neff, *La satire des femmes dans la poésie lyrique française du moyen âge*, quoted in Albistur and Armogathe, *Histoire*, pp. 59–60.

17. Albistur and Armogathe, *Histoire*, p. 67.

18. See Joan Kelly, "Early Feminist Theory"; Eric Hicks, *Le débat sur Le roman de la rose* (Paris: Champion, 1977); and Charles F. Ward, *The Epistles on the Romance of the Rose and Other Documents in the Debate* (Chicago: University of Chicago Press, 1911).

19. E.g., the Council of Basle (1431–1439) and the Council of Constance (1414–1418).

20. Christine de Pisan, *The Book of the City of Ladies*, trans. Earl Jeffrey Richards (New York: Persea, 1982).

among "feminists," humanists, and the clergy are often considered as being at the source of the most important manifestations of women's writing in the Renaissance (Marguerite de Navarre, Louise Labé, etc.). As Joan Kelly puts it,

> Feminist theorizing arose in the fifteenth century, in intimate association with and in reaction to the new secular culture of the modern European state. It emerged as the voice of literate women who felt themselves and all women maligned and newly oppressed by that culture, but who were empowered by it at the same time to speak out in their defense. Christine de Pisan was the first such feminist thinker, and the four-century-long debate that she sparked, known as the *querelle des femmes,* became the vehicle through which most early feminist thinking evolved.[21]

Everyone was talking about woman in the fourteenth and fifteenth centuries . . . and by the sixteenth century, *women* were talking, writing, and publishing at the Court, in the salons—and at home.[22]

The concrete, historically empirical links between the rise of women's voices and the larger, conceptual changes referred to by a Goux or Foucault remain, of course, to be documented. But at the very least, it is clear that from 1300 to 1600, "woman" was put into discursive circulation in entirely new ways.[23]

If woman remained somewhat "triumphant" even into the early seventeenth century,[24] by 1650, "the classical order had triumphed"[25] and the male pen set out in earnest to quiet all the talk about "the female." While arguments in print between men and women about the relative humanity of woman certainly continued throughout the seventeenth and eighteenth centuries, the women who took part in those arguments were not, or at least did not perceive themselves as, involved in a women's movement, in a specifically activist, ideological, immediate battle over the rights of women.

As Kelly has so clearly argued, the *querelle des femmes,* begun in the

---

21. Kelly, "Early Feminist Theory," p. 5.

22. Also see Joan Kelly-Gadol, "Did Women Have a Renaissance?" in *Becoming Visible: Women in European History,* ed. Renate Bridenthal and Claudia Koonz (Boston: Houghton Mifflin, 1977), pp. 137–64.

23. How this veritable explosion of rhetoric around woman may be related to other major conceptual changes is also an open question. For example, Kristeva has shown that it was during the period 1300–1500 that the dominant modes of symbolization in the West were changing radically from the symbol to the sign. Cf. Julia Kristeva, *Le texte du roman* (The Hague: Mouton, 1970), p. 28.

24. See Ian MacLean, *Woman Triumphant: Feminism in French Literature, 1610–1652* (Oxford: Clarendon, 1977).

25. Albistur and Armogathe, *Histoire,* p. 192.

fifteenth century, was to continue in essentially the same mode into the late eighteenth century; only then would "a new radical content" begin "to transform the thematic concerns of the old debate."[26] Whatever the potentially "feminist" breakthroughs of *les précieuses,* of exceptional women like Mme de Sévigné, of a Cartesian feminist like Poullain de la Barre, of a Mme Riccoboni or Tencin—or even of a Diderot—"woman" in their time was not *the* discursive issue of intellectual and political debate as she had been at the threshold of the Renaissance and would be again at the threshold of modernity.

There was not, in fact, another discursive explosion of comparable proportions precisely on the topic of woman until the middle of the nineteenth century in France. The first traces of activist feminism per se accompanied the French Revolution, but it was not until the Saint-Simoniens (1829–1834) built up a cult around woman that there arose a discursivity on woman equal in its obsession to that of the fourteenth and fifteenth centuries. And, once again, it was largely through the efforts of one woman that words were set in motion: Flora Tristan began what is sometimes called modern, existential feminism, and from that point forward women were to become increasingly active in national, intellectual, and political life. The period from 1800 to 1848 produced as many women writers as had the entire eighteenth century; and the "women of '48," the "socialists of 1880," and so on began a tradition of feminism in France concerned primarily with the problem of how to provide women with the status of subjects in history.[27]

Can it be that this new phase in women's discursive activity in the nineteenth century bears no relationship to the localization by philosophers of the second major epistemological break in the history of the West? That is, could it be that the "two major transitions in Western thought" might be directly linked to the subject (of) woman? Could not,

---

26. Kelly, "Early Feminist Theory," p. 6.

27. In England (but for Mary Wollstonecraft's *Vindication of the Rights of Women* [1792]), it was during approximately the same period (1840–1920) that women were the most discursively present. See, for example, Rogers's *The Troublesome Helpmate* (pp. 189–225) on the journalistic wars of the late nineteenth century. See also, on the growth of the women's movement and socialism, the Introduction to Ann Snitow, Christine Stansell, and Sharon Thompson, eds., *Powers of Desire* (New York: Monthly Review Press, 1983), esp. pp. 13–21. Jacques Derrida, insisting that there are continuities between the women's movements of the nineteenth and twentieth centuries, has asked "whether a program, or locus of begetting, was not already in place in the nineteenth century for all those configurations to which the feminist struggle of the second half of the twentieth century was to commit itself and then to develop." (See Jacques Derrida and Christie V. McDonald, "Choreographies," *Diacritics* 12 [Summer 1982]: 67.)

for example, the great Utopian theories of the nineteenth century be a kind of ultimate effort to do without *the* Other? Such major conceptual changes as the breakdown of the sign, the questioning of the Subject and his quest for the Object, could only come about in a culture once again radically changing its conception of conceptualization: the loss of *the* Quest, the disappearance of *the* Object.

All of this remains to be documented, of course. The proponents of such a system, however, might perceive "feminism" not simply as being the "symptom" or "result" of a contemporary crisis in legitimation and meaning, but indeed as providing the *internal coherence* of history itself. Most important, the causal links in this system of transitions would not be male images of women throughout history, but *the history of women's discursivity*. That history would have to take as its starting point the rather startling observation that feminism is the only -ism of all the -isms invented throughout Western history which allows for the fact that women not only speak but have something *to say*.[28]

Recognizing that women speak at all has always been an ambiguous parenthesis in Western systems of thought right up through the twentieth century. A contemporary example is this now rather infamous observation by Lévi-Strauss: "Of course, it may be disturbing to some to have women conceived as mere parts of a meaningful system. However, one should keep in mind that the processes by which phonemes and words have lost—even though in an illusory manner—their character of value, to become reduced to pure signs, will never lead to the same results in matters concerning women. For words do not speak, while women do; as producers of signs, women can never be reduced to the status of symbols or tokens."[29] Lévi-Strauss will, of course, forget his rapidly inserted (and rather embarrassing) observation in order to allow for operations of the system whose rich contributions to the human sciences have been nevertheless indispensable. Examples could be multiplied.

Let us follow this line of reasoning a bit further.

The responses of men to a woman-speaking-with-knowledge-and-authority is familiar enough in the realm of the private and is being increasingly documented in the realm of the public. It would seem that the sound of a woman's authoritative voice can have only two effects on male

28. See Hélène Cixous, "Le sexe ou la tête," *Cahiers du GRIF* 13 (October 1976), for a discussion of this opposition—much stronger in French—between *parler* and *dire*. Women have always spoken ("too much," say the Masters), but they never have anything *to say*.
29. Claude Lévi-Strauss, *Structural Anthropology*, trans. Claire Jacobson and Brooke Grundgest Schoepf (London: Basic Books, 1963), p. 61.

desire: a deadly or sexually electrifying one.[30] As Sarah Kofman and others have shown, in either case (the phallic shrew versus the S&M mistress), women's discourse is always perceived as unclean, transitory, of no ultimate import, *impropre*.[31] For a feminist sensitive to this question, it soon becomes evident that Man's response in both private and public to a woman who *knows* (anything) has most consistently been one of paranoia.

Male paranoia involves, fundamentally, the fear of the loss either of all boundaries or of those boundaries becoming too painfully constrictive. And this encounter with boundaries is almost always described by men as an encounter with what is called "God"—that being who has no boundaries. The case of President Schreber, for instance, is not only a classical example of male paranoia, but can also serve here as a perfect representation of the crisis of knowledge intrinsic to modernity. In this, one of Freud's most famous cases, Schreber (also) believed that the world was coming to an end: "Schreber became convinced of the imminence of a great catastrophe, of the end of the world."[32] He alone could restore it to its lost state of bliss (*Seligkeit*—both *jouissance* and death), but only by transforming himself into a "woman." Therefore, "Schreber inverses the phallocentric circuit in order to place himself in the region (space) of 'receptivity' ";[33] or, rather, he must become totally self-sufficient—he must become his own mother and father, totally self-productive: "when I speak of my duty to go deeper into voluptuous pleasures, I never mean by that sexual desires towards other human beings (women) and even less sexual commerce, but I imagine myself man and woman in one person in the process of making love to myself . . . but that has nothing to do with the idea of masturbation."[34] This ultimate denial of sexual difference is attributed by Freud to Schreber's (repressed) passive homosexuality—his desire to be God's wife. It might also be linked to the *necessity* of his becoming God's son (Christ the Savior)—that ultimately feminine fig-

30. This has been amply documented, for example, in feminist studies of erotic literature. See, for example, Anne-Marie Dardigna, *Les châteaux d'éros*.

31. Lecture by Sarah Kofman, Reid Hall, Paris, France, May 28, 1980; published as part of *L'énigme de la femme dans les textes de Freud* (Paris: Galilée, 1980). An interesting recent variation on this process is the curious idealization followed by rapid dismissal of feminist theory by male academics in the United States.

32. Sigmund Freud, "Psychoanalytic Notes on an Autobiographical Account of a Case of Paranoia," in vol. 12 of *The Complete Psychological Works*, p. 68.

33. Alain Cohen, "Proust and the President Schreber," in "Graphesis," *Yale French Studies* 52 (1975): 201.

34. Ibid., p. 202. In another vein, Susan Suleiman has diagnosed the contemporary "self-engendered text" as a complex manifestation of male paranoia in "Reading Robbe-Grillet: Sadism and Text in *Projet pour une révolution à New York*," *Romanic Review* 68:1 (January 1977): 43–62.

ure.[35] That is, the desire to be both woman and spirit (both matter and form, self-created—an automaton?) may be the only way to avoid becoming the *object* of the *Other's* (female's) desire; it allows the complete abandonment of object-love, an existence in-between, in a perpetual state of "passion."

If we were to adhere to the causal system outlined above, is it not possible that the periodic coming to the surface of male homosexuality (through the savior of Christ?)[36] and/or the sudden explosion of new theoretical systems (through a new mastery of the unnameable when not its fetishization?)[37] could be directly linked to the presence of the Woman's word—whether in the European transition from the Middle Ages to the Renaissance or, more visibly, in the nineteenth and twentieth centuries?[38]

Limiting ourselves here only to the epistemological crisis of the late nineteenth century, and whether or not one is tempted by these various chains of causality—local crises, internationalization, capitalism, scientific progress, feminism—it is clear that the master discourses in the West are increasingly perceived as no longer adequate for explaining the world: words and things no longer coincide, and all identities have been thrown into question.

Freud was one of the first to recognize this new world out of joint. If we turn to his paper on the unconscious, we find that there it is schizophrenia (rather than paranoia) that has the most to do with separation of words and things: "the predominance of what has to do with words over what has to do with things"[39]—just as in dream-work. In his late paper on "Words and Things," Freud follows up on his work on schizophrenia and aphasia (1891) by showing that the breakdown in the link between word-presentations and thing-presentations is a breakdown in the symbolic function, a form of " 'agnostic' disturbance."[40] What is involved is the breakdown in the metaphorical function (condensation) between the two

35. See Cohen on Schreber's relationship with his father. On Christ as a female figure, see Luce Irigaray, *Amante marine* (Paris: Editions de Minuit, 1980).

36. Even Nietzsche saves Christ.

37. We know from Freud that the desire to theorize may be seen as a primary mechanism of paranoia: Freud, "Preface to Reik's 'Ritual and Psychoanalytic Studies,'" *The Complete Psychological Works*, vol. 17, p. 261.

38. Freud remarks in passing in his study of Schreber, "The strikingly prominent features in the causation of paranoia, especially among males, are social humiliations and slights." (*The Complete Psychological Works*, vol. 12, p. 60.) It is difficult here not to think of how men have historically perceived and described feminists and their social interactions with men.

39. Freud, "Assessment of the Unconscious," *The Complete Psychological Works*, vol. 14, p. 200.

40. Ibid., pp. 214–15.

and a resultant emphatic repetition of isolated operants: acoustic, tactile, written, etc. This crisis in figurability will retain his interest throughout his later works, especially those concerning the function of the sacred. It is perhaps no accident, then, that even our most contemporary anti-Freudian analyses retain the word "schizophrenia" to describe the libidinal economy of contemporary Western culture.[41]

Whatever word one uses to describe the breakdown of the master discourses, it is clearly a question of a breakdown in the symbolic function, an inability of words to give form to the world—a crisis in the function of the *techne*. Whether or not one wants to attribute this "agnosis" to a precise event or historical situation, the fact remains that the war between *Res* (God and thing) and *Verba* (His son and word) has increasingly become a violent battle among jealous gods over the powers of pro-creation; over that space which has begun to threaten all forms of authorship (paternity). Is this only the logical end point of those master discourses? An exploration of the space forming them (connoted as feminine)? Or is it more visibly linked to a certain sexual etiology? Might it not be that the inscription of the "feminine," as essential to nineteenth- and twentieth-century accounts of the world, is a way of combating (or socializing) male paranoia as it inscribes itself within the crisis of monotheism—a kind of response, this time, to the demise of Christian discourse rather than its expansion?

In any case, what fiction has always done—the incorporation and rejection of that space as grounds for figurability—new theoretical discourses, with rapidly increasing frequency, have also been doing. Seeing themselves as no longer isolated in a system of loans and debts to former master truths, these new discourses in formation have foregrounded a *physis*, a space no longer passive but both active and passive, undulating, folded over upon itself, permeable: the self-contained space of eroticism.

If this space is maternal—and I think it is (if only for the male body and imagination)—what can be the feminist relationship to this desperate search through the maternal body characterizing our modernity? It is hard to say, for feminism itself, as Julia Kristeva has pointed out, has been until very recently primarily about time, not space.[42] For, again, feminism is a product of as well as a reaction against the humanist and Enlightenment thought rejected by the newborn discourses of the nineteenth century. What's more, feminism may be seen as the final secularization of the West.

41. Gilles Deleuze and Félix Guattari, *Anti-Oedipus: Capitalism and Schizophrenia*, trans. Robert Hurley, Mark Seem, and Helen R. Lare (New York: Viking, 1977).
42. See Kristeva, "Women's Time."

Contemporary thought in France, taking on the problematics of modernity, is, on the contrary, concerned almost wholly with somehow reintegrating the sacred into the Western symbolic system before it collapses.

What would have happened, then, if Eurydice had thrown herself defiantly in front of Orpheus—loudly refusing to follow obediently behind him toward the light at the end of the cavern? On the other hand, what might happen if women join together with the male philosophers to think the new spaces of modernity by imagining Woman as incarnating those spaces? Do they not risk reuniting with the very Law they set out to fight? Clytemnestra and Egysthes may join together to kill Agamemnon, but there will always be an Orestes to revenge the violence done his father. And, of course, there are the furies.

I invoke these highly speculative questions only because it seems to me that the most important theoretical knots encountered by feminist theorists today are not primarily tied to the repetitive riddles of causality but to *modernity itself*—to its truths, its myths, and its fears. For instance, I think that we can agree with Roland Barthes and others that at the forefront of modernity is the battle against those systems of mediation which have (over)determined our history: Money, the Phallus, and the Concept as privileged operators of meaning.[43] To that extent, feminism is certainly *intrinsic* to modernity. It has, however, also been pointed out that those mediators are *metaphors* at the basis of Western culture itself, and therefore at the foundation of Judaic thought, which forms the bedrock of that culture. Any foreclosure or denial of those mediators can therefore be seen to invite a bizarre form of antisemitism.[44] On the other hand, those mediators are, most important, *images,* and, as we have seen, it is the very principle of Judaic law itself eventually to ban all essentially iconic images in its movement toward utopia.[45] To the extent that feminism is primarily a battle against what are perceived as "false images" of women, it is necessarily bound to some of the most complex epistemological and religious contradictions of contemporary Western culture. That is, the feminist gesture is as much a derivative of the law it is fighting as are its Others— and what is at stake at all of our intersections is, precisely, not to lose sight of that fact.

Those texts of modernity attempting to work through the crises in

43. See Barthes, *Sollers écrivain.*
44. Julia Kristeva, "L'antisémitisme aujourd'hui," *Art presse* (January 1979).
45. See the discussion (Chapter 1, above) of Jean Joseph Goux, *Economie et symbolique* and *Les iconoclastes.*

legitimation and figuration outlined here cannot avoid putting "woman" into circulation if they are *seriously* at work. But "woman" according to whom? The connotations obligatorily assigned to her are in the process of being rearranged, displaced—and replaced. Most important, in this process, "woman" becomes women—or, oddly enough, the first person pronoun, used by both men and women. The resultant gynesis has already attracted the attention of French and American feminists attempting to define a female specificity. My questions obviously differ from that project. For it is, in a sense, impossible to know what, if anything, these discourses have to do with women—we would have had to have been considered as speaking subjects by those discourses from their beginnings in order to start with such definitions. What is of interest is nothing less really than a new kind of *querelle des femmes:* a strangely new and urgent emphasis on "woman," a willing blindness to the *endoxes* of its history and contemporary contexts; the uses of woman as part of a strategy of radical reading and writing—the urgently explicit and unavoidable attempts of modernity to think the unnameable (God or Woman?) before it thinks "us." Who?

GYNESIS II

INTERFACINGS

A surface regarded as the common boundary of two bodies or faces.

5

The Speaking Subject:
The Positivities of Alienation[1]

> Everyone is the other, and no one is himself. The *"they,"* which
> supplies the answer to the question of *"who"* of everyday *Da-sein*, is the *"nobody"* to whom every *Dasein* has already surren-dered itself in being-among-one-another.
>
> Martin Heidegger, *Sein und Zeit*

The "Other" has been a major preoccupation of French thought for the last fifty years. In the United States, at least until very recently, that term has most often evoked Sartrean phenomenology and the inevitability of intersubjective warfare. But while Americans were busy reading Sartre, intellectuals in France were rereading Heidegger and Nietzsche, becoming obsessed with Mallarmé and the texts of such writers as Georges Bataille and Maurice Blanchot, and requestioning Hegel's mas-ter/slave dialectic as elaborated in Kojève's reading. These rereadings and the theoretical outburst of what is loosely called, in retrospect, "struc-turalist theory" (including Russian Formalism), interlocked unevenly, but progressed together steadily toward a radical redefinition of "alterity" which directly refuted that of Sartre. The phenomenological "Self" and "Other" came to be seen as belonging with all of those Cartesian models of

1. I am aware of how scandalous it is to use these "old words"—"positivities" and "alienation"—to qualify a general philosophical movement intent on exposing and unravel-ing positivism and phenomenological theories of alienation (*Entäusserung* in Hegel). It is not certain whether these two words seem best to qualify a "certain teleology" of contemporary French thought because of an extreme case of *paleonomy* (see Derrida, *Margins of Philosophy;* and Derrida, *Dissemination,* trans. Barbara Johnson [Chicago: University of Chicago Press, 1981], and *Positions,* trans. Alan Bass [Chicago: University of Chicago Press, 1981]) or whether the fact of such a general emphasis could seem obvious only to the feminist reader.

rational and scientific knowledge where "certainty" is located in the ego—as "predator of the Other." And it is this ego, no matter what its sex or ideological position, that came to be seen as responsible for our modern technological nightmare. It is also this ego that the fictions of modernity (Artaud, Joyce, Mallarmé, Beckett come to mind) have been seen as attempting to explode. The result of this recognition has been an accelerating exploration of Man's non-coincidence-with-himself through new and radical theories of alterity.

In its structuralist version, at least in terms of literary theory, this refutation of the humanist self (that is, Man) often took on some of the same forms as American "new criticism": pointing to the illusions of intentionality, psychology, expressivity, and to the fallacy of communication. But, in France, this voiding of the person was more expansive: it was accompanied, most significantly, by a quickening return to Freud through Lacanian psychoanalysis: a new road for exploring Man's seemingly hopeless alienation from his "self." In what seems retrospectively a very short period of time, Man's non-coincidence-with-himself became *positivized.*

The object here is not to review the rich and varied work toward new conceptions of the speaking subject as it has been and still is being pursued in linguistics, semiotics, psychoanalysis, and philsoophy.[2] But it is important to remember, and wonder at, the fact that this complex and far-reaching theoretical dismantling of the knowing and finally imperialistic speaking subject did not reproduce itself in Anglo-American theory, and most especially not in the United States.[3] There, even putting traditional humanist studies aside, from behavioral psychology to performative linguistics, Man's rational control over himself, his language, and his actions is still assumed to be possible—and is still considered desirable.

Psychoanalysis in France took the lead in attempting to redefine and resituate the mechanisms of intersubjectivity—at the symbolic intersections of the Oedipus complex and language. Otherness is always already present in the Same ("person") because it is the subject's entry into the language of the Other that informs "him." The Other is the signifier's treasure; the unconscious is the discourse of the Other—to repeat only two of Lacan's most famous aphorisms. For Lacanian theorists, it is the

2. For a general, historical introduction to this question, especially with regard to philosophy in France, see Descombes, *Modern French Philosophy;* for a more psychoanalytic and linguistic approach, see, for example, Julia Kristeva's early article, "Le sujet en procès," in *Polylogue.*

3. This work has enjoyed much wider acceptance in England than in America, especially in fields outside literary studies, as narrowly defined. Journals such as *Screen* (cinema) and *M/F* (feminist theory) have been in dialogue with this work for some time.

subject's never-completed break away from the holistic space and rhythm of the maternal body into the time and syntax of patriarchal language that brings about the recognition of sexual difference. The fact that, because we speak, the break is never complete, produces the symptoms of what has been increasingly called in the twentieth century, especially through Marxist thought, "alienation." But if that alienation from the self has always existed—because human beings have always been born of woman (at least until recently)—it is only today, Lacanians would argue, that we can understand Man's alienation with the tools of modern linguistics. The subject who speaks is composed of language itself; and, for post-Heideggerian theorists such as Lacan, it is only by listening through the cracks in the language of communication that the presubjective, prelogical, and open spaces of Heidegger's *Dasein* may "come to light." Ultimately, for them, it is only the analyst who can hear exactly how the speaking subject came not to be himself.

According to these writers, since this process of inner division and infinite splitting (*Spaltung*) is "universal" (and will remain so as long as "Man" is born of "Woman" and speaks), real historical progress, to be brought about by rational-subjects-in-history, must be seen as a myth. If Lacan himself did not believe in progress, neither have most of his followers.[4] There is, of course, the remote possibility that the non- or not-yet-subjects who are seen as closest to the presubjective, maternal space (women, according to many analysts) will begin to speak—but then, Lacan might say, that is not language, but rather still only a symptom of language: *lalangue*.[5] The combination of Althusserian Marxist theory with Lacanian psychoanalysis in the 1960s did somewhat reduce this pessimism with regard to Man's progress-in-history; but throughout the various metamorphoses in this particular attempt not to leave history behind completely, any "progress" remained visible only at the level of a very privileged space of language: the "artistic text."

It was, in fact, within this privileged written space that psychoanalysis

---

4. On Lacan on Progress, see, for example, his "Entretien avec des étudiants," Yale University, November 24, 1975, published in *Scilicet*, no. 6/7 (1975): 37. See also, for example, Wladimir Granoff: "Neither Freud nor analysis is able to be weighed with respect to the introduction of changes in society" (*La pensée et le féminin* [Paris: Editions de Minuit, 1976], p. 206); or Eugénie Lemoine-Luccioni in more specific reference to sexual difference as the privileged object of psychoanalytic inquiry: "No sexual revolution will be able to move these dividing lines, not that which passes between man and woman, nor that which divides woman" (*Partage des femmes*, p. 9).

5. I refer to the inevitable male subject and female non-subject in Lacanian theory. On the qualities of *lalangue* in relationship to women, see, for example, Eugénie Lemoine-Luccioni, *Le rêve du cosmonaute* (Paris: Editions du Seuil, 1980), p. 132.

was to meet up with philosophy, however different the paths taken by various "schools" of the latter might have been and in spite of their internal disaccords. In contrast to psychoanalysis, however, philosophy's main speakers will maintain that theories of intersubjectivity, however radical their redefinitions of "subject" and "object" might be, are theoretically and politically inadequate and must be left behind. For example, with Jacques Derrida, the privileged operator beyond the human subject was to be the movements of écriture grating against the larger conceptual, philosophical outline of any given epoch.[6] For Michel Foucault, it was to be discourse within a particular epistemological network of power-sources.[7] For Gilles Deleuze and Félix Guattari, it was to be the machinations of desire (for Lyotard, libido) within any given cultural heritage.[8] All of these philosophical movements were to become violently opposed to the stable, Oedipal, intersubjective assumptions of that Lacanian psychoanalysis which in many ways made them possible.

For example, within the first of these philosophical gestures (Derrida), against the imperial subject-even-with-an-unconscious, it is the less Lacanian, more radical side of Heidegger and the gently theoretical side of Blanchot that sowed most of the seeds for what is now called in France "the ideology of écriture." For Heidegger, the human subject in the modern world has come to be not-himself because he has simply forgotten how to let Being be in language. "Modern Man" must slow down. He is no longer astonished by the quiddity of things: the redness of red, the wordness of a word. The Sartrean position of "existence before [Heidegger's] essence" would be, from this perspective, just one more step in Man's drive for mastery over physis; his forgetfulness of the potentially gentle, poetic union of technē with physis. According to Heidegger, the *object* of Man's perception must be released from its bondage before Man as subject can be liberated. Man must become but a listener and respondent to the speech-thought of *Dasein,* by exercising great care, infinite patience, and wise passivity. For Heidegger and his followers, history has shown that only the poet, at least in our modern world, has managed to do so.[9]

---

6. For an introduction to the force and specificities of the word "écriture," see Gayatri Spivak's introduction to Derrida's *Of Grammatology* (Baltimore: Johns Hopkins University Press, 1976).

7. See, for example, his "The Discourse on Language," an appendix to *The Archeology of Knowledge* (New York: Harper & Row, 1976).

8. For the clearest introduction to Deleuze and Guattari, see Foucault's "Theatrum Philosophicum," *Critique* 282 (1970). See also, for example, Jean-François Lyotard's *Economie libidinale* (Paris: Editions de Minuit, 1974).

9. See, for example, *Sein und Zeit,* translated as *Being and Time* by John Macquarrie and Edward Robinson (New York: Harper & Row, 1962); "Ce qu'est et comment se détermine la

Heidegger's insistence, however, on the necessity of this particular form of "alienation" *only so as to be able,* later, to move toward *Eigentlichkeit*—a re-self-possession—will be deconstructed and rewritten by Derrida through the echo chamber of Maurice Blanchot's readings and writings. For Blanchot, the "subject of writing" can in fact never repossess himself, can never move beyond original self-*estrange*ment: language remains his master. It may seem that the writer controls his words, but it is really he who is controlled, caught, emptied out, and held in passive fascination by words and their shadows: "The work requires of the writer that he lose everything he might construe as his own 'nature,' that he lose all character and that, ceasing to be linked to others and to himself by the decision which makes him an 'I,' he becomes the empty place where the impersonal affirmation emerges."[10] Blanchot adopts Heidegger's ethic of "respon-sion"; his "reader" and "writer" merge. His reader can only listen to language; and his writer can only relinquish his own self-reading to unite with the reader within and through the impersonal consciousness of lan-guage. For him, as for Heidegger, the nonsubject unites with a nonobject (often called "l'absente," an "absent female"), in a continuous fall toward "the identical neutrality of the abyss" (Mallarmé). The "alienation" nega-tivized by the Man of progress has become the "strangeness" positivized by the Writer, and the alternating alterity of reader (as) writer continually re-marks the specificities of écriture.

For Blanchot, therefore, " 'The relationship of another to myself is not a relationship between [two] subjects'."[11] Derrida will begin with this ob-servation and will echo it many times, in many forms, especially in his early work devoted to sketching in detail the spaces of écriture. For him, wher-ever there exists the traditional subject present to himself in relationship to an object, there exists metaphysics and its attendant phallo-logocentric representations.

Citing (Siting? Sighting?) Derrida out of textual "context" is always a risky business for anyone sensitive to what is involved in doing so, and immediately calls for a barrage of parentheses and inverted commas to mark the fragile validity of being sure enough of what Derrida means to quote only parts of what he writes.[12] But here we are on relatively solid

---

physis" in *Questions II* (Paris: Gallimard, 1968), pp. 165–276; and *Die Frage nach der Technik,* translated as "The Question concerning Technology" in *"The Question concerning Technology" and Other Essays*.

10. Maurice Blanchot, *The Space of Literature,* pp. 25, 55; see also Paul de Man, "Impersonal-ity in Blanchot," in *Blindness and Insight.*

11. Blanchot, *L'entretien infini* (Paris: Gallimard, 1969), p. 99.

12. A great many American critics have expressed their impatience with the Derridean

ground. For of all Derrida's inter-positions, the redefinition of alterity through a collapsing of the metaphysical categories of the Same and the Other (including those of psychoanalysis where the Other is simply ingested by the Same) and the battle with the Father-Author are his oldest, most consistent and explicit topics.

In what is perhaps Derrida's longest and most complex meditation on alterity, "Violence and Metaphysics: An Essay on the Thought of Emmanuel Levinas,"[13] Derrida emphasizes the ways in which Levinas's thought sketches a radically new kind of ethical relationship, a nonviolent form of alterity which could begin to undo the hold transcendence and metaphysics maintain on us.[14] According to Derrida, Heidegger did not go far enough in rethinking the "Other," for, as Derrida-with-Levinas continue to write, Heidegger ultimately remained at the interior of the Greek and Platonic tradition ruled by vision and the metaphor of light.[15] That is, he continued to assume "the spatial pair inside-outside (but is this, in all its aspects, a *spatial* pair?) which gives life to the opposition of subject and object."[16] For Derrida, ontology, along with phenomenology, through a lack of respect for the Other (their own category), through their refusal to radically rethink alterity, remain philosophies of Western violence.[17] Writing with Levinas, Derrida shows how the entire history of the concept of *autrui* (which, he reminds us, may not even be a concept, that is, may not be Greek),[18] must, to begin with, be re-thought at the crossroads of the Greek (Same and Other) and the Jew (infinitely Other).

Ecriture is where the potentialities of this new nonviolent alterity have been traced by Derrida. It is there, for example, that there is no "Father-Author" to kill: "The specificity of writing would thus be intimately bound to the absence of the Father."[19] Writing, as écriture, is an orphan, written by No-One. In what is now one of his best-known formulations, he explains that there is no such thing as a sovereign subject of écriture:

---

process. It is that very resistance to taking the time necessary for understanding, the resistance to being patient enough to wait for meaning, that Derrida shows to be at the core of our dominant ways of knowing in the West.

13. Derrida, *Writing and Difference*, p. 79 and passim.

14. Ibid., p. 83. Not even the most important texts of Levinas can be adequately addressed in this study. The reader might want to refer to the following essay, written from a perspective different from mine: Catherine Chalier, *Figures du féminin: Lecture d'Emmanuel Levinas* (Paris: La Nuit Surveillée, 1982).

15. Also see Luce Irigaray on this question in *Speculum*, especially the last section.

16. Derrida, *Writing and Difference*, p. 88.

17. Ibid., p. 91.

18. Ibid., esp. pp. 104–105.

19. Derrida, *Dissemination*, p. 77.

the classical notion of the author is just that—classical—and must be deconstructed if alterity is to be truly reinvented. The subject of écriture would thus be seen as but "a *system* of relations between strata: the Mystic Pad, the psyche, society, the world," for "within that scene, on that stage, the punctual simplicity of the classical subject is not to be found."[20] Derrida will show, throughout all of his readings-with-others, that any one writing subject in any text is indeed unfindable and most especially he himself is impossible to "pin down." For Derrida, there are always in any text at least "two texts, two hands, two visions, two ways of listening. Together simultaneously and separately."[21] Writing is alterity in language, and conceived in this way, it offers ethical possibilities as yet undreamt of in the West.

Derrida does not, of course, insist only upon Blanchot, Heidegger, and Levinas. Excavating Husserl's "absolute subjectivity," for example, he shows how it escapes Husserl's own hands because "there is no constituting subjectivity. The very concept of constitution itself must be deconstructed."[22] Wandering through Bataille's proposals for a new kind of sovereignty, Derrida gently pushes the proposals out from under the umbrella of Hegelian mastery where Bataille's sovereign sometimes remains: "For sovereignty has no identity, is not *self, for itself, toward itself, near itself.*"[23] In his article, "Signature, Event, Context," Derrida shows how assumptions about writing, context, author, source, intention, and communication, as articulated by J. L. Austin's performative linguistics, are but a series of metaphysical clichés and commonplaces. When John Searle (the son) comes to Austin's (the father's) defense, Derrida playfully, indeed gleefully, metamorphoses "Searle" into an "anonymous society": SARL (*Société anonyme à responsabilité limitée*). Even a signature is no guarantee of authenticity. For Derrida, the proper, that is, paternal name itself is one of the first things to become totally improper, improbable, and strangely Other.[24]

---

20. Derrida, *Writing and Difference*, pp. 226–27. In a later interview with Jean-Louis Houdebine and Guy Scarpetta, published in *Positions*, Derrida reminds us that he is not saying that there is *no* subject of writing (or no subject), but that "it is solely necessary to reconsider the problem of the effect of subjectivity such as it is produced by the structure of the text" (p. 88).

21. Derrida, *Margins of Philosophy*, p. 65.

22. Derrida, *Speech and Phenomena, and Other Essays on Husserl's Theory of Signs*, trans. David B. Allison (Evanston, Ill.: Northwestern University Press, 1973), p. 85, n. 9.

23. Derrida, *Writing and Difference*, p. 265.

24. See Derrida's "Signature, Event, Context" in *Margins of Philosophy*; John R. Searle's reply, "Reiterating the Differences," *Glyph* I (1977); and Derrida, "Limited Inc.," *Glyph* II (also published separately [Baltimore: Johns Hopkins, 1977]).

Contemporary articulations of the demise of the Cartesian subject in France—whether through Lacan's "Other," Derrida's "écriture," Foucault's "discourse," or Deleuze and Guattari's "machines"—all seem to come back, by various routes, to a widespread fascination with something "neuter." The concept has its most immediate roots in Nietzsche and Heidegger. The latter, in particular, evoked the "neuter" by emphasizing that the German word *man* signifies both "oneness" and "theyness," within a consistent movement toward valorizing the latter semantic layer. The famous Heideggerian "they" is an(other) anonymous society of "ones" to which any "I" must inevitably yield his existence.

What is interesting, for our purposes here, about the insistent use of the term "neuter" by many of the writers mentioned thus far is its wide association with modernity. Tzvetan Todorov, for example, in discussing the work of Blanchot and Barthes, explains the frequent and explicit use of the term "neuter" by both writers as an indication of their desire to go beyond the subject-object dyad; that is, as an indication of a desire intrinsic to modernity. Todorov concludes that "the unity, as well as the modernity, of these two contemporary approaches to literature lies, I suggest, in the fact that they lead us to view the other as essentially different from the self, as the other in itself—in that they open the way for an era of generalized alterity and exteriorization." This era of generalized alterity involves what Todorov sees as an "absence of self and presence of 'otherness'"; he does not feel this major trend in contemporary thought to be accidental, either, for "perhaps it is through literature that one can read most clearly the characteristics of our time."[25]

Indeed, it does seem that the concept of neuter—or anonymity as it is sometimes called—has captured the imagination of the most interesting contemporary (male) writers thinking about modernity in France. Some of them use the term "neuter" explicitly; others circle around it and even try to avoid it. For Blanchot, this "neuter" designates very specifically the strange alterity of writing. Françoise Collin has explained Blanchot's use of the term with reference to "difference"—a loaded word in this context, one to which we shall return shortly: "The neuter [*Le neutre*] is difference and literature as difference is the language of the Neuter or neuter language. Difference is not diversity inscribed in the general but the repetition and displacement of the Same, that is, that which separates from while resembling itself, without resemblance implying the presence of an

---

25. Todorov, "Reflections on Literature in Contemporary France," p. 531. Readers will be interested in an article that appears in the same issue: Maurice Natanson, "Phenomenology, Anonymity, and Alienation," pp. 533–46.

original to which its copy would refer."[26] For Barthes, this neuter is also "the language of writing" as well as what he calls (in reference to "himself") the modern "vacancy of the 'self'—a self which, if it has not been entirely annihilated, can at least no longer be clearly located." For him, the neuter is neither active (male) nor passive (female); it is rather an "amoral oscillation," the contrary of an opposition. Neuter writing would be what he calls white writing, exempt from the exhibitionism of literary theatre—indeed, exempt from the intimidations of mastery of any kind.[27]

Derrida also writes of the neuter. Although he insistently warns against the dangers of "neutralization" as intrinsic to the *Aufhebung* of metaphysics, he does endorse a certain neutral process "beyond" neutralization: the procedure of "neither . . . nor," a lack of position, an uneven, unlocalizable oscillation. Reading Blanchot or Bataille against "themselves," he shows that their neuter is not traditionally neutral. While reminding us that the "undecidable" (neither . . . nor) is only the first and tenuous phase of a larger process, he cautions that this first neuter phase may also be as interminable as are the texts of metaphysics.[28]

For those philosophers more concerned with the neuter anonymity of the "world" than of the "text," the movement toward evacuating personal pronouns, toward the *on dit,* the "one says" of modernity, remains just as strong. "Neuter" could just as accurately characterize the pansexual body caught up in the modern discursive power networks described by a Foucault as the equally neuter "singularities" dreamt by a Deleuze and Guattari. For both Deleuze and Guattari, "singularity"—not to be confused with individualism—is "pre-individual, non-personal, a-conceptual. It is completely indifferent to the individual and to the collective, to the personal and to the impersonal, to the particular and to the general—and to their opposition. It is *neuter*."[29] For Deleuze, the "splendor" of the anonymous pronoun "One,"[30] the "neuter singularity" of modernity, is best apprehended through the philosophy of paradox. For him, only the paradox can move us into pure "becoming" beyond the fixed sexual identities of intersubjectivity, of subject and object. And finally he exemplifies this process through the image of "the little girl," and most especially, in a

26. Françoise Collin, *Maurice Blanchot et la question de l'écriture* (Paris: Gallimard, 1971), p. 220.

27. Roland Barthes, *Roland Barthes* (Paris: Editions du Seuil, 1975), pp. 135–36.

28. See, in particular, *Positions* (esp. pp. 41–44); *Dissemination* (esp. note on p. 207); and the end of "From Restricted to General Economy . . ." in *Writing and Difference,* esp. pp. 273–77.

29. Gilles Deleuze, *Logique du sens* (Paris: Editions de Minuit, 1969), p. 67.

30. Gilles Deleuze, *Différence et répétition* (Paris: Presses Universitaires, 1968), p. 4.

return to the text from the world, through the wanderings of Lewis Carroll's Alice: "All of these reversals, such as they appear through infinite identity, have the same consequence: the contesting of the personal identity of Alice, the loss of the proper name [. . .] The paradox is first of all that which destroys good sense as the unique sense, but afterward that which destroys common sense as the assignation of fixed identities."[31]

At some point, the feminist reader, while optimistically following the retreat of the all-too-human subject in these writers, may begin to wonder, nonetheless, about gender; or, rather, about the lack thereof throughout this splendid and neuter anonymity of both the text and the world. For parallel to the valorization of a neuter-in-language-without-subject, there has been a regenderization of the space where alterity is to be re-explored in language. The assurance of any given subject's sexual identity may have become the wrong question for modernity, but there seems to be no question for these writers that the space of alterity to be explored always already must connote the female.

The feminist philosopher Michelle Le Doeff has suggested that the contemporary obsession with *autruisme,* "Other-ism," may be linked to that of liberal *altruism* as the historical lot of women: "A masculine for himself, a feminine completely for the other."[32] This explanation is certainly plausible, especially given what Le Doeff points out to be the ideology of altruism common to many of the eighteenth- and even nineteenth-century texts that serve as foundations for deconstructions and archaeologies.

But Julia Kristeva, among others, has suggested a more radical connection. Beyond Freudian and Lacanian recognitions that the first significant Other is always the mother (to be replaced by "other women" in interminable succession for the male), Kristeva has repeatedly pointed out that the Other is always, in fact, the "other sex": "The difference between 'I' and 'you' turns out to be coextensive with the *sexual difference,* and every perturbation of the allocutionary polarity brings about or follows interferences between the two sexes. It is one way to show that the sexual difference is correlative to differences between discursive instances: that the 'other' is the 'other sex'."[33] The space "outside of" the conscious subject has always connoted the feminine in the history of Western thought—and any movement into alterity is a movement into that female

---

31. Deleuze, *Logique du sens,* pp. 11–12.

32. Le Doeff, *L'imaginaire philosophique,* p. 202.

33. Julia Kristeva, *La révolution du langage poétique,* p. 326. All further page references in text.

space; any attempt to give a place to that alterity within discourse involves a putting into discourse of "woman." If an autonomous "I" or "he" can no longer exist, then only an anonymous "she" can be seen to—as Heidegger might say—*ex-sist:* "he is a subject without genital jouissance, she is genitality and disseminated power without subject" (Kristeva, p. 488).

These new kinds of explorations into female alterity operate in both theory and fiction; indeed, it is those explorations that have so confused the boundaries between the two. Not only are the abstract spaces of alterity in contemporary thought gendered female (Freud-Lacan's "unconscious," Derrida's "écriture," Deleuze's "machines," Foucault's "madness"), but so too are the main characters of its theoretical fictions. Evidence for this ranges from the privileging by psychoanalysis of the focus on female hysterics to the emphasis by contemporary philosophy on those bodies which have escaped Western society's definition of "the normal male": the insane, the criminal, the male homosexual. In modern "fiction," the expanse of female alterity also extends from spaces, through pronouns, to characters. But it is at the actantial level, in fact—particularly when the convention of characters is only barely retained—that the movement back and forth among these levels is clearest. As Kristeva puts it, "The feminine other appears clearly in the feminine characters, that is, when, put to death as addressee, 'you' becomes a fictional third person: 'she'" (Kristeva, p. 327). "She" can be a psychologized woman but also, at the same time, the very mechanism, the very substance of the male writer's death as subject.

No one, for example, has described this process, the correspondence between the female qualities of alterity and the "female" of character, so explicitly as has Michel Leiris. Always writing at the very edges of traditional narrative, he addresses himself to a woman, but "only because she is absent"; "she" is not in any way "an object," but rather the "melancholic substance" of that which is missing for "him": that which forces him to desire, that is, to write. The function of writing is, for him, to "fill a void or at least to situate, with respect to the most lucid part of ourselves, the place where gapes this incommensurable abyss."[34] And that place, the emptiness of that abyss in his self, is female.

It is no accident, then, given the extent to which modernity privileges these explorations of alterity, that the *M(other)* has become a major obsession of contemporary French thought.[35] Returning to Lacan, Kristeva

34. Michel Leiris, *L'âge d'homme* (Paris: Gallimard [Folio], 1939), pp. 156–57.
35. As a parenthesis. It would appear that the unique Female-Other-As-Mother—to the exclusion of women-subjects who are not mothers (for they are "men")—is as tenacious in contemporary theory as ever. I was surprised to come across the following statement by

continues her discussion on the gender of the Other: "Moreover, the first 'other' with whom 'I'—the son—initiate a genuine dialogue is the mother. Privileged addressee, the mother is above all the other sex; she is therefore doubly justified in constituting this pole of alterity through which the allocution constitutes itself, and which fiction is going to usurp, absorb, and dissolve" (Kristeva, p. 326). And not only fiction. For Lacan and psychoanalysis, the mother is constitutive of the subject; for Derrida, she is the only possible *survivante,* the "survivor" as "more than alive," of any écriture; for Deleuze, it is the rejection of the mother that is the founding fantasy of the West.[36] For all of these writers, the mother must be rediscovered, differently, if we are to move beyond the repetitive dilemmas of our Oedipal, Western culture. It would seem, in fact, to be the mother who has the language, the maternal tongue, necessary for all of these writers in modernity; or at least that language which according to Lacan escapes the self, the Cartesian ego—the *lalangue* of literature. And here we come full circle, for, as Georg Groddeck once pointed out, the mother's language is that of the neuter *ça,* the "it," the "id" of the unconscious—the language beyond the always already determined gender of the self.[37]

In 1970, the famous case of Louis Wolfson, *Le schizo et les langues,* was published in France (Deleuze wrote the introduction).[38] Wolfson's mother's presence and voice caused him so much anguish, irritated him so deeply, that "everything belonging to her linguistic register"[39]—English to begin with—became unbearable to him. Wolfson learned four foreign languages and transcoded them into an elaborate secret language of his own, cutting up his maternal tongue in a mysterious and sophisticated way, so as to avoid having to speak or hear this "maternal tongue" directly, from anyone. His remarkable textual account of the process was heralded

---

Michel Serres in an interview he gave to *Marie-Claire* concerning his book, *Le parasite:* "For me, there are only two sexes . . . and they are not the man and the woman. I believe that the two fundamental sexes are the mother and the others. The man and the woman, that's completely superficial. There is the mother—those women who were mothers and those who will become mothers—and all the others." *Marie-Claire* (May 1981): 327–32.

36. Lacan's mother is everywhere; Derrida's *survivante* is especially present in *Glas* (Paris: Galilée, 1974); Deleuze's "oral mother" is presented at length in *Présentation de Sacher-Masoch* (Paris: Editions de Minuit, 1967).

37. See, for example, Groddeck's *Le livre du ça,* trans. L. Jumel (Paris: Gallimard, 1978). Derrida will consciously feminize the neuter *ça* (it) in a different way in *Glas:* there, the *ça* will become *sa,* the feminine possessive, as well as the abbreviation for "signifier."

38. Louis Wolfson, *Le schizo et les langues* (Paris: Gallimard, 1970).

39. The expression is Josué Harari's in "Critical Factions/Critical Fictions," in *Textual Strategies,* ed. Josué Harari (Ithaca: Cornell University Press, 1979), pp. 54–56.

in France as exemplary of modernity's rejection of the Cartesian subject, the sign, and representation. Here were the mechanisms of modern fiction writing laid bare.

The fact that it was a maternal voice (of a "guilty mother") at the basis of this "ear fear" (Nietzsche) does not retain the attention of any of the writers who commented on Wolfson's text. But it must retain the attention of the feminist critic who is sensitive to the positivities of alienation at which we have been looking. For, to the extent that all fiction is a cutting up of the maternal tongue, is written in "foreign languages," might not literature, at least historically, have been one of men's few socialized responses to the unbearable mother's tongue?[40] Could that be one of the reasons why contemporary theoretical explorations of necessarily maternal, female "Otherness" so closely resemble fictions, just as contemporary fictions so often resemble theory? Could it possibly be that the new philosophically valorized "neuter anonymity" of the text or world—a valorization of singularities beyond sexual difference—is but a new attempt to escape the rising voices of women? (The mysterious Heideggerian "they" or the unlocalizable Deleuzian "One," in their conspiracies against the Cartesian ego, do sound strangely paranoid.) And perhaps most important, is that which comes before or after the human subject of the same "substance" for the woman writer as for the male writer?

Such questions, especially those concerning what women's relationship to the alterities of modernity is or might be, may be unanswerable for some time to come. One woman writer, Clarice Lispector, has at least attempted to begin asking these difficult questions. In her *La passion de G.H.*, the "I," through confrontations with what is "before the human," seems indeed to have been radically altered, to have glimpsed something resembling the new space the men have been exploring: "What my whole being ignored—that was the neuter. And the neuter was that life which I had previously called nothingness. The neuter was hell."[41]

---

40. The reader may be interested in Geoffrey H. Hartman's theory, in response to Derrida, of "great art" as an "ear wound": see *Saving the Text* (Baltimore: Johns Hopkins University Press, 1981). The question raised here is obviously not without relation to the discussion of male paranoia in Chapter 4 (above).

41. Clarice Lispector, *La passion de G.H.* (Paris: des Femmes, 1978), p. 97.

6

Thinking the Unrepresentable: The Displacement of Difference

> All these signs can be ascribed to a generalized anti-Hegelianism: difference and repetition have taken the place of the identical and of the negative of identity and of contradiction.
>
> Gilles Deleuze, *Différence et répétition*

"Representation" is one of those words that have assumed such currency in France since the early 1960s that it has now become difficult to talk about it as if it could still mean anything. Or, rather, it has become so clear what the word "representation" means that we can no longer innocently write the expression "to talk about something." For example, to the extent that I am here *representing* something called "contemporary French thought," I am complicitous with a system of presenting the world that is as old as Plato. I assume the absence of "contemporary French thought" so as better to render it present again, now, under the control of a "subject who is supposed to know." I re-present it, I copy it, attempting to find an invariant meaning that can then be placed before my reader for acceptance or rejection. If I did not do so, my only task would be to write one sentence: Please just read all the originals for yourselves.

The process of representation, the sorting out of identity and difference, is the process of analysis: naming, controlling, remembering, understanding. A process so seemingly natural to us as to be beyond question. Yet, in France it has been diagnosed as being at the very roots of our Western drive to know all, and shown to be inseparable from the imperial speaking subject whose demise we touched upon in the last chapter; it has been denounced as complicitous with a violence as old as Western history itself.[1]

Representation is the condition that confirms the possibility of an imitation (mimesis) based on the dichotomy of presence and absence and, more generally, on the dichotomies of dialectical thinking (negativity). Representation, mimesis, and the dialectic are inseparable; they designate together a way of thinking as old as the West, a way of thinking which French thought, through German philosophy, has been attempting to rethink since the turn of the century. Between 1930 and 1960, the dialectic and its modes of representation, as elaborated by the neo-Hegelians and redefined by the phenomenologists, were the major focus of French intellectuals and represented a major hope for reconstructing the world. Maurice Merleau-Ponty, for example, was to write in 1946 that the dialectical integration of the irrational into a larger and more expansive rationality was the task of the twentieth century.[2] An understanding of negativity—either as represented by the "Idealist" or as redefined by the "Marxist"—promised to make possible a general science of contradiction—a science capable of comprehending and ultimately changing a henceforth worldwide battle between masters and slaves.

But there soon surfaced in France a movement toward redefining the functions of mediation elaborated by traditional Hegelians and Marxists, as well as a quickening sense of urgency about looking again at the relationship between those two systems of thought. That movement, which came into its full maturity after 1968, still pursues its quest for a nondialectical, nonrepresentational, nonmimetic mode of conceptuality. The reasons for this turnabout in French intellectual history are doubtless complex, perhaps unknowable. But the radical change cannot be simply attributed to "Parisian fashion," as so often happens in American intellectual circles. Like the student uprisings in the late 1960s and early 1970s, this outburst of energy seemed to manifest itself in several countries, under several banners. Broad conditions and processes such as the intelligentsia's

1. It is not my project in this book to pursue a philosophical investigation into the intricacies of representation. It is helpful to remember, however, that in German philosophy, "representation" is generally designated by three related words: *Darstellung* in the sense of exposition or *mise en scène; Vorstellung* as the process of bringing or placing something before oneself to see and make one's own; *Repräsentation* as the notion that here is something "inside" a given subject's head—the idea as image—which merely needs to be expressed on the "outside," voiced, to become real. All of these imply the initial absence of what is being made present again. *Vorstellung,* in particular, designates the possibility of bringing back what is past, recovering it, copying it, imitating it.

2. Maurice Merleau-Ponty, *Sense and Non-Sense,* trans. Hubert L. Dreyfus and Patricia Allen Dreyfus (Evanston, Ill.: Northwestern University Press, 1964), p. 63.

rediscovery of the Soviet Gulags and their emphasis, in aftershock, on the 1930s (the Moscow Trials, Hitler-Stalin Pact, etc.); the Cultural Revolution in China, the louder voices of the Third World, and general Western economic abundance; as well as more local events such as the deceptions of the Algerian War, Sartre's break with the Communist Party, the late discovery in France of the Frankfurt School, and 1968 are often cited as reasons. Whatever the reasons, a redefinition of the dialectic as inherent to theories of representation came to be seen as a major priority in a world where reversing the positive and negative poles of any given system seemed to have no effect on that system's economy of violence. The tone of arguments over who was or was not "dialectical enough" changed. What Walter Benjamin called the "Angel of History" had begun to infiltrate the ranks of the "Revolutionary Intellectual" within the storm of twentieth-century intellectual inquiry.[3]

In France, Lacanian psychoanalysis was one of the first of these major schools of thought to meet up with the dialectic as a system of mediation. Lacan's was one of the first new systems of French thought to move into a spatial logic different from that both of history and of the knowing-subject-in history. In an intensive dialogue with Hegel, mediated by Kojève, he both retained and dismissed various elements of that "system of contradictions" leading to "absolute knowledge." For example, he kept, following Freud, a network of tripartite topologies (demand, desire, and need; real, imaginary, and symbolic; etc.) within an emphasis on the mechanisms of intersubjectivity. He also retained a dialectic of presence and absence now based in sexuality; for Lacan, the difference of contradiction is the difference between having or being the phallus, between having or being the signifier for another signifier: the logic of castration. To do away with the possibility of mediating presence and absence is, according to Lacan, nothing less than to do away with the social contract itself. And the Father (the dead father)—or rather the phallus—will be seen as the only mediator possible in patriarchal culture.

Lacan also maintained, within his system of representation, a form of the "inner self" (through an analysis of Hegel's *belle âme*) to be rendered present for the analyst through different series of *negations* (*Verneinung,*

---

3. See Walter Benjamin's captivating description of Klee's "Angelus Novus" in the ninth of his "Theses on the Philosophy of History," *Illuminations,* ed. Hannah Arendt (New York: Schocken, 1969), pp. 257–58. I often think of the radical change in question here as a resurfacing of the unresolved contradictions inherent in the work of Benjamin himself. In fact, a reconsideration of the internal quarrels of the Frankfurt School, in the light of contemporary French thought, is long overdue. Particularly relevant would be a close reading of the Adorno-Benjamin correspondence.

Verleugnung): the name of that "inner self" is the unconscious. But this "inner self" is problematized beyond recognition in Lacan. In fact, it is not "inner" but externalized in the space of signification. Lacan was one of the first to lay bare the complicity between traditional concepts of the self and the psychology of representation—a psychology which found its most welcome home in the United States.[4] The tripartite systems of Hegel and Freud began to separate in Lacan, for the Lacanian subject is not the knowing self but itself an imaginary construct launched by desire and trapped between the real and the symbolic. For Lacan, there is little correspondence between the subject of dialectics, "who knows what he wants," and the Freudian subject, caught in a knot of desires: "In this respect: that desire becomes bound up with the desire of the Other, but that in this loop lies the desire to know."[5]

Lacan retains the Hegelian concept of the *Aufhebung,* but he twists it into a knot in the way that was announced by Freud's famous sentence, "Negation is a way of taking cognizance of what is repressed; indeed it is already a lifting of the repression, though not, of course, an acceptance of what is repressed."[6] Lacan's is a sort of Aufhebung, but one that cannot totally conserve (in) the present. Lacan rescued the dialectic process from the Hegelian dialectical system with its moralistic psychology; as well as from traditional Marxist theory with what he saw as its Feuerbachian heritage[7] and its mechanistic externalization of negativity only into the realm of socioeconomics. What Lacan did, in fact, was renew an ancient insistence on a space where there is no contradiction; a space whose displacement is governed by a quaternary rather than tripartite logic, one that was soon taken up by new philosophies: a logic of the real, imaginary, symbolic, and "the subject in his reality."[8] This subject, no longer a stationary *Cogito,* is put into movement around the four corners of a square, both there (*da*) and not there (*fort*) according to a series of displacements

---

4. See, for example, Lacan, *Ecrits: A Selection,* pp. 37–38, and *Ecrits,* pp. 397–98.

5. Jacques Lacan, "The Subversion of the Subject and the Dialectic of Desire in the Freudian Unconscious," in *Ecrits: A Selection,* p. 301.

6. Sigmund Freud, "Die Verneinung (Negation)," in vol. 19 of *The Complete Psychological Works,* pp. 235–36. However an exploration of the relationship of Lacan's thought to dialectics might be approached, one would have to begin with Freud's article on negation; Hyppolite's reading of it (Jean Hyppolite, "Commentaire parlé sur la Verneinung de Freud" in Lacan, *Ecrits,* pp. 879–87); and Lacan's "Réponse" (*Ecrits,* pp. 381–99). An introduction to this overall argument on negativity is Anthony Wilden, *The Language of the Self* (New York: Delta, 1968).

7. For an interesting discussion of Feuerbach and Marx, see Jean-Joseph Goux's "Le temple d'utopie," in *Les iconoclastes,* pp. 31–51.

8. Jacques Lacan, "On a Question Preliminary to Any Possible Treatment of Psychosis," in *Ecrits: A Selection,* p. 196.

over which "it" has no control: the substitution and displacement of signifiers, the differential process of language.⁹

Most important for our concerns here is the fact that this twisting of the normally orderly dialectical system was due to Lacan's recognition of and insistence on that which escapes any possible dialectic of representation: what he calls the "Real" and Bataille calls the "sacred."¹⁰ In order to understand the process of gynesis, it is important to remember that the various attempts to join Freud with dialectical thinking have differed substantially according to whether or not they situate themselves "before" or "after" Lacan; and, among those that come "after," according to whether or not they respect his radical subterfuge of the traditionally conceived dialectical process through his emphasis on this Real.

The Real must be treated carefully. For not to handle it carefully is to misjudge the force of Lacan's twisting of the dialectic and to return to a nineteenth-century Freud through the back door. For example, in what is an otherwise highly cogent analysis of the possible contributions of Lacanian theory to historical materialism, Fredric Jameson first "brackets" the notion of the Real and then, finally, decides that "it is not terribly difficult to say what is meant by the Real in Lacan. It is simply history itself."¹¹ This conclusion, if suggestive, is clearly false. For if the Real *is* anything, it is certainly not history—nor "reality," nor a "text."¹² The closest Lacan has ever come, to my knowledge, to giving the Real an ontological foundation is in the following statement:

> Mathematization alone achieves a real—and that is because it is compatible with our discourse, the discourse of analysis—a real that has nothing to do with what traditional knowledge has stood up to, and which is not what it believes, reality, but truly a fantasy.
>
> The real, I would say, is the mystery of the speaking body; it's the mystery of the unconscious.¹³

In Lacanian literature, the "Real" designates that which is categorically unrepresentable, nonhuman, at the limits of the known; it is emptiness,

9. For example, on the determination of the subject's destiny through the displacement of signifiers, see Lacan, *Ecrits*, p. 30.

10. In some ways, the "Real" might be seen as the object and telos of psychoanalysis itself.

11. Fredric Jameson, "Imaginary and Symbolic in Lacan: Marxism, Psychoanalytic Criticism, and the Problem of the Subject," *Yale French Studies* 55/56 (1977): 384.

12. Jean-François de Sauverzac quotes the following, but without giving a reference: "Reality is the ready-to-wear of fantasy . . . [the real] is when one knocks into oneself" (*Nouvelles Littéraires*, September 17–24, 1981, p. 32). My thanks to Leon Roudiez for pointing out this quotation to me.

13. Lacan, "Ronds de Ficelle" in *Le Séminaire Livre XX: Encore* (Paris: Editions du Seuil, 1975), p. 118.

the scream, the zero point of death, the proximity of jouissance.[14] To bracket the Real for the sake of argument, and then define it as history, is to rephenomenologize and degenderize—and attempt to *dialectize*—the most subversive element of Lacan's four-cornered topology, in the most traditional of ways.[15] That this can even be logically and coherently attempted is witness to Lacan's debt to dialectical thinking. At the same time, it is precisely with the topic of the Real, the irrepresentable "escape valve" of any system, the "black hole of knowledge," that Lacan sidesteps the Dialectic and its Representations, contests History and its Truths.

Finally, Lacan's twisting of the dialectical knot cannot be simply relegated to what is generally referred to as the ideology of structuralism; if nothing else, it has served, as least in France, to open the door to antistructuralist philosophies. For the concept of "structure" as it has come to be understood by the readers of "French structuralism" is entirely compatible with the dialectics of traditional representation and its system of originals and copies, presences and absences, especially to the extent that they both maintain an "ideal reader." The structural project involves only a kind of "freezing" of the dialectic in order to establish a model. It involves a kind of snapshot of a system in movement in order to find an invariant code that, while inoperative when the system is in motion, can be used again and again in any series of snapshots as long as the ideal reader or viewer stays the same. Take away that hypothetical Cogito, as Lacan began to do, and the entire system collapses. Structuralism is not that so-called methodology which does away with the subject, but an advanced—perhaps the last—*science* of the dialectics of representation. It is the grammar of dialectics, without the necessary intonation.[16]

14. *Feminine* jouissance, actually. But we will return to that problem shortly.

15. At the risk of unfairly singling out Jameson again in this study, I should just mention here that it is often at those points where the phenomenological Marxist discovers Lacan that the least radical part of Lacan's work, that part most enmeshed in our dominant culture of mimesis and representation, is reinforced. Jameson echoes, in a footnote, one of the most repeated (and clichéd) assertions of vulgar Lacanianism: "This is also the place to observe that the feminist attacks on Lacan, and on the Lacanian doctrine of the Signifier, which seem largely inspired by A. G. Wilden, 'The Critique of Phallocentrism' (in *System and Structure* [London: Tavistock, 1972], pp. 278–301) tend to be vitiated by their confusion of the penis as an organ of the body with the phallus as a signifier" (pp. 352–53). That the ultimately conservative "phallacies" of this so-called "confusion" have been dealt with at great length for at least twenty years, and not only by feminists, is not mentioned by Jameson.

16. Indeed, the entire so-called "structuralist controversy" could be seen as a hysterical response to modernity's threatened collapse of the dialectic and its representations. Particularly unfortunate was the passion for labeling *everyone* a structuralist, from Althusser to Lévi-Strauss. See, for example, the introduction to *The Structuralist Controversy*, ed. Richard Macksey and Eugenio Donato (Baltimore: Johns Hopkins University Press, 1972). It is also curious to see how many of the same names show up again in the "post-structuralist" canon. For a lucid and helpful discussion of these issues, see Philip Lewis, "The Post-structuralist Condition," *Diacritics* 12 (Spring 1982).

The fate of the dialectic in contemporary French thought was decided, along with that of the speaking subject, with increasing rapidity when philosophy met up with Lacanian psychoanalysis. This meeting was explosive—most certainly because it was a meeting with Nietzsche, who, "in any case [. . .] burned for us, even before we were born, the intermingled promises of the dialectic and anthropology."[17] For Nietzsche, there are not two (or more) kinds of dialectics, but just one with variations, one which has been Western Man's disease since Plato. For Nietzsche there are no opposites, just as there is no imperial subject; and to continue to see the world or the world's texts as governed by contradiction, where one term is inevitably valorized, can lead to nothing but nihilism and the alternating slavery of both "masters" and "slaves."

The new philosophies in France heeded, either directly or indirectly, Nietzsche's words. For all of them, to paraphrase Barthes, the textual body's most erotic zone came to be no longer where there is contradiction—most especially, where there is the presence or absence of something; but rather anywhere the overall garment has left *gaps*—whether the garment be history, the world, or the text. From that moment begins a distrust, and erotization, of the text, as well as of the world, which can no longer be reduced to what Man *sees* or is presented with (*Vorstellung*). And it is through the gaps in the knowable world-text that meaning is shown to be simultaneously present and absent (if only in the flash of a *coup de dès*); where it is shown to escape the control of the Aufhebung through a process beyond representation. Nietzsche: "Insidious Questions: When we are confronted with any manifestation which someone has permitted us to see, we may ask: what is it meant to conceal? What is it meant to draw our attention from? What prejudice does it seek to raise? and again, how far does the subtlety of the dissimulation go? and in what respect is the man mistaken?"[18]

This textual politics of distrust, and the search for the "hole in the text," led to an intensive rereading of the philosophical canon in a search either for what had been left out or for that process which exceeded what had been left for Man to see.[19] In all cases, the new philosophies were to conclude that this "unrepresentable factor" can perhaps be formulated, but

17. Foucault, *The Order of Things*, p. 263.

18. Friedrich Nietzsche, *The Dawn of Day*, section 523, in *The Complete Works of Friedrich Nietzsche*, vol. 9, ed. Oscar Levy (New York: Gordon, 1974).

19. The concern for the gap or hole in the text crosses wide disciplinary boundaries, from Foucault's "madness" to Riffaterre's "hole in the doughnut" (and the semiosis beyond mimesis). Umberto Eco has diagnosed the "gap," "hole," the decentering of any artistic system as definitional of modernity: *L'oeuvre ouverte*, trans. Roux (Paris: Editions du Seuil, 1965).

not represented, for it is the space of nonresemblance between the signifier and the signified.

The work of Louis Althusser deserves special mention here. Althusser, a member of the Communist Party, was, along with Etienne Balibar and Lyotard in his early work, one of the last philosophers of his generation in France to attempt to save Marxist dialectics from the fate of The Dialectic. His entire career was devoted, in fact, to the theoretical problem of how to problematize Marx's dialectic long enough to do so without jeopardizing Marxian politics: "So I think that, in its approximation, this metaphorical expression—the 'inversion' of the dialectic—does not pose the problem of the *nature of the objects* to which a *single method* should be applied (the world of the Idea for Hegel—the real world for Marx), but rather the problem of the *nature of the dialectic* considered itself, that is, the problem of *its specific structures*; not the problem of the inversion of the 'sense' of the dialectic, but that of the *transformation of its structures*."[20] Althusser, anxious to leave phenomenology behind while coming to terms with this problem, ultimately shifted his and many others' emphasis away from the existential subject toward his now well-known definition of ideology: The "representation" of "the Imaginary relationship of individuals to their real conditions of existence."[21] For students of Althusserian philosophy, the "truth" of Marxism is no longer to be found in economics, history, or the existential consciousness, but in a series of "false representations"; Marx's "dialectic" *itself* was a false representation of Hegel's. In fact, Marx's dialectic does not yet exist. Marx's own logic can only be found through a symptomatic reading of the logic of his texts; a true dialectical materialism would be what Marx didn't say. Pierre Macherey, an Althusserian literary critic, has developed an entire theory of literary production around this conclusion: "Can we make this silence speak? What is the unspoken saying? What does it mean? To what extent is dissimilation a way of speaking? Can something that has hidden *itself* be recalled to our presence? Silence as the source of expression. Is what I am really saying what I am not saying? Hence the main risk run by those who would say everything. After

20. Louis Althusser, *For Marx,* trans. Ben Brewster (New York: Pantheon, 1969), p. 93. See also his "On the Materialist Dialectic" (pp. 161–224). Althusser's reading of Marx is often compared to Lacan's reading of Freud because of their common emphasis on what the two Great Fathers did *not* say.

21. Louis Althusser, *Lenin and Philosophy* (New York: Monthly Review, 1971), p. 162. I should mention that the term "ideology" has now become as distrusted in France as the word "representation." An entire history of the word's semantic trajectory would have to be undertaken before we might be able to understand why.

all, perhaps the work is not hiding what it does not say; this is simply *missing* [*cela lui manque*]."[22]

Althusser and his immediate followers never ventured closer to Lacan's twisting of the dialectic than the concept of ideology and the notion that there is "in the text" another text which up until now Western Man has been unable to read because of its "invisibility." Lacan's direct subversion of the speaking subject was left out of their analysis completely. The task of attempting a new kind of materialist reading and writing of that other, so called invisible text, through radical reinterpretation of the speaking subject, fell to the group *Tel Quel:* there, a new post-Lacanian theory of the speaking subject came to be seen as essential to the development of a nonmechanistic, nonmimetic materialism beyond representation.[23] The texts Western Man has not been able to read were, for the early Tel Quel group, first and foremost those texts where the subject is submitted to a materialist practice (rather than praxis), a practice rendering the subject unrecognizable: textual écriture.[24] Concentrating on the texts of Bataille, Mallarmé, Sade, Lautréamont, Nietzsche, and others, this group of writers and philosophers searched intensively for that geometrical space where both meaning and its subject disappear and explode into the "black hole" of Lacan's Real.

Providing a history here of the theoretical innovations of Tel Quel would be pushing far beyond the goals and limits of this text.[25] But it is important to emphasize that until approximately 1974, the collective search of Tel Quel, in all of its diversity, for a new scientific theory of writing and reading exercised considerable influence in linguistics, philosophy, and literary theory.[26] After 1974, many of the individual members of that

22. Pierre Macherey, *A Theory of Literary Production* (London: Routledge & Kegan Paul, 1978), p. 86. Also see James H. Kavanagh's essay "Marxism's Althusser: Toward a Politics of Literary Theory," as well as the interview with Etienne Balibar and Pierre Macherey in *Diacritics* 12 (Spring 1982).

23. See, for example, an early work by Philippe Sollers, *Sur le matérialisme* (Paris: Editions du Seuil, 1974), esp. p. 89 on Althusser.

24. See Philippe Sollers, *Logiques* (Paris: Editions du Seuil, 1968), esp. p. 9.

25. While there is as yet no reliable overall history of the "Tel Quel group" (which still exists), the English reader can refer to: Leon S. Roudiez, "Twelve Points from Tel Quel," *L'esprit créateur* 14:4 (Winter 1974); Stephen Heath, *The Nouveau Roman* (London: Elek, 1972). A consideration of *Tel Quel* as a journal, within a general theory of "cultural renewal," can be found in Danielle Scouras, "Toward a 'New Culture': *Il Politecnico, Tel Quel,* and Cultural Renewal" (diss., Columbia University, 1981).

26. The desire for a *scientific* theory of literature, common to both "Marxist" and "structuro-linguistic" literary criticism during the 1960s and early 1970s in France, has not been adequately analyzed. Some see it as a desire to relegitimize the arts in a world of science—or perhaps it was a desire to shore up the delegitimized position of the intellectual in Europe as a "leader." For two different discussions around this problem, see, for example, "Les intellectuels et le pouvoir: Entretien M. Foucault–G. Deleuze," *L'arc* 49 (1972; reissued 1980); and Julia Kristeva, "Un nouveau type d'intellectuel," *Tel Quel* 74 (Winter 1977).

group followed definitively different textual and political paths. But all of them, whether or not they left Marx and Lacan behind, continued their search for the "Other Text"—the one beyond representation.

After the early work of the Tel Quel group, very little attention was paid by the philosophers either to sorting out the various dialectics or to following the textual intricacies of Lacan's subversion of the speaking subject. In fact, philosophy and psychoanalysis became allergic to one another. While assuming that the dialectic and the subject are to be rethought, dialectics very quickly become One Dialectic, and Lacan's psychoanalysis the last possible representation of Oedipus.[27]

The two philosophers I am privileging in this study—Jacques Derrida and Gilles Deleuze—launched their very different subversions of both the Dialectic and Oedipus by taking Nature and Culture, Identity and Difference, out of contradiction. Beginning with the fundamental theory of écriture he developed while working with Tel Quel, Derrida placed the Dialectic and the structure of Oedipus at the base of the phallogocentrism that has concealed and debased the differential process of writing within the representational worlds of the text. Deleuze, in line with Foucault (for whom madness is the other text—the one that does not exist), and in conjunction with Félix Guattari, disconnected the Dialectic and Oedipus from the binary machine that fuels them, calling for a liberation of difference from the sedentary texts of this representational world.

If Lacan's exclusive emphasis on "mental life" was already a movement away from words and things as they seem naturally reflected one by the other, Derrida's insistence on "textual life" broke whatever mirrors we had left; or rather, he displaced and distorted those mirrors so thoroughly that entering into a text with Derrida is like getting lost in a funhouse where no One is at home.

The image created by the mirror of mimesis—that of presence and absence (and the certainty that we know which is which)—is where Derrida begins. It is beginning to be well known that through a series of readings in Heidegger with Nietzsche, or of Nietzsche through Heidegger, Derrida lays *Presence* at the very foundation of Western systems of representation; but the implications of the insight have hardly been explored at all. With Heidegger, he goes back further than just German

27. It is our inheritance of the nineteenth-century concept of the family—our consecrated human representation of Dialectical Oedipus—which is often seen as fundamental to our twentieth-century straitjacket. At least theoretically—for here is a point where "experience" and "knowledge" truly conflict. For a synthesis, see Jacques Donzelot, *The Policing of Families,* trans. Robert Hurley (New York: Pantheon, 1979).

etymology (*Sein*) to the Greek syntax and semantics where philo-sophy was born: "presence" or "being" is there *ousia* or *parousia,* signifying "homestead," "being-at-home," and "integral, unmediated presentness." In its dynamic element, this *ousia* is *physis.* Neither sense can be replaced by what the Greeks called existence (Heidegger's ex-sistence)—to be "outside of," "external to Being." Derrida traces Heidegger's oscillating attitude toward this double problematic by unraveling from Heidegger's hopes for Man's eventual homecoming his other, more radical, announcement of a new kind of ontology beyond the dialectics of presence and absence. In Derrida's view, Heidegger decisively exposed the ways in which philosophy has always authorized itself through presence, the present of experience. For Derrida, it is not that one should therefore prefer absence, but rather that one should prefer to think about why all of Western philosophy could not think difference differently from the way it did. He writes that it is necessary to "think our relation to (the entire past of) the history of philosophy otherwise than in the style of dialectical negativity, which—as a tributary of the vulgar concept of time—posits an other present as the negation of the present past-retained-uplifted in the *Aufhebung,* where it yields its *truth.*"[28] Derrida's entire project, in all of its multiplicity, has been to render manifest the writing-as-difference that has always already disturbed the self-presence of phonetic theories of language within metaphysical systems of representation.

Most familiar to the American reader is no doubt Derrida's *Of Grammatology,* in which he outlines this project through a close reading of Lévi-Strauss and Rousseau. The metaphysics of presence governs all of the binary oppositions in Western thought, beginning with the fundamental opposition between Nature and Culture. And so "if, premeditating the theme of writing, I began by speaking of the substitution of mothers, it is because, as Rousseau will himself say, 'more depends on this than you realize.'"[29] For the myth of presence is, first of all, the myth of nature-before-culture, the natural goodness of the Maternal—a presence that has never existed but only been dreamt of. To maintain this utopian dream, Western Man has erased, debased, what Derrida calls the archi-écriture: the originary violence of naming which has always already inflected any so-called nature. And that erasure has been possible only because of the dialectical logic of representation which has governed us: "The horizon of

28. Derrida, "*Ousia* and *Gramme,*" in *Margins of Philosophy,* p. 38.
29. Derrida, *Of Grammatology,* p. 146. For an introduction to the *Grammatology,* see that by Gayatri Spivak (in *Of Grammatology*); or, for another view, cf. Paul de Man, "The Rhetoric of Blindness: Jacques Derrida's Reading of Rousseau," in *Blindness and Insight.*

absolute knowledge is the effacement of writing in the logos, the retrieval of the trace in parousia, the reappropriation of difference, the accomplishment of what I have elsewhere called the *metaphysics of the proper* [*le propre*—self-possession, propriety, property, cleanliness]."[30]

From this starting point, Derrida follows Heidegger's precedent of giving to concealment ontological precedence over the unconcealed, unveiled *truth*—(*Alētheia*):[31] "A text is not a text unless it hides from the first comer, from the first glance, the law of its composition and the rules of its game."[32] The text dis-similates. Beyond what the text "means," beyond its inclusion of the absent in the present, of the past in the now, of the outside in the inside; beyond the "naïveté of representation"—is "the productive movement of the effect of difference: the strange graphic of differance."[33] In dis-similating itself, the text disseminates and scatters to the winds our own illusions as to some one meaning glued to the voice-over of the text we think we have been reading.

In order to render manifest the text's difference-from-itself, Derrida first traces for us the process by which we come to be so sure that we know what a word "says" and "means." That sureness comes from our assumption that there is a semantic kernel to any given word-concept which can always be recovered through analysis. Just as Marx hoped to discover the "rational kernel" of his dialectic within the "mystical shell" of Hegel's speculative philosophy, we are sure that a word must have a rational, unchanging kernel of meaning in spite of its multiple, mysticizing wrappings.[34] For example, we believe that "Santa Claus," when spoken, is "Santa-Claus" and not "Saint Eclaus," "Santac Laws," or even "sand her claws." We can only make that assumption—and pursue our (childhood) beliefs—because of the identity and difference of dialectical mutual exclusion—a representational mode of thinking which, according to Derrida, is the cornerstone of Western theories of language.

30. Derrida, *Of Grammatology*, p. 26.

31. See especially Heidegger's "On the Essence of Truth," trans. R. F. C. Hull and A. Crick, in *Existence and Being*, ed. Werner Broch (Chicago: Henry Regnery, 1950). For Derrida, the most telling metaphor in the eternal arguments around truth and illusion is the metaphor of *optics*. The metaphor of the *camera obscura* is essential to dialectical thought—and, as Derrida and his disciples will show, to psychoanalysis. See, for example, Lacan, *Ecrits*, p. 647 and passim; for a critique, Sarah Kofman, *Caméra obscura, de l'idéologie* (Paris: Galilée, 1973) or, once again, Luce Irigaray's *Speculum de l'autre femme*.

32. Derrida, *Dissemination*, p. 63.

33. Derrida, *Of Grammatology*, p. 296.

34. Cf. Karl Marx, *Capital*, trans. E. and C. Paul, 2 vols. (London: J. M. Dent & Sons, 1930), esp. the afterword to vol. 2 of the second German edition. N. Abraham and M. Torok's *L'écorce et le noyau* (Paris: Flammarion, 1978) plays with this metaphor.

Derrida recognizes, however, that to oppose this dominant and ethno-centric logic of reason would only be to fall prey to its own logic: "one cannot speak out against it except by being for it, [. . .] one can protest it only from within it; and within its domain, Reason leaves us only the recourse to stratagems and strategies."[35] We are thus left by Derrida to the adventures of a certain wandering, without telos or finality, without domi-nation or mastery.[36] In order to pry apart the metaphysical oppositions that have chained us, we must begin to follow the movements of dif-ference-in-motion (*physis*) before it is chained by truth, syntax, and sign. Derrida's dissemination *solicits* physis instead of ordering it and, in the process, catches philosophy at its own game.[37] The Dialectic henceforth becomes, in truth, a Zig-Zag.

Just a few words at this point on "Derrida" and "Marx." If Marx turned Hegel on his head, Derrida has sent both spinning in the same direction. In the work that he has published, however, Derrida makes very few references to Marx and even fewer to Marx-and-Hegel. Any speculation as to his specific or personal position on the problematic would be hopeless from the beginning. It is not that he "hasn't had time" to subject Marx to the same "protocol of reading" as he has applied to Husserl, Heidegger, Nietzsche, etc.;[38] such a conclusion underestimates his notion of strategy "as opposed to" opposition. In "Positions" (his third interview, originally published in 1971), Derrida is deliberately provocative in reference to his sidestepping of Marx: "Do me the credit of believing that the 'lacunae' to which you alluded are explicitly calculated to mark the sites of a theoretical exploration which remains, *for me*, at least, *still to come*. And they are indeed lacunae, not objections; they have a specific and deliberate status, I even dare say a certain efficacity."[39]

In *Ja, ou le faux bond* (the second part of his fourth interview, published five years later), Derrida again reiterates the necessity to move slowly; rejects "dogmatic Marxism" as well as so-called "post-Marxism"; empha-sizes that the relationship between the concept of "Marxism" and our "metaphysical tradition" still remains to be problematized—and only then posits that "as a 'philosophical system,' if Marxism (a hypothesis to be complicated) would present itself in this way, it would entail, *as* [does]

35. Derrida, *Writing and Difference*, p. 36.
36. On "strategy," see, especially, *Margins of Philosophy*, p. 7.
37. See *Dissemination*, p. 53.
38. *Of Grammatology*, Gayatri Spivak's note, p. 318.
39. Derrida, *Positions*, trans. Alan Bass, p. 62.

every system, possibilities for deconstruction and even auto-deconstruction which must be taken into account practically, politically."[40]

Derrida is clearly aware that deconstructing "Marx" today would be a totally different gesture from deconstructing "Hegel," "Husserl," "Heidegger," "Nietzsche," etc.—both practically and politically. If American and French Marxist critics can have so insistently objected to Derrida's "anti-Marxism," is it not because he has rendered, at least for the time being, "Marx" (his texts? "Marxism"?) thoroughly unreadable through his deconstructions of The Dialectic? Derrida's "efficacious lacuna" seems to be all we are left with where the "rational kernel" should have been after the "mystical shell" was peeled away. In a characteristic *faux bond,* Derrida's zig-zag seems to have been curiously on target.[41]

For Derrida, then, the Dialectic of representation is any conceptual logic, based in binary opposition, with or without a mediating third element, which through negativity and the contradiction of identity and difference brings about a representation, a mimesis productive of Universal Truth, thereby erasing the movement of *différance.*[42] He will link the Dialectic to its specific manifestations within logics such as those of Christianity (as opposed to Judaic thought)[43] and the Family, as well as to its dependent concepts: the sign,[44] the metaphor,[45] the Cogito,[46] and castration.[47] As we shall see later, his zig-zag through all trinities to be deconstructed metamorphoses into various spatial figures that, like Lacan's topology mentioned earlier, are based in a *quaternary* logic. Most particularly, there is the logic of the chiasma. At the crossroads of the chiasma, there is no center, neither presence nor absence. There is, however, the possibility of a "gap," a space of slippage, where meaning escapes through a process never to be seen as such: a "certain dialectics."[48] Any attribute

---

40. Derrida, "Ja, ou le faux bond," *Digraphe* 11 (April 1977): 118.
41. Derrida has been increasingly explicit about this strategy. See, for example, *Les fins de l'homme,* pp. 526–28. For the most condensed consideration of the Dialectic, see the left-hand margin of *Glas.* Specific passages on negativity and the dialectic are scattered throughout his published work: for example, "Cogito and the History of Madness," esp. p. 308, n. 4; "The Theatre of Cruelty and the Closure of Representation," esp. pp. 245–47; "From Restricted to General Economy," esp. pp. 275–76—all in *Writing and Difference;* or "The Pit and the Pyramid," esp. pp. 76–78, and, of course, "Différance," in *Margins of Philosophy.*
42. We shall return to this word in Gynesis III.
43. E.g., in *Glas,* p. 64: "there is therefore no Jewish 'for oneself,' near-to-oneself."
44. E.g., *Margins of Philosophy,* pp. 75–77.
45. See "White Mythology" in *Margins of Philosophy.*
46. See especially "The Ends of Man," in *Margins of Philosophy,* and "Cogito and the History of Madness," in *Writing and Difference.*
47. See especially "Outwork, prefacing" and "Dissemination," in *Dissemination.*
48. *Writing and Difference,* p. 246.

that empirical, common sense might have believed to exist at this center, which is not a center, becomes both there and not there, in and out of the folds of the text, caught in Derrida's chiasmatic net.

That attribute, which is always already never there where we believed it was, is the "transcendental signifier" and its signified. And it will be with a zig-zag through Lacan that Derrida will most precisely show that The Signifier for Lacan—the Phallus—is not *ever* where we think it is. For Derrida, castration is never simple—nor, for that matter, is Derrida's relationship to a psychoanalysis that is most definitely after Lacan.[49] We shall return more specifically to some of the words Derrida has put into play to designate the workings of that strange place *between* psychoanalysis and philosophy, the place of the "Other Text." His dissemination of all concepts leads back, in fact, very quickly to that space where there is no contradiction but only a transposition-of-spaces-in-difference—the unconscious—even while Derrida is already, always, deconstructing by "encrypting" that "inner space" itself.[50]

For what Derrida *is* working on has no name or place—at least not yet. Lacan's Real? Not exactly. The trace of différance is even more thoroughly unnameable, unrepresentable, than Lacan's Real: "There is no *name* for it at all."[51] Neither inner nor outer, it is in-between (*entre*), it enters (*entre*), it inter-venes between all metaphysical oppositions. And, as we shall see later, "When the middle of an opposition is not the passageway of a mediation, there is every chance that the opposition is not pertinent. The consequences are boundless."[52]

If one is already working with several signatures when focusing on Jacques Derrida, with Gilles Deleuze the problem of the proper name becomes even more visible. —Literally, first of all, because his intellectual collaboration with Félix Guattari since 1969 has remained a steadfast one. But even if their first publication together (*Anti-Oedipus*, 1972) was to bring about a certain change of "style," Deleuze's multiplicity was already apparent in the diversity of his previous writings as a, strictly speaking, "professional philosopher": the proper names in his titles—Nietzsche, Spinoza, Kant, Bergson, Proust, Sacher-Masoch, Lewis Carroll—testify

49. See, for example, pp. 107–13, n. 44, in *Positions*, trans. Alan Bass, for Derrida's most explicit critique of Lacan. (See also his "The Purveyor of Truth," *Yale French Studies* 52 (1975).

50. See, for example, "Fors," introduction to N. Abraham and M. Torok's *Cryptonymie: Le verbier de l'homme aux loups* (Paris: Aubier-Flammarion, 1976).

51. *Margins of Philosophy*, p. 26.

52. Ibid., pp. 255–56, n.

to his disdain from the beginning for any homogenized canon of signatures.

Secondly, with Deleuze, one enters not only a funhouse, but an entire carnival of science and fiction. In all of his books, there is a scrambling of discursive, disciplinary codes certain to unsettle any academic reading. For example, in reference to Deleuze and Guattari's 1980 book, *Mille plateaux,* Catherine Clément remarks something that could be said about most of his books, whether or not his is the only signature: it is a book of history, economy, ethnology, politics, aesthetics, linguistics. And a book of philosophy? "It's philosophy. Or maybe not. It's writing, and thinking. Chagrined people—those with thin skin, you know?—will worry in their corner, smaller and smaller. The others, philosophers or not, will amuse themselves. And even seriously."[53]

Seriously. For some, especially in the United States, this adverb is irrelevant to Deleuze and Guattari. That judgment, in my opinion, is, however, oversimple and unfortunate. First, Deleuze and Guattari *are* very "serious." Perhaps they are not serious in the French sense (grave, without laughter, reasonable), since their work is also frivolous, gay, and light (perhaps even futile), but they are most certainly not joking. This is clear if only because of the wide impact they have had on contemporary thought and, most especially, on its students everywhere. In the United States, where theory from France enters through language and literature departments, that impact has tended to be academically minimized with words like "utopian," "anarchistic," and "perverse." This is in part perhaps because Deleuze and Guattari take you further and further out of the text, not deeper into it. It is also because their books are often categorized and then quickly dismissed as but frivolous by-products of 1968. But it is mostly true because Deleuze and Guattari are virulently anti-academic academics, with a hatred of the "faculties" impossible to contain within prescribed public, academic discourse. The private has always been their politics, and they tend to ignore the professionalistic demand to censor what they have to say.[54]

Deleuze and Guattari occupy precarious positions at the intersections and interfacings of the questions—both French-American and feminist—in this book: 1) because of the status of their work in the United States, where they are ignored or dismissed by the majority of academics and

53. Catherine Clément, "Postface 1980: De l'anti-Oedipe aux Mille plateaux," *L'arc* 49 (Nouvelle Edition 1980): 97; see also *Mille plateaux.*

54. See, e.g., Gilles Deleuze on the assassination of his generation with the history of philosophy in "I Have Nothing to Admit," *Semiotext(e)* 2:3 (1977).

fervently worshiped by a vocal (male) student minority; 2) because of their idealistic posture toward the United States, and the fact that they are the only writers in France who have consistently taken American literature and culture as their model; 3) because they are two of the rare male theorists in France who are publicly supportive of feminism and particularly of the feminist movement in France (even if French women are often told they are going about things in the "wrong way"); 4) because there are as yet no women theorists in either France or the United States who have published extensively as their "disciples" (as opposed to Lacan and Derrida);[55] and 5) because, in spite of their sympathy for feminism and their iconoclasm often parallel to that of feminists, their own work, and that of their male followers, puts forth some surprisingly stereotyped genderizations and images of women.

Deleuze and Guattari's work, especially Deleuze's early work, is of particular importance for us, then, in part because of these contradictions; but also because theirs is an uncompromising "philosophy of questions," just as feminism today must be.[56] And, further, Deleuze's most insistent problem-question has always been: How and why does the "binary machine" work?

> It is false [to say that] the binary machine only exists for reasons of convenience. It is said that "base two" is the easiest. But in reality the binary machine is an important piece of the apparatuses of power. As many dichotomies as necessary will be established in order to stick everyone to the wall, to push everyone in a hole [. . .] Binary machines of social classes, of sexes, man-woman, of ages, child-adult, of races, black-white, of sectors, public-private, of subjectifications, among our own kind—not our kind.[57]

For Deleuze, as for Derrida, the binary machine is at the foundations of the dialectic and its representations. For him, representation is also the form of Western philosophy, that form which, above all, presupposes a *cogitatio natura universalis*: the subject that authorizes itself with the statement, "but everyone knows . . .": "*Everybody knows, no one can deny* [*it*], that's the form of representation and the discourse of representing."[58]

The *cogito* is only one of several "transcendental illusions" of representa-

---

55. The one exception to this being Braidotti, "Féminisme et philosophie," where Deleuze's work, as a "tool box" for feminist theory, is thoroughly unpacked.

56. For Deleuze, a theory is but a question developed to the extreme limits of all of its implications. Cf. Gilles Deleuze, *Empirisme et subjectivité* (Paris: PUF, 1953), esp. p. 119.

57. Deleuze and Parnet, *Dialogues,* pp. 29, 155–56.

58. Deleuze, *Différence et répétition,* p. 170.

tion described by Deleuze. Inseparable from it are also the ways in which "difference" has been violently subordinated to resemblance through negativity and the analogies of judgment;[59] that is, through the movement of the dialectic—and, most particularly, the dialectic of the master and slave. What is crucial for Deleuze is Nietzsche's observation that neither the master nor the slave has ever been able to take difference into account; that the dialectic renders everyone a slave. For him, opposition in the place of difference is negative, reactive; the subject of the dialectic is a sad man, against life, avid to judge, measure, limit it rather than to live it. For him, dialectics is "the thinking of the slave, expressing the reactive life in itself and the becoming reactive of the universe."[60]

Deleuze wants to develop, rather, a *philosophie du oui*, a philosophy of affirmation that is not dependent on two negations; an affirmation that *differs* from negation without opposing it.[61] Taking difference out of contradiction with opposition is Deleuze's most extensive strategy-with-Nietzsche against representation; a question finally of perpetually moving difference into difference-with-itself. Deleuze's *différenciant de la différence,* the differentiating of difference, affirmative beyond contradiction, is a difference *without concept,* without place, without mediation, and always in movement.[62] It is an intensively different kind of difference that Deleuze wants to bring to the surface of life, a difference distinguished from itself without distinguishing itself.[63]

Deleuze will consequently take on all machines of representation which refuse this affirmative difference, and most especially those of Oedipus, Hegel, and Marx. For Deleuze, pyschoanalysis is the last avatar of the anthropological representation of sexuality, "psychoanalysis as a gadget, Oedipus as a reterritorialization, a retimbering of modern man on the 'rock' of castration."[64] Psychoanalysis has produced an unconscious that is negative, "an enemy"; it can teach us only about lack and the law; it has in fact confused the "lack" of castration with the "emptiness" of desire: "the result: castrate the mother and be castrated; kill the father and be killed" within the world of images, the world of fantasy.[65]

But psychoanalysis is not the only sedentary binary machine challenged

---

59. Ibid., esp. pp. 341–46.
60. Gilles Deleuze, "Le surhomme: Contre la dialectique," in *Nietzsche et la philosophie* (Paris: Presses Universitaires de France, 1962), p. 224.
61. Ibid., p. 216.
62. See, especially, Deleuze, *Différence et répétition,* pp. 16–17, 41, 78.
63. See "La différence en elle-même," in *Différence et répétition,* p. 43.
64. Deleuze and Guattari, *Anti-Oedipus,* p. 308.
65. See, for example, "De la pensée," in *Logique du sens,* pp. 253–60.

by Deleuze. As pointed out by Jean-François Lyotard in reference to *Anti-Oedipus,* what Deleuze and Guattari subvert most profoundly is in fact Marxism:

> . . . the two Elders [Marx and Freud] are in fact put under the same banner: in their works, every way that the libidinal economy communicates with the political economy is truly a transforming force and thus a potential departure; on the contrary, that by which the libidinal conceals the political in Freud or the political the libidinal in Marx must be leaped out of and danced upon. Thus, as the visible axis of the book, everything that is *unconsciously* political in psychoanalysis will be profoundly subverted, Anti-Oedipus being Anti-State, rupture with the despotic configuration unconsciously present in psychoanalysis. But parallel to that, everything unconsciously libidinal in Marxism will be detached, a libido imprisoned in the religious scaffolding of dialectical politics or economic catastrophism, a libido repressed in the uninterrupted analyses of commodity fetishism or of the naturality of work.[66]

Production, recuperation, negativity, guilt, anguish, analysis—common to the sedentary dialectical machines of Marx and Freud—are to be transformed by forcing both machines to their breaking point. For Deleuze and Guattari, it is new kinds of desiring machines, as opposed to Oedipus or the State, which can help us to produce a new kind of unconscious, a generalized unconscious, more in tune with a modernity beyond representation.

In its emphasis on the need to liberate difference from the dialectic and to introduce movement into the stable, and in its war against all tripartite machines of representation (Oedipus, dialectics, the sign), the work of Deleuze and Guattari has strong affinities with that of Derrida. But the resemblance ends there, not only because of Deleuze and Guattari's neo-empiricism, but also because of a curious mixture of "life" and "writing": the text and its modalities of concealment are given no ontological priority within their surface-machinations. The text, any text, any part of a text, is for them but one of the partial objects in the unconscious still to be invented. The key words of their strategy are not careful patience, but speed; not undecidables, but paradoxes; not traces, but rhizomes. Theirs too is a quaternary logic capable of accounting for thought as event rather than as signification; but it is a logic so deterritorialized, so rapid, as to be beyond any textual écriture.

The problem for Deleuze and Guattari is not one of how to weave

66. See Jean-François Lyotard, "Energumen Capitalism," *Semiotext(e)* 2:3 (1977): 12.

together, or even disentangle, but of how to break apart, of how to release and quicken the flow outward of any element which has already begun to exceed any given system of representation. This element is what they call the paradoxical element, one in excess, with no proper place or identity, an empty place.[67] This empty space, this element x—unrepresentable, unnameable—escapes in a movement destructive to signification. The most promising strategy for Deleuze and Guattari, once this movement has been produced, is not, however, to meditate on the meaning thus destroyed, as some Derridians might do, but to move away quickly, forget it, produce a new meaning before polarization can again set in: "to make the empty space circulate, to make pre-individual and non-personal singularities speak, in short, to produce meaning is the task today."[68]

The unconscious-yet-to-be-produced is the only space for Deleuze where the unnameable element x might freely circulate in a kind of "chaosmos."[69] Often described as a Real-in-flux, it is where No-One reigns. The privileged points of entry into the Real-in-flux are the famous Deleuzian "escape lines": lines for an escape into life. The Real-in-flux is life itself for Deleuze and Guattari, an "experimentation-life." It can also be writing, but only as parts-of-writing-connected-with-life, never as immanent in textuality or écriture.[70]

Finally, the "escape lines," royal road to the Real, are never in dualistic positions but, as we might expect, always already between. This "between" is not, however, exactly the same as Derrida's "between," for it is not a space of oscillation, but a space of "absolute speed." It is a process that, by shooting through the gaps in the texts of the world, might produce new worlds, new life, escaping presence and absence, the life-only-as-subordinate-to-death of representation.[71]

> In reality, there is neither union (*waçl*) nor separation (*façl*), just as there is neither distancing (*bu'd*) nor approaching (*gurb*) . . . There is union without unification, approaching without proximity, and distancing without any idea of distance and proximity.
>
> Ibn ʿArabî, *Le Traité de l'Unité* (mystical text, c. twelfth–thirteenth century)

67. *Logique du sens,* p. 265.
68. Ibid., p. 91.
69. Ibid., p. 206.
70. On écriture, see Deleuze and Parnet, *Dialogues,* pp. 61–63.
71. On Deleuze and Guattari's "between," see, for example, "Intermezzo," the last page of Catherine Clément's "Postface 1980."

> For nothing destroys description so much as words, and yet
> there is nothing more necessary than to place before the eyes of
> men certain things the existence of which is neither provable nor
> probable, but which, for this very reason, pious and scholarly
> men treat to a certain extent as existent in order that they may be
> led a step further toward their being and their becoming [toward
> being born].
> Albertus Secundus (epigraph to Hermann Hesse's *The Glass
> Bead Game*)

The displacement and indeed destructuration of the dialectic in France
are, for our purposes here, where the process of gynesis and its relationship to modernity as well as feminist theory become clearest. For, as
with the demise of the Cartesian ego, that which is beyond the Father,
overflowing the dialectics of representation, unrepresentable, will be gendered as feminine.

To destructure or attempt to subvert the dialectic is to put the function
of mediation into question. As we have seen briefly, Lacan was the first to
displace, slightly, the mediator in patriarchal culture—the Father—from
"reality" to the "symbolic," as well as the first to reconceptualize and
reemphasize spaces "exceeding" the dialectic, twisting the dialectic into a
knot. But those efforts did not bring about the Father's disappearance-in-
representation. On the contrary. For the psychoanalyst, any state existing
before the mediation of the name-of-the-Father continues to be considered as the state of primary narcissism represented by the mother and
child. Any state where that mediation has been foreclosed or bypassed is
an entry into psychosis, represented by a feminized dialogue with God
(the case of Schreber).[72] For Lacan, not to recognize the phallus as belonging to the Father—as mediator between the mother and child in all of
us—is to open the door to delirious metonymy in the Real; or to mass
hysteria: what sex am I, anyway?

Philosophers were not to underestimate the power of that Lacanian
conclusion and its implications for philosophy. They were also not unaware that any denial on their part of the dialectics-of-presence-and-ab-
sence (castration) would implicate them (unmercifully) in the psychoanalytic structure. Their strategy, then, was to be one of displacement, not
confrontation. The Aufhebung, recognized as mediating between culture
and nature, difference and identity, is also seen as that which fundamen-

---

72. See, especially, Lacan, "On a Question Preliminary to Any Possible Treatment of
Psychosis," in *Ecrits: A Selection*, p. 179 and passim.

tally defines male and female through hierarchization: "The *Aufhebung* is very precisely the relationship of copulation to sexual difference."[73] They will therefore displace the Aufhebung of mediation even further, set about a total reconceptualization of difference beyond contradiction and, in so doing, self-consciously throw both sexes, and their sexual organs, into a metonymic confusion of gender. The phallus-as-Aufhebung becomes in their texts little more than one partial object among others. Both "men's" and "women's" bodies become truly cut up, fragmented bodies: penises, anuses, breasts, vaginas are cut from the images of their representations in order, eventually, to imagine a new kind of body. But as we might expect and as Derrida writes: "Remains—the mother."[74] For this newly invented body in their work is in-between, undecidable, or, at the very minimum, in absolute speed. Not exactly neuter, it is nonetheless borderline asexual. It is, strangely enough, a perfect Freudian representation of the mother's body for the infant, the mother as *primum movens* of the infant's sexual anxiety.

It is no accident that the interrogative return to our sources of knowledge must also be a return to the mother's body.

This in-between body obviously poses certain new questions for the feminist reader. For the traditional feminist question has been about the phallus: Is not the phallus a figment only of the *male* imagination? Who decided it to be The Mediator? Why does The Mediator have to be the phallus? Why can it not be the breast or . . . The philosophers would seem to agree. And yet, their first steps toward asking those same questions, by removing the phallus from its sacred attachment to the male body, seem to have created a new body even more unrecognizable. The woman reader, in any case, knows that it is most certainly not hers.

Whose phallus is it, anyway? The Father's? The Mother's? Or does it belong to a body in-between?

Derrida's strategy for posing and then subverting when not short-circuiting these questions may be summed up by the words oscillation and undecidable. For example, one of Derrida's disciples, Sarah Kofman, begins to ask certain questions with regard to the Cerisy Colloquium "Les fins de l'homme":[75] ". . . one might ask oneself if, by keeping for this colloquium a title so strongly marked by metaphysical humanism, one does not run the risk of arousing suspicions that a need to *master* dif-

---

73. Derrida, *Glas*, p. 127.
74. Ibid., p. 132.
75. Sarah Kofman, "Ça cloche," in *Les fins de l'homme*, pp. 89–117. All further page references in text.

ferences is still lurking there. All differences, but especially, since the scene in twelve years has been displaced, *the sexual difference* [. . . How can we escape] the suspicion that this colloquium is designed to rescue, assist, set upright again (in every sense) man, understood no longer as *anthropos*, the universal man, sexually neuter, but as *aner* or *vir?*" (p. 90). She continues, however: "It seems that the subtitle of this colloquium: 'around the works of Derrida' allows us to erase immediately any such suspicion . . ." (p. 90). For Derrida—unlike "Freud" (for example, pp. 91–98) and "feminism" (for example, p. 91)—has continually denounced the phallocentrism of any (male) we. His strategy of denunciation is that of oscillation—a "feminine oscillation" represented by woman, an oscillation that, according to Kofman, all phallocrats have tried to fix into a stable position of opposition (pp. 97–98). This strategy of oscillation is, of course, a strategy of generalized *fetishism*—"to the profit of the feminine" (pp. 99–100). Kofman goes no further, but simply calls for "the end of all oppositions, that of man as well as of woman, to the advantage of a 'feminine jouissance,' if by feminine one understands undecidable oscillation" (p. 111). A generalized undecidability is a generalized fetishism is a generalized feminity—beyond phallocentrism. It is also—and this is never mentioned in Kofman's article—a generalization of *male paranoia.*[76]

Is it only a coincidence, then, that President Schreber represents for Deleuze and Guattari their ideal "body without organs"? While denouncing paranoia as opposed to the liberation of schizophrenia, Schreber, praised as-the-schizophrenic-before-Freud's-paranoia, is retained as the model for the body without organs, a body in oscillation, a *female* body, which is nonetheless not a woman as opposed to man.[77]

This is where our feminist questions have certainly already begun. But our questions cannot be our traditional ones, for the phallus has already been "burned" along with the Dialectic and anthropology. What then is this strange body? Might not the confusion of boundaries, between inside and outside, surface and depth, lead us to Melanie Klein's work on the Good and Bad Mother?[78] Are the spaces of primary narcissism, or of psychosis, the only way to escape the Oedipus complex? Could it be that,

---

76. Derrida, in his response to Kofman, is certainly aware, however, of that danger: "I am neither positing generalized fetishism as an ideal, nor do I valorize it as such . . ." Kofman, "Ça cloche," p. 114.

77. On Schreber's female body-without-organs see Deleuze and Guattari, *Anti-Oedipus*, pp. 8, 12–19, 56–57. We will return to it later.

78. Melanie Klein, *The Writings of Melanie Klein* (London: Hogarth, 1975–1980).

outside of Oedipus and the Dialectic, there can be nothing other than a woman-without-organs-in-oscillation? If woman is indeed the phallus for Man, as Lacanian theory would have it, are the male philosophers fighting over it? And, most important, what are we going to do about the word "representation"? For it is, at the very least, obvious to the feminist reader that it is in those texts chosen as exemplary by the theorists of the-process-beyond-representation that some of the cruelest presentations of women's bodies and destinies remain. What new can be done with this presentation-beyond-representation which has been diagnosed as modernity? And where can the feminist emphasis on the texts of modernity be marked: on the "potentially liberating" process beyond the traditional images-of-our-dead-bodies; or on the nontraditional presentations of the process that still brings about those deaths?

In any case, it is clear that psychoanalysis and philosophy, especially in France, have themselves polarized into a rather Oedipal structure: as Joyce might put it, psychoanalysis has increasingly come to be about saving "the Time of the Father" and philosophy about saving "the Space of the Mother." This dichotomy mimes another which is of immediate interest here in reference to the mother's body: psychoanalysis and mysticism.

As contemporary philosophers are quick to point out, Freud himself was allergic to philosophy, as well as to music and anything "Dionysian." For him, philosophy was inherently mystical rather than "scientific," and to be avoided at all costs. This allergy on the part of Freud is not without context. German mysticism, initiated by Master Eckhart in the thirteenth and fourteenth centuries, after various permutations resurfaced in force in the nineteenth century: "This first wave, after having ebbed, manifested itself again at the beginning of the 19th century, at the moment of the great return to mysticism promised by nascent romanticism, of which Franz von Baader was the promoter. It was he who pulled Eckhart from purgatory and, after having discovered him in Munich, he revealed him to German idealism, beginning with Hegel (1824)."[79] German intellectuals came to equate both Hegel and Nietzsche with mysticism; Freud certainly did so, even while he himself had been profoundly and early influenced by Goethe and the cult of Nature. Gradually, however, Freud was to renounce all "mystical temptations" with wonted vehemence. Most interesting in the present connection is his particular notion of mysticism, encapsulated within one of the last sentences he wrote: "Mysticism: the obscure auto-

79. See Paul-Laurent Assoun, "Freud et la mystique," in "Résurgences et dérivées de la mystique," special issue of *Nouvelle revue de la psychanalyse*, vol. 22 (Fall 1980): 44. I highly recommend the entire issue to any feminist concerned by the questions raised here.

perception of the reign, beyond the Ego, of the Id."[80] This is important because Freud borrowed the term "Id" from Groddeck, who used it to mean Natural Nature, Eternal Mother, Essential Woman, Primordial Energy. For Freud, any conceptual system that valorizes that maternal space, the *Id*, is mystical. The territorial battles he thus began with those colleagues more interested in the Mother than in the Father (Jung, Groddeck, Ernest Jones, Otto Rank) trace to this day a solid dividing line between paternalistic Freud and his maternalistic Others (D. W. Winnicott, Klein, Jung, etc.).[81]

If this series of internal and external divisions—first between the scientific Freud and his early Goethian temptations; then between Freudian psychoanalysis and German Idealism (and philosophy for Freud); and finally between Freudian psychoanalysis and its excommunicated psychoanalytic "mystics of the maternal"—is already complicated, it becomes even more so when we look at the more precise coordinates of mystical discourse: the Mother, Death, and the Unknown.

Even a cursory examination of religious and lay mystical currents reveals a series of ideas we have already come across in our explorations thus far.[82] For example, mystical discourse would seem to include: 1) an antirationality founded in paradoxical and apophatic logic (e.g., pp. 8, 158); 2) a posture of antiknowledge (p. 23); 3) experiences "without" a subject (p. 41); 4) an experience where, divorced from words, *"the Thing would speak by itself"* (p. 63); 5) where the Other is without a face for identity (p. 124); 6) where an unresolved paradox leads to confusion between the inside and the outside (pp. 168, 60); 7) where the ego is exploded onto the surfaces of the body (p. 167); 8) where language is not one of communication but of "transmutation at the interior of terms" (p. 23); 9) where there is an emphasis on giving rather than exchanging (p. 31); 10) where there is an obsession with that which survives death (pp. 81–82) and especially with cadavers (p. 9); 11) where there is a paranoid hatred of the world tending to crystallize in sects of the "elect" (pp. 32, 18–19, 29–32); 12) where there exists an alienation from any form of commitment (in the existential sense) (p. 205); 13) where there reigns a profound pessimism about changing

---

80. Cited by Assoun (ibid.) as from Freud, *Gesammelte Werke*, vol. 17.

81. The reader will no doubt note that it tends to be these "theorists of the maternal" who have found a home in the United States. Could this be because, in these theories, the libido is characterized as sexually neutral rather than exclusively male? In France, Jung is just now beginning to find a certain reading audience in psychoanalytic circles outside Lacanian influence. The group "Confrontations" has recognized this influx and some of its members are going back to reconsider the infantile Imago that combines the Mother and Father in one organic figure: *le Père-Mère*, the Father-Mother.

82. *Nouvelle revue de la psychanalyse*'s special issue, "Résurgences," summarizes well the recent literature on psychoanalysis, philosophy, and mysticism. Page numbers in text refer to this issue.

anything: i.e., "there is *no future*" (pp. 206–7); 14) where the sex must be female to bring about a resurrection of spirit (p. 14).[83]

It would be difficult, given these references, not to perceive a series of connections with contemporary psychoanalysis and, especially, with philosophy in France. American critics, at least, have not failed to point out those connections. Some attribute this to an immediate "mystical" literary tradition (the Surrealists, Bataille, Heidegger, etc.), and in so doing, retain the negative connotations that have been attached to the word "mysticism," especially since Sartrean existentialism. But others, including the writers we are interested in, have questioned the *rejection* of mysticism. According to the psychoanalyst Guy Rosolato, the scientific denial of mysticism invites "a *scission* between scientific activity and the use one can make of it, between a rational domain about which one is concerned and a domain of the unknown which one leaves aside as the responsibility of others, either in order to disinterest oneself in it or else to adopt its myths in a paradoxical co-existence."[84] It would seem, indeed, that one of the lessons of the late twentieth century has been that human beings are unable to live without a certain experience of the sacred. To ignore or deny that experience is therefore to invite, among other things, a return of traditional religions—or of their equivalents (including terrorism) in a lay universe. Feminism, as a philosophy of questions, must be particularly attentive to this problem. For mysticism, as experience, is about saving the *Mother* from and instead of the Father.[85] To the extent that feminism is necessarily involved in that gesture, the question becomes, how do we want to save her? Our approach, in any case, cannot be to decide *between* paternalistic psychoanalysis and what Freud saw as its antithesis: maternalistic mysticism or philosophy.

This is where the male writers we are focusing on, and the women theorists who are their disciples, are of particular relevance. For mysticism is often defined as the "pretension to do without an intermediary" (*Le Littré*). Theorists, writers of modernity are attempting precisely, each in

---

83. Once again, I emphasize the collection, "Résurgences," for the sake of economy. Anyone interested in pursuing the subject would most certainly want to begin with the most important work done in France on the mystical experience/text: that of Michel de Certeau. See, especially, "L'enonciation mystique," *Recherches de science religieuse* 64 (1976): 183–215; and *La possession de Loudun* (Paris: Julliard-Gallimard, Collection Archives, 1970). For an overview of his work, see "Folie du nom et mystique du sujet: Surin," in *Folle vérité*, ed. Julia Kristeva (Paris: Editions du Seuil, 1979), pp. 274–304.

84. *Nouvelle revue de la psychanalyse*, "Résurgences," p. 33.

85. Feminism and mysticism have a long common history of which, no doubt, the Saint-Simoniens provide one of the most important episodes. Today, that branch of feminism most intent on reviving the cult of the Maternal Goddess—usually of Jungian inspiration—is still strong. See. e.g., Mary Daly's *Beyond God the Father: Toward a Philosophy of Women's Liberation* (Boston: Beacon, 1973).

different ways, not to do away with mediation but rather to redefine and displace that intermediary beyond the myths of both nature and culture, beyond the boundaries of narcissism and psychosis. *Between* the dialectic and mysticism, they are attempting to found new discursive spaces for the sacred.

The problem is, of course, that this leads to an explosive putting into discourse of the maternal, of "woman" and her attributes. None of the writers we are focusing on, however, nor any of the major women theorists in France, can seem to get beyond gynesis as it transpires within a *male* economy. This has led, among other things, to a certain repetition: almost as if psychoanalysis, based in Freud, relegated what it could not think about to a philosophy which, outside of returning to the Father, can only write fiction. Within that repetition, the difference—if we may use that word—between the men and women theorists, whatever their attitude toward psychoanalysis, is that the former have confused sexual difference (faced with the new, monstrous maternal body they have invented) while the women have infused it with new signification (in part by becoming mothers themselves?)

A Marxist critic has written about general problems of mediation with reference to Benjamin and Derridean deconstruction.[86] His concluding question is more than relevant here; for it would seem that the late twentieth century is, in fact, *"in medias res,* caught in the middle of differences *about* the middle ground that may *not* be capable of med-iation (*Ver-mittlung*) [. . .] [We] differ [. . .] on how to differ. Should then the pious attempt of the would-be mediator (the Goethean *Mittler*) be gaily abandoned and heterogeneity positively affirmed? But doesn't the shared need to awaken from the nightmare of history point symptomatically beyond local quarrels and sectarian cliques to the common interest?"[87] Most certainly yes.

But it is highly probable that "we" (?) won't awaken from that nightmare until male theorists awaken from their illusion that "masculinity imagines itself poorly or imagines itself, at the most, only by feminizing itself";[88] until men speak their sexuality instead of speaking about it—or about "ours." Until that moment, the "common interest" will remain male—and "woman's difference" will continue to be seen as the only solution to the problem of how to rethink the unrepresentable.

86. Irving Wohlfarth, "Walter Benjamin's Image of Interpretation," *New German Critique* 17 (Spring 1979): 70–99.

87. Ibid., pp. 96–97.

88. Philippe Lacoue-Labarthe, "L'imprésentable," *Poétique* 21 (1975), p. 74.

7

The Demise of Experience:
Fiction as Stranger than Truth?

A labyrinthian man never looks for the truth, but only for his
Ariadne.

Nietzsche

Truth is not an unveiling which destroys the secret, but the
revelation which does it justice.

Walter Benjamin

The ancient problem of the relationship between what in
everyday language we call "experience" of "reality" and what we then
decide to call "knowledge" about it (let alone knowing the "truth" about
it) has resurfaced with a vengeance in the twentieth century. Radical critics
of dominant Western culture have been urgently concerned, since at least
the turn of the century, with the problem of how to continue criticism in a
modern world where it is understood not only that what is being criticized
is already an ideological, symbolic construction, but also that it is therefore already a lie. So then, where might be found the truth? From the arts,
especially modernist and postmodernist fiction, to the philosophies, a
deep dissatisfaction with science has led to a radical reevaluation of the
relationships between what Walter Benjamin called "direct, lived experience" (*Erlebnis,* "shock") as opposed to retrospective, "privileged, inward
experience" (*Erfahrung,* "aura").[1] That the relationship between the two is
no longer obvious; that, in any case, it can no longer be seen as reflective,
natural, or unmediated, is now certain. As Gilles Deleuze has explained,
we are talking about an era of generalized anti-Platonism, where it is no

1. See in particular Benjamin's *Charles Baudelaire: A Lyric Poet in the Era of High Capitalism,* trans. Harry Zohn (London: NLB, 1973).

longer only models and their copies that are put into play, privileged; but also the *simulacrum,* traditionally seen as false, bad, and ugly because it does not resemble enough the Original *or* its copies.

In fact, "One defines modernity by the potency of the *simulacrum.*"[2] The power and full implications of this statement are only slowly becoming more tangible to those still thinking in a psychologized and representational mode (and almost everyone is), especially with regard to their own experience. For example, media and computer technology are no longer so limited in scope: most of us can at least begin to glimpse the ways in which the components of "our lives" have already been imagined, repeated, erased, spliced to other "lives"; ways which are not only out of our own control, but under no-One's control at all, except perhaps that of technology itself.

In French thought over the past thirty years, the question of exactly how "experience," "knowledge," and "truth" are so out of kilter for modernity has not been swept aside as it has tended to be in Anglo-American theory.[3] The effort to rethink and experiment with the ways in which reality, as imaginary and symbolic construction, can today be experienced, known, and finally changed has been constant. This has entailed, for the most part, the attempt to move beyond mechanistic cause/effect theories based in reflection; this has been done by privileging different kinds of "cultural cement": ideology, the unconscious, language, and therefore writing. In effect, for many contemporary theorists and writers, to be radical in our culture may require new kinds of mental acrobatics: for example, to be radical may no longer be to work for the side that is "right," speaks the "truth," is most "just." It may in fact be to work rather for the *Pseudos,* for "the highest power of falsehood";[4] it may be to opt for overwhelming falsehood, thereby confusing and finally destroying the oppressive system of representation which would have us believe not only in its subsystems of models (the real, the first) versus simulacra (the unreal, inauthentic), good versus bad, true versus false; but would also have us believe in a world ultimately obsessed with self-destruction.

It is, in fact, most likely obvious by now to the reader that, following our writers, lost in the folds of the fabricated and delegitimized narratives that surround us, disarmed of the *cogito* and the dialectics of representa-

---

2. See Gilles Deleuze, "Simulacre et philosophie antique," in *Logique du sens,* p. 306.
3. Marcelin Pleynet has put it this way: "Our experience remains the captive of a knowledge which is no longer really our experience; our knowledge is embarrassed by an experience which has not yet become knowledge." "La levée de l'interprétation des signes," in *Art et littérature* (Paris: Editions du Seuil, 1977).
4. Deleuze, *Logique du sens,* p. 303.

tion, any question of "truth" in and for modernity can only be a tentative one. It will therefore only concern us here to the extent that a certain definition of truth, based in a highly personal, naturalized "reality," is not only intrinsic to but also the last line of defense for feminism as hermeneutic. Feminism, while infinite in its variations, is finally rooted in the belief that women's truth-in-experience-and-reality is and has always been different from men's and that it as well as its artifacts and productions have consequently been devalued and always already delegitimized in patriarchal culture. Feminists tend to see the fact that Man, men, are experiencing a form of delegitimation today either as a positive step toward demystifying the politics of male sexuality in patriarchy or as nothing other than another complex ruse of patriarchal reason. As with the other questions in this study, it is not certain that the choice is that clear-cut.

It is certainly not clear if we look closely at the writers in France rethinking truth-in-modernity. Their major battle, in the wake of Heidegger, Nietzsche, and Freud, has been to unravel the illusion that some kind of universal truth exists which can be proven by some so-called universal experience. This stand against the historically solid alliance between truth and experience has been a stand against humanism—a positive step for women in most ways, but with a twist. For these writers, truth, therefore, can equal neither "experience" nor "reality" as those words have been philosophically understood in the West since Plato—and therefore any discourse rooting itself in either one is, in truth, an ancient, uselessly repetitious fiction.

The history of universal truth is the history of metaphysics and its attendant definitions of the Good and the Moral: from Plato's *esse verum* to Aristotle's *eikos;* from the theological *propositio* of the Middle Ages to Positivist *Logic;* from Hegel's *Absolute* to the Phenomenological *Experience.* Heidegger, closest to the writers we are concerned with, was to place major emphasis on this long, common history. His best-known analysis of metaphysical truth as *Alētheia* (the unveiled), that of Plato's myth of the cave, makes clear the continuity in Western definitions of the Truth: the unveiling, bringing to light of that which had been lost, hidden, veiled, badly "represented." Truth in the West has always been defined as "exactitude of representation" in which "man thinks everything according to 'ideas' and appreciates all reality according to values."[5] The stripping of veils, the ascendant "striptease toward the Idea," ordered by Man-in-

5. Martin Heidegger, "La doctrine de Platon sur la vérité," in *Questions II,* pp. 143–44, 162. The reader will also want to refer to "On the Essence of Truth" in *Existence and Being;* as well as to "Logos" and "Alētheia" in *Early Greek Thinking,* trans. David Farrell Krell and Frank A. Capuzzi (New York: Harper & Row, 1975).

command, is what Heidegger tells us has led to the twentieth century's dominantly pragmatic, when not imperialistic, posture toward knowledge, as well as to a conjunction between the movement toward pure Idea and the "ought to" of teleology, futurity, and obligation. According to Heidegger, if we are to survive the twentieth century, Man can no longer be the "opener of truth" but must find a way to become the opening *for* it. Heidegger will eventually turn to the poets to find that "way."

Before Heidegger, Nietzsche and Freud had already spread enormous doubt about our ability to reach Truth through the ascendancy of judgment. For Nietzsche, truth is Man's oldest illusion. Even more important, why is it that Man has so fervently desired the Truth? *"Why not rather untruth? And uncertainty? Even ignorance?"*[6] The shock of recognition that Western Truth, and the Western desire for Truth, have been a terrible error is what Nietzsche leaves for the twentieth century to gain the hard way.

Freud regards truth, of course, as even more difficult to locate, untenable-as-judgment, and it is in his work that truth finds its first concrete displacements, away from experience, away from reality: "It has not been possible to demonstrate in other connections that the human intellect has a particularly fine flair for the truth. We have rather found, on the contrary, that our intellect very easily goes astray without any warning, and that nothing is more easily believed by us than what, without reference to the truth, comes to meet our wishful illusions."[7] For psychoanalysis, truth can consist only of parcels of "truth" from the past which return to us deformed, disconnected; they return from and through the unconscious into the fictions of our present lives. If, therefore, psychoanalysis as a science is to have any truth-value, it is from this recognition that we can have no access to the truths of our illusions except through an understanding of the logic of the unconscious.

Truth as veiled. Truth as error. Truth as partial and delayed, as that which we do not want to know. With those threads, the theorists of and in modernity began to weave new intellectual patterns, searching for the potential spaces of a "truth" that would be neither true nor false; for a "truth" that would be *in-vrai-semblable*, implausible, improbable, incredible, thereby making *vrai-semblance* the code word for our metaphysical heritage.[8] While this project is certainly not foreign to twentieth-century

6. Nietzsche, *Beyond Good and Evil*, trans. Helen Zimmern (New York: Macmillan, 1924), p. 5.
7. Freud, *Moses and Monotheism*, trans. James Strachey (London: Hogarth, 1974), p. 129.
8. From a psychoanalytic perspective, Jean-Michel Ribettes has maintained that

Anglo-American explorations in logic (e.g., Bertrand Russell), it has found its most radical directions and support in post-existential France.

I shall not follow in detail the battles between Lacanian psychoanalysis and Nietzschean philosophies over the stakes and status of "truth" for modernity.[9] But it is interesting to note those points on which psychoanalysis and philosophy in France would seem to agree: that 1) truth and falsehood have been and must continue to be taken out of opposition; 2) reality defined as representation can no longer play the major part in reformulating a new approach to "truth" if we are to avoid the repetitious violence of moralistic thinking; 3) no one can *tell* the truth—at least not all of it; and, finally, 4) henceforth, "truth" can only be thought through that which subverts it: the "real" for Lacan; "écriture" for Derrida; and the "becoming of difference" for Deleuze.[10]

This series of doubt-full debates around the possible positions of "truth" for modernity largely centers around the problem of "fiction," both written and oral, even as this latter distinction is already being broken down.[11] The metaphysical opposition of fiction versus truth makes no more sense; but to call it nonsense only throws us back to another opposition. Is fiction (coded as such, as a written text) a key to truth? Or is any truth always already a fiction (written or otherwise)? This debate obviously has important consequences for any literary, cultural, and political

---

vraisemblance, exactitude of representation, is also particularly *male,* belonging as it does to an obsessional rather than hysterical economy. "Le phalsus (Vrai/semblant/vraisemblance du texte obsessionnel)," in *Folle vérité,* ed. Julia Kristeva (Paris: Editions du Seuil, 1979), pp. 116–70.

9. For an introduction to some of the questions involved, see Barbara Johnson's "The Frame of Reference: Poe, Lacan, Derrida." For an overview of the polemic between Lacan and Derrida, also see Spivak's introduction to Derrida, *Of Grammatology,* esp. pp. lxiii–lxvii.

10. On "truth" in Lacan, one would want to look especially at his "Au-delà du 'Principe de réalité'" and "La science et la vérité," in *Ecrits;* the opening pages of *Télévision* (Paris: Editions du Seuil, 1973); "Radiophonie" (on the *semblant*), *Scilicet* 2/3 (Paris: Editions du Seuil, n.d.); and "Le savoir et la vérité," in *Encore.* For an overview of the problems of *la vérité, la vraisemblance,* and *le semblant* in psychoanalysis, I have found the collection of essays in *Folle vérité* (ed. Kristeva) very useful. On the position of "truth" in Derrida, besides "The Purveyor of Truth," see especially *Positions,* trans. Alan Bass, pp. 111–13, n. 44; and *Spurs/Eperons.* In Deleuze, cf., e.g.: *Différence et répétition,* pp. 198–217; and *Nietzsche,* pp. 108–11.

The contemporary polemic surrounding truth and fiction is obviously not limited to these writers. Cf., for example, Barthes's early *Critique et vérité* (Paris: Editions du Seuil, 1966).

11. The Derridean wearing-away of both the common and the uncommon distinctions between speech and writing owes much to Freud. The reader might want to refer to Naomi Schor, "Le détail chez Freud," *Littérature,* no. 37 (February 1980) for a reading, in the wake of Derrida, of how, in Freud, the detail in a written text is seen as a disseminator of fiction while, orally, it is revelatory of truth.

criticism concerned with how to situate texts as a force for change in the "reality" of the world—especially since these texts have caught up with psychoanalysis and philosophy in France. For "truth" is traditionally "to be right"; in French, it is to have reason (*avoir raison*). Traditionally, where reason is lost, things are wrong, insane. A cultural critic who judges a fiction as not true judges it as being beyond reason—which is all it ever set out to be in the traditional scheme of things. To judge a text as wrong, as not having reason, is not to disrupt anything, but is instead, in a terrible twist, to confirm the viability of the original metaphysical opposition.[12] Clearly, traditional acts of literary criticism based in this kind of judgment are henceforth seen to be caught in a strange, mutually congratulatory relationship with the text they are judging.[13]

In any case, according to our writers, the true can no longer be linked to traditional notions of experience-in-the-world, those notions having reached their highest point in Hegel's definition of experience as discourse *within* a subject-conscious-of-himself: "*Inasmuch as the new true object issues from it,* this *dialectical* movement which consciousness exercises on itself and which affects both its knowledge and its object, is precisely what is called *experience* [*Erfahrung*]."[14] Experience in this sense can only be an *appropriation* of the "real," thus transforming it into "reality" by and for the Cartesian Subject. The phenomenology of existentialism, for example, came to be seen in Europe as the last anthropological system of thought to have attempted to bridge the gap between the *percipio* and the *cogito*: the fact that we *live* in one world where we can see only "fragments" while we *think* in another world according to the knowledge that we can obtain about the whole that we can never see. The phenomenologists attempted to found the cogito in the percipio in order to understand how meaning comes to be and then judge that meaning according to moral standards. But ultimately, that transcendental gesture accounts for their sole reliance

12. To begin unraveling this problematic more slowly, one might start with Foucault and Derrida's polemic over Descartes: Foucault, *Madness and Civilization,* trans. Richard Howard (New York: Mentor, 1967); Derrida, "Cogito and the History of Madness," in *Writing and Difference;* Foucault, "Mon corps, ce papier, ce feu," appendix to the second edition of *Folie et déraison.* Also of import is Shoshana Felman's *La folie et la chose littéraire,* where insanity *is* the literary substance.

13. Anglo-American feminist criticism is particularly prone to distinctions between Truth and Falsehood, Right and Wrong, Sane and Insane—or Honesty and Dishonesty. For example: "*The Great Gatsby* is a dishonest book because the culture from which it derives and which it reflects is radically dishonest" (Fetterley, *The Resisting Reader,* p. 94).

14. Hegel, *Phenomenology of Spirit,* trans. A. V. Miller (Oxford: Clarendon, 1977), p. 55. The reader might want to refer to Heidegger, *Hegel's Concept of Experience* (New York: Harper & Row, 1970).

on the ethic of *praxis*: the only possible truth *now* is that truth based in the living present—for *me*—in the immediacy of true experience.

It is clear that this "me" around which the world turns was to become totally unacceptable to post-existential France. The concept of experience was radically displaced: "experience" came to be thought of as that process which exceeds mastery, as the "silence" of discourse, as that which disturbs the subject-present-to-itself.[15] The emphasis has been placed on that which continually undermines any credulity or belief based in experience-only-to-be-then-expressed-in-language: on ideology, desire, the unconscious, fiction as anti-knowledge. For the theorists of modernity, only an empiricist could believe that language expresses-without-loss-of-reality, that it can faithfully translate experience, that it makes no *difference*.

Empiricism—the "science of experience"—is, of course, that doctrine which holds that all knowledge originates in direct experience of what is commonly called reality, without theory, and undisturbed by language. That is, where language is superfluous to life.

Whatever the fundmentally empirical foundations of psychoanalysis in practice (that is, as based in vision), Lacan's entire "return to Freud" was in reaction against empiricism: empiricism was seen by Lacan as being at the very roots of Anglo-American conservative, normative, recuperative psychologies (such as behaviorism). The only possible place for "experience," according to Lacan, is in the experiential and experimental language of the "analytical experience" as analogous to fiction.

The philosophers, however, did not find it quite so easy, or productive, to reject empiricism so quickly. In fact, empiricism is in some ways posited by them as a beginning from which to question philosophy most radically—as its opposite.

For example, in Derrida's work, experience has always equaled presence, transparency, egotism, meaning, and, therefore, violence.[16] Like any other metaphysical commonplace, however, experience cannot simply be done away with or denied, but must be used under erasure because of its relationship to the history of philosophy as a nonphilosophy, an anti-philosophy.[17] Empiricism is philosophically incapable of justifying itself: "But

---

15. The reader has probably already recognized the presence here of Georges Bataille: see *L'expérience intérieure* (Paris: Gallimard, 1970–1973). On Bataille's notion of experience, see Kristeva's "L'expérience et la pratique," in *Polylogue,* and Derrida's "From Restricted to General Economy," in *Writing and Difference.*

16. Cf. Derrida, *Writing and Difference,* pp. 132–33, 152; *Of Grammatology,* pp. 60–61; and *Positions,* trans. Alan Bass, p. 30.

17. Derrida, *Of Grammatology,* p. 60.

this incapacitation, when resolutely assumed, contests the resolution and coherence of the logos (philosophy) at its root, instead of letting itself be questioned by the logos. Therefore, nothing can so profoundly *solicit* the Greek logos—philosophy—than this irruption of the totally-other; and nothing can to such an extent reawaken the logos to its origin as to its mortality, its other."[18] As the Other of philosophy, empiricism constitutes a point of departure, exorbitant in its exteriority, for Derridean deconstruction—until the very concept of empiricism itself begins to self-destruct: "To *exceed* the metaphysical orb is an attempt to get out of the orbit (*orbita*), to think the entirety of the classical conceptual oppositions, particularly the one within which the value of empiricism is held. [. . .] The opening of the question, the departure from the closure of a self-evidence, the putting into doubt of a system of oppositions, all these movements necessarily have the form of empiricism and of errancy. [. . .] We must begin *wherever we are* . . ."[19] Those moments when the Derridean strategy opens the text to so-called empirical events—biography, historical anecdotes, and so on—are, from their beginnings, the most radical moments the reader can experience in philosophy—the openings toward the writing that can begin to split open any closed philosophical system.

Like Derrida, Deleuze sees empiricism as an anti-philosophy. Unlike Derrida, however, Deleuze does not put empirical experience under erasure but, with a non-self-reflexively exorbitant leap, explodes it beyond any possible or at least any believable representation of "reality": empiricism is not Deleuze's philosophical doctrine, but his ode to Anglo-American philosophy and literature. For him, empiricism operates against the concept of "the principle," the principles of philosophy, through an insistence on "life" and the ways it can force systems to their breaking point: "if one sees something there which traverses life, but which thinking finds repugnant, in that case thinking must be forced to think it, to make of it thinking's point of hallucination, an experimentation which does violence to thinking . . ."[20] It is ultimately Deleuze's "escape lines" away from founding principles that provide new pathways for this necessary hallucination; new ways towards *becoming*—the only ways Deleuze would risk changing what *is* (philosophy).

18. *Writing and Difference,* p. 152.
19. *Of Grammatology,* p. 162.
20. Deleuze and Parnet, *Dialogues,* pp. 68–72.

Faced with this demise of "conscious experience" in the world, the feminist reader will perhaps find some more questions.

She will most certainly welcome the demise of Truth—Man's Truth. She will agree that the dream of unveiling the Truth-in-its-entirety, so as to shine in its veracity, has turned into a nightmare (created by men); that, in fact, it is Man's *apocalypse* (etymologically to dis-cover, un-cover, to reveal the secret).[21] But, on the other hand, she will also understand that it is not enough to *oppose* Man's Truth; the very conceptual systems that have posited it must be undermined. And, finally, she will begin to recognize that many of those conceptual systems are intrinsic to feminist thinking whether or not openly declared: systems of defining the self, perception, judgment, and, therefore, morality.[22]

"Morality" is perhaps that which most stubbornly adheres to Truth-in-judgment. What is true is also good. What is false is bad. *Ethics*—the discipline devoted to deciding what is good and bad—will be one of the first *systems* to be rejected as an institution, after Freud and Nietzsche, by psychoanalysis and philosophy in France. For Lacan, psychoanalysis must become allergic to any form of ethics—for to indulge in morality (or in any form of social reformation) is to fall prey to (American) normalizing pedagogy.[23] For the philosophers, ethics is inseparable from the history of philosophy. Both Greek and Christian, ethics is the language of priests. If Deleuzians have for the most part avoided the problem, creating an ethic for every new occasion, Derrideans have recently been a bit more sensitive to the necessity of necessity: "There is therefore a duty—or, if you wish, a duty is being decided upon, a duty which is *final* in every sense of the expression, the duty of the question, of the maintenance of the question of the ends, or the questions of the end of philosophy. That is the answer."[24] Given that *ethos* means *heim,* at home, as in Plato's cavern, the point may be not to rush out of the cavern with everyone else, but rather to stay, to

---

21. See Derrida on the "Apocalypse": "D'un ton apocalyptique adopté naguère en philosophie," in *Les fins de l'homme,* pp. 445–87.

22. The relationship of feminism to moral and moralistic thinking has recently become the site of new feminist questions in France, especially through the work of the study group "Le Sexisme Ordinaire" of *Les temps modernes.* For an introduction to the problem, see the issue of *Les cahiers du GRIF* "Jouir," vol. 26 (March 1983), esp. Françoise Petitot, "Inter-dire," pp. 89–92. That the question of feminism's relationship to traditional morality has not been adequately posed in this country is evidenced by internal splits in the women's movement over S/M, pornography, censorship, etc.

23. See, for example, "La direction de la cure." Lacan himself delayed the publication of his *Ethique de la psychoanalyse* (published in a "pirate edition") for fear it would be positivized.

24. *Les fins de l'homme,* p. 169.

render it strange, uncanny—to develop an *ethos unheimlich* by questioning the writing on the walls of the cave itself.[25]

The *true*, then, is to be thought strangely by modernity, outside of the metaphysical categories of opposition—or between them. This approach involves, first and foremost, a relinquishing of mastery, indeed a valorization of nonmastery. And, as we know, a lack of mastery has, historically, always connoted the feminine.[26] Secondly, the *true*, to be isolated in those processes anterior to or, in some cases, beyond the Truth as produced by the *technē*, is that which can never be seen, which never presents itself as such but rather captures, points, withdraws, hides itself in its veils: and that *true* is seen as being "woman"—the "nontruth" or "partial true" of Truth. Or, for others, "woman" is precisely that element which disturbs even that presupposition (Truth as castrated).

Whatever the strange intricacies of these new wanderings through the demise of Truth-in-Experience, "woman" is that element most *discursively present*. Julia Kristeva has called this new element in modernity a *vréel*—a kind of "she-truth":

> We can today perceive, by listening to the discourses that speak to us as contemporaries as well as to the approaches which try to speak of the source and progression of those discourses, that the great upheaval of speaking beings today can be summarized in this way: the *truth* [*vérité*] which they are seeking (which they are trying to tell), is the *real* [*réel*]—"Vréel" then. An obsessive fear since the beginning of time, this experience is becoming today, if not one of the masses, at least massive, weighty; even more so because no common code is there to neutralize it by justifying it. [. . .] The ancient question returns: how to render the vréel more likely, more representable [*vraisemblable*]?[27]

The only way, of course, to render this "vréel" *vraisemblable,* seemingly true, is to put it into discourse in new ways: hence the *gynesis* whose potential spaces we have had to outline so schematically here. The demise of the Subject, of the Dialectic, and of Truth has left modernity with a *void* that it is vaguely aware must be spoken differently and strangely: as woman, through gynesis.

What can be the feminist's response to these manifestations of gynesis and its strange body? Is not her first impulse to deny it?—to charge that

---

25. Ibid., p. 172.
26. Cf., for example, Gilbert and Gubar's *Madwoman in the Attic,* p. 10.
27. Kristeva, *Folle vérité,* p. 11. The neologism, *vréel,* suggests the words *vrai*(truth), *réel* (real), and *elle* (she).

these "processes beyond representation" are but part of a new ruse invented by Man to avoid, once again, his own truth and experience? But, on the other hand, in order to demonstrate that, are we not just as obliged, as feminists, to put the signifier woman into circulation, ourselves to engage in gynesis? Whose ruse is it *then?* And whose *gynesis?*

It is too easy to put gynesis down to "idealism" as somehow opposed to feminism, a true "materialism." As long as we do not explore the boundaries of and possible common spaces between modernity and feminism; as long as we do not recognize new kinds of artificial, symbolic constructions of the subject, representation, and (especially) experience, we will be engaging in what are ultimately conservative and dated polemics, not radical theory and practice. It becomes particularly tempting at times of extreme political crisis to abandon this challenge of our century and revert to a "natural view of things": reality is what I see, hear, and touch. Nothing could be more reactionary—or pointless—in postmodern culture. As Jane Gallop has so succinctly put it, "Belief in simple referentiality is not only unpoetic but also ultimately politically conservative, because it cannot recognize that the reality to which it appeals is a traditional ideological construction, whether one terms it phallomorphic, or metaphysical, or bourgeois, or something else. The politics of experience is inevitably a conservative politics for it cannot help but conserve traditional ideological constructs which are not recognized as such but are taken for the 'real.'"[28]

To question how thought-in-modernity and feminism itself may both be inscribing woman as the ultimate truth of and for modernity is, for the feminist today, to risk becoming entangled in her own apocalypse.

But then, that is a risk intrinsic to modernity itself—and I think it is a risk worth taking.

To do so, however, feminists must *take* the risk, must "dive into the wreck" of Western culture rather than push it aside:

> We are, I am, you are
> by cowardice or courage
> the one who find our way
> back to this scene
> carrying a knife, a camera
> a book of myths
> in which
> our names do not appear.[29]

28. Jane Gallop, *"Quand nos lèvres s'écrivent:* Irigaray's Body Politic," *Romanic Review* 74:1 (January 1983): 83.

29. From Adrienne Rich's "Diving into the Wreck," *Diving into the Wreck, Poems 1971–1972* (New York: W. W. Norton & Company, Inc., 1973).

GYNESIS III

INTERTEXTS

Field of signification where there has been a transposition of one
or more systems of signs into another, accompanied by new
articulations of the enunciative and denotative position.

8

Toward the Hysterical Body: Jacques Lacan and His Others

> On the whole, a woman is much more than that. She is the
> necessary representation for that which constitutes in every dis-
> course this *Weibliche* as the nomination of the fundamental
> necessity for the constitution of articulated discourse.
>
> Wladimir Granoff, *La pensée et le féminin*

> . . . the substance of the repressed being on the side of the
> feminine.
>
> Sigmund Freud, letter to W. Fliess

The fact that woman and her obligatory connotations are
essential to the functioning of psychoanalytic theory has never been denied
by those caught up in the conflicting winds of the polemical tornado that
psychoanalysis always seems to produce. Less often emphasized until recently, however, has been the fact that psychoanalysis was founded as a
science on *women*—that is, on women hysterics. It was Freud's work with
Jean-Martin Charcot in Paris on the iconography of hysteria that was to
lead to his first full-length study with Josef Breuer, *Studies in Hysteria*, and,
indeed, to his use of the word psychoanalysis itself. As Stephen Heath
puts it, "The discourse of hysteria is not just a beginning of psychoanalysis, it is, in its forcing of the signifying matter, a fundamental condition."[1]

Of course, Freud was the first to admit that *men* could also be hysterics
(much to the surprise of the Viennese Medical Society), and he would

1. Heath, "Difference," p. 55. Also see his *The Sexual Fix* (London: MacMillan, 1982).

continually insist that, indeed, "we have been in the habit of taking as the subject of our investigation the male child."[2] Within this strange gap between the female bodies at the inceptions of psychoanalysis and the male subject taken as its norm, and especially within the resultant syntax, lies the power (and, for some, the faults) of psychoanalysis itself. "The hysteric is a woman who can also be a man" becomes, in a hallucinatory conceptual leap, the very definition of hysteria as an object of psychoanalytic knowledge. Through this gap, itself hysterical, slipped the confusion between women and "woman," a confusion which in turn generated a perpetual oscillation that has never been able to move beyond its first contradictory articulation. Indeed, when Michèle Montrelay today posits a "speech said to be 'hysterical' but which should rather be qualified as feminine" because "all women enjoy the use of their uterus," we are back with the Viennese Medical Society in spite of Freud's very precise (and then shocking) objections.[3] It is no wonder, then, that psychoanalysis is ultimately about "saving the name of the father"—for without him, who could possibly know what (whose body) we are talking about anyway?

This oscillation among female bodies, male subjects, and the words used to describe both extends to Freudian analysts themselves; and, of course, Lacan was the first to recognize that. His portrait of the analyst is not very different from that of the hysteric: in fact, he finds the analyst to be "a perfect hysteric, that is, without symptoms, except from time to time mistakes in gender."[4] This oscillation has, in reference to Lacan's reference, also and perhaps inevitably become part of the public mythology surrounding Lacan himself: Lacan—*le père sévère,* the thundering father with a falsetto voice. Catherine Clément has written of him as a shaman with "the powers of travesty which will make of him a something else, not a man, not a woman, superhuman."[5] It is almost as if, through his relentless return to Freud, Lacan was himself forced to *incarnate* the gaps in the immaculate conception at the foundations of psychoanalytic theory itself: female body, male subject, an oscillating name. He even repeated, strangely, Freud's itinerary: like Freud, "Lacan only interested himself, in the beginning, in women."[6] The Papin Sisters, Saint Teresa, Marcelle,

2. Sigmund Freud, "Some Psychical Consequences of the Anatomical Distinction between the Sexes," *The Complete Psychological Works,* vol. 19, p. 249.

3. Montrelay, *L'ombre et le nom,* p. 28.

4. Lacan, "Séminaire," *Ornicar?* 12/13 (November 16, 1976): 12. Also see *Encore,* p. 41. Granoff has developed this thesis at length in *La pensée et le féminin.*

5. Catherine Clément, *Vies et légendes de Jacques Lacan* (Paris: Bernard Grasset, 1981), p. 235.

6. Ibid., pp. 70, 75.

Aimée, Hadewijch d'Anvers, right up to "the lady analysts," all provided the bodies for Lacan's theoretical metonymy. And yet he founded his school, he posited his theories of absolute sexual difference, but never moved beyond the *male subject* as absolute metaphor. In taking psychoanalytic theory further than anyone before him, he, like Freud, was never able to fathom the "dark continent" of female sexuality.

This strange repetition-in-Freudian-syntax is of interest here only inasmuch as it was syntax itself that Lacan attempted to stretch to its breaking point in his seminars; a breaking point which he named "feminine jouissance" and with which he and so many others have identified. I will not be concerned here with Lacan's "images of women" or with his railings against feminists—those have been increasingly treated elsewhere.[7] Rather, I shall examine how this breaking-of-syntax leads to gynesis and to that strange feminine body which, no longer that of Charcot's photographic hysteric, has rematerialized as *iso-graphic*: as *writing*. The fact that psychoanalytic discourse seems unable to exist outside this oscillation between the female body and the male subject is worth pondering, however. Is it not strange how Lacan's oral and self-consciously male contestations of Order and Syntax have finally relegated that which is "feminine" to another hysterical body: the *written* text? It is almost as if he were but a frail link between Freud's hysterics and the hysterical texts of modernity, both unsure of their sex and iconoclastic to the extreme.

Among Cartesian orphans, Lacan is certainly one of the best-known explorers of the spatial contours of gynesis. He is an inventor of new spaces, or rather a reorganizer of those spaces we already know, so as to emphasize their unsuspected productivity. Barbara Johnson has linked together Lacan with Derrida in their attempts to displace the Euclidean model of understanding, to re-explore the boundaries of what can be comprehended.[8] Johnson describes this project in terms of developing new ways of seeing—and, I would add, of not seeing. For, as Lacan will say of the unconscious, "The word 'everywhere' fits an unperceived thing as well as 'nowhere.'"[9] "Everywhere" and "nowhere" would indeed describe well the places not only of the unconscious but of those other spaces whose comprehension Lacan and his others show to be so utterly impossible. From the logic of Borromean knots to "literature" itself, those spaces

7. The most comprehensive and intelligent critiques of Lacan's "images of women" may be found in *Feminist Issues*. For an example of Lacan's posture toward "Les dames du MLF" (Mouvement de libération des femmes), see *Encore*, pp. 54, 69.

8. Johnson, "The Frame of Reference: Poe, Lacan, Derrida," p. 482.

9. Lacan, *Télévision*, p. 15.

escape any comprehension even if, ultimately, they may be apprehended. That this distinction between comprehending and apprehending involves new relationships to *physis,* that is, new methods of capturing "truth," will come as no surprise; nor can it be unexpected, therefore, that this attention to *physis* involves new relationships to the feminine as well.

We have already looked briefly at some of the ways in which Lacan's work, to the extent that it is engaged in the project of modernity, is linked to gynesis. It is in his *Séminaire XX: Encore*[10] that these links are most explicit—and his new feminine spaces most pervasive. There he elaborates, elaborately, how and why "woman" is that which escapes any form of universal logic, how and why "woman is not All." He shows how, as opposed to Universal Man (the Self of humanist thought), "woman" may be seen as the anti-universal *par excellence.* Generally considered as his major contribution to knowledge about the "dark continent of female sexuality," *Encore* has been the object of numerous studies.[11] Yet, what is most surprising about this seminar is that it is not ostensibly about women at all: except for Saint Teresa, "the ladies of the MLF," and women analysts, *women* are absent. The titles of the sessions reflect this: we find there, among other things, jouissance, Jakobson, the signifier, love and love letters, Aristotle, Freud, God, knowledge, the Baroque, knots, rats in labyrinths; but only one "woman"—who is not a woman but the woman. We will return to her shortly.

This is not surprising if we remember Lacan's primary hypothesis, a hypothesis repeated in the early pages of the seminar: "Men, women and children, these are only signifiers" (p. 34). He reminds us of this founding hypothesis throughout *Encore*—in the event that we might be tempted to rephenomenologize these words. We are the children, boys and girls, riding on a train pulling into Lacan's station: the boys will see a door marked "Ladies" and the girls one marked "Gentlemen." The chance that the boy and the girl might see the same word or the same words in the opposite order is, of course, not excluded. The fact that we are seated in the order we are remains, however, beyond our control—it has been

10. The connotations of the title, *Encore,* are numerous. There is first, of course, its theatrical bravado to be accounted for. And *encore* in French has multiple significations: for example, "still" (as in "to still be doing something"); "what's more"; "so what?"; and, most important, the simple "more." It most generally suggests some kind of combination of repetition and supplement. There is also the phonetic play with *en corps* (in the flesh)—as enacted by Hélène Cixous in her fiction-novel *Là*—as well as "*Enc(re)/Or*" (golden ink). All further page references to *Encore* are given in the text.
11. In English, for example, see Heath's "Difference."

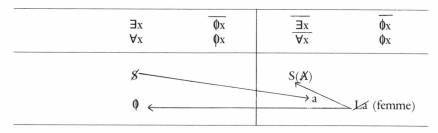

$\exists x \,\overline{\emptyset x}$ = The Primitive Father
$\forall x \,\emptyset x$ = The Phallic Function

$\overline{\exists x} \,\overline{\emptyset x}$ = The Woman as Not All
$\overline{\forall x} \,\emptyset x$ = The Woman in the Phallic Function

Figure 1. (From Jacques Lacan, Le Séminaire Livre XX *[Paris: Edition du Seuil, 1975]. Reproduced by permission of M. Jacques-Alain Miller and Editions du Seuil.)*

determined for us by our culture, and again by Lacan. So much for Nature.

This obligatory cultural seating arrangement leads us into the major postulate of the seminar—a postulate constructed around four points: jouissance, the Other, the sign, and love (p. 40). Postulate: There is no sexual relation: the only basis of analytic discourse is that "there is no— that it is impossible to pose—sexual relation" (p. 14). This is "the only truth" of psychoanalysis, even if psychoanalysis was not the first to re-mark it (p. 17). Two bodies marked male and female, carried along in a signifying chain, can never meet; they never have and they never will, according to Lacan.

Lacan's most graphic statement in *Encore* will perhaps clarify this hope-less situation and allow us to explore with him some new spaces. The left-hand side of Figure 1 (above) represents the "male part" of speaking subjects and the right-hand side the "female part." According to Lacan, any speaking subject can inscribe himself or herself on either side. The formulas at the top of the graph represent "ideal" situations—"outside of history" as Lacan would say—while the bottom half represents the itiner-ary of speaking subjects as sexed in history and culture.[12] Those who are sexed male must cope with Universal Man: the primitive father who de-nied castration, $\exists x \,\overline{\emptyset x}$. Those bodies sexed male may or may not deny it,

12. *Encore*, p. 73. In spite of Lacan's own lengthy warnings about the dangers of resorting to graphs, the distinctions and interrelationships between the top and the bottom halves of the graph are never questioned, nor is the fact that one assumes the other.

hence the possibility of also having $\forall x \; \phi x$. On the right side of the graph, we might expect to find Universal Woman: but, Lacan tells us, she does not exist. She is always already "barred." Beyond that distinction, the same two possibilities exist as to castration: $\overline{\exists x \; \phi x}$ or $\overline{\forall x} \; \phi x$. This "woman," who is never universal, is represented in the lower half of the graph by $\overline{La}$. What is this woman, then? "There is no woman except she who is excluded by the nature of things which is the nature of words, and it must be said that if there is something about which women themselves complain enough for the moment, it's certainly about that—simply, they [women] don't know what they're saying, that's the whole difference between them and me" (p. 68). Or again,

> [. . .] that means that when no matter what speaking subject falls in under the banner of women, this proceeds from the fact that he is founding himself as being not-all, by placing himself in the phallic function [to be the phallus]. That is what defines the . . . the what?—woman exactly, with this exception, that Woman [*La* femme] can only be written by barring the *La*. There is no Woman [*La femme*], with a definite article for designating the universal. There is no Woman because—I have already ventured the term, and why should I think twice about it—with regard to her essence, she is not all. (p. 68)

She is not All with regard to her essence; in essence, she is not All.[13] Woman is divided, multiple, everywhere and nowhere on Lacan's graph. Does *Le Tout,* an "All," exist for the right side of the graph? Of course; it is the Mother. Here is where Lacan's distinction between woman and the mother becomes insistent. If it is true that woman can enter into the sexual relation only under the sign of motherhood, that does not mean that she *is* a mother. A mother is a woman-with-child, her "hole is corked," and she has become All. For Lacan, woman as absent subject is not the Mother: "and don't speak to me about the secondary sex characteristics of the woman, because, until a new order, it is those of the mother which prevail in her. Nothing distinguishes woman as a sexual being, if not precisely her sex, her sexual organs" (p. 13).

Woman is not All. *Women* are not All? The distance between the singular and plural is quickly traversed. For Lacan, women have a "particular function in the symbolic order"; a "dead-end position"; with a "second

13. Many defenders of Lacan have remarked that feminist objections to this observation are misguided—for, they say, this is exactly what feminism is about: the belief that women must not be abstracted, idealized. For example, Catherine Clément: "Lacan, by working on a tiny article of the language—the 'the' [*la*]—claimed as his own a very old issue for women, and he knew it" (Clément, *Vies et légendes,* p. 77). I am tempted to add: that is all the difference between him and us.

degree relationship" to the symbolic order.[14] And a woman does not and cannot know anything about any of this, according to Lacan. She is a woman to the extent "that she cannot find herself" (p. 94); she does not correspond to a self-in-language: "there is always something about and in her which escapes discourse" (p. 34); she must be taken as "One-less" (p. 116).

The fact that woman is not All has, of course, particular consequences for men—for Man, who can, if only ideally, be All. For one thing, this fact would seem to account for Don Juan as a universal phenomenon: "Women, from the moment there are names, can be put on a list and be counted [. . .] If woman were not not-all, if in her body she were not not-all as a sexed being, nothing of all this would hold" (p. 15).

Of course, "One [men] can also put oneself [themselves] on the side of the not-all. There are men who are there as well as women. This happens. And who by the same token are quite comfortable there. Despite, I will not say their phallus, but despite that which encumbers them under this title they glimpse, they experiment with the idea that there must be a jouissance that is beyond. These are what one calls mystics" (p. 70).

Caught between Don Juan and male mystics—let us go back to Figure 1. The man-in-the-world (left side of the graph: $), a nonetheless-divided-subject, supported by the phallus (φ), can never know this woman-not-all. His desire passes through the *objet petit a,* the "small object o," that object which can be anything, the object of his desire: "A look, that of Beatrice, three times nothing, a batting of the eyelashes and the exquisite loss that results: it is there that the Other looms [. . .]"[15] Man is convinced that the object of his desire is the woman, but it is really the "object o": and that is the basis of his timeless and polymorphous perversity (pp. 67–68).

The reader will notice that the "small object o" is not, however, the object of women's desire. Both their desire and its object(s) are divided, dispersed. One object of women's desire remains in the sphere of "woman" S(Å), the other in the sphere of "man" (φ). The first is jouissance S(Å) and the other is the phallus (φ). She desires both; she never corresponds to One (Ⱡɑ). When the phallus rules, according to Lacan, she is a "phallic woman" (and can be dismissed along with Queen Victoria). Her constant and simultaneous desire for jouissance, however—S(Å)—will constitute the center piece of Lacan's seminar.

What is signified by this S(Å)? A as Å is, first of all, Lacan's famous

14. Lacan, "Sosie," in *Séminaire II* (Paris: Editions du Seuil, 1978), pp. 304–305.
15. Lacan, *Télévision,* p. 40.

Other—the "signifier's treasure," this time barred.[16] The function of the bar through the A is the same as for La: A is a limit, an impossible situation which can never be reached, and thus, in Lacanian terms, merits representing something to which women relate (p. 75). Given that the Other in Lacan's discourse is always woman ("The Other in my language can therefore only be the Other sex"; pp. 39–40), does that mean that this S(A) is *another* woman then? No.

Let us go back. Woman is not All. She is excluded by the nature of things, that is to say, of words. There is something *chez elle*, about and in her, that escapes discourse. But Lacan does not stop there. For if woman is not All, she nevertheless has access to what he calls a "supplementary jouissance"—beyond Man, beyond the Phallus (p. 68).

Of this supplementary jouissance, it would seem women can know nothing: "she has a jouissance, this *she* who does not exist and does not signify anything. She has a jouissance about which maybe she herself knows nothing, except that she feels it—that, she knows. She knows it, of course, when it happens. But it doesn't happen to all [women]" (p. 69). She doesn't "breathe a word about it" (p. 56), nor do the "women analysts" (pp. 54, 69).

This "extra jouissance," beyond phallic jouissance, is nonutilitarian (p. 10) and has nothing to do with love (p. 11). It has to do with the space of the Other (p. 14). It is, in fact, a *substance,* different from but not unrelated to "the quite expansive substance, complement of the other" described as "modern space": a "pure space, just as one says pure spirit" (p. 25). It is the substance discovered by Freud in the discourse of the hysteric (p. 41) and, most important, it is of the order of the infinite; it cannot be understood consciously, dialectically, or in terms of Man's Truth—for it is what we have always called "God."[17]

Lacan announces from the very beginning of the seminar that he will prove that "God" does in fact exist in the modern world—and that It would be the very substance of the Other sex (p. 44). This is in fact announced by the cover chosen for the published seminar itself: "you only

16. Lacan, "The Subversion of the Subject and the Dialectic of Desire in the Freudian Unconscious," in *Ecrits: A Selection,* p. 304.

17. It is no accident that hysteria is again evoked, sending us back to the oscillation between female body and the male subject. "Once you are dealing with an infinite ensemble, you cannot possibly posit that the not-all entails the existence of something produced by a negation, by a contradiction. You can, at the very most, posit it as an undetermined existence. [. . .] It is between the $\exists x$ and the $\overline{\exists x}$ that this indetermination is suspended, between an existence that can find itself to affirm itself [Man], and woman in that she cannot find herself [at all]" (*Encore,* p. 94).

have to go look at the statue of Bernini in Rome to understand right away that she [St. Teresa] is coming [*qu'elle jouit*], there is no doubt about it. And what is the source of this jouissance? It is clear that the essential testimony of mystics is precisely to say that they experience this jouissance, but don't know anything about it" (pp. 70–71). Stephen Heath points out that this reliance on an image (constructed by a man) falsifies Lacan's argument from the beginning.[18] But it seems to me that the emphasis is more on what we cannot see, on how what we cannot see cannot be symbolic because it is feminine. Lacan chides Charcot for wanting to bring the invisible, nonsymbolic, and therefore mystical experience back to visibility, for "If you look closely, it is not that at all" (p. 71). If we look closely, we will see that woman's jouissance as supplement, as "God," is just as invisible as is woman's vagina; we will see it as that which has an *effect* on the symbolic but cannot *be* symbolic. Woman's supplement makes up for her lack, but it, like her lack, cannot be seen. Psychoanalysis is truly a science of the invisible—a science of the S(Ⱥ) as the limit of any discourse, and especially of Lacan's own. For, by his own admission, he himself will believe in woman's jouissance (and therefore in "God") only as long as what links them (the "extra") can be *explained by him* (p. 71).

Feminine jouissance is therefore posited by Lacan as an ultimate limit to any discourse articulated by Man. It is, however, only the first of a series of such limits, which, through metonymy, will all be gendered as feminine.

The limit of any discourse for Lacan is also the "true." Truth (capital T) can or could only exist as long as there is or was a belief in Universal Woman. Freud, for example, maintained Woman as the equivalent of Truth (p. 115) with his question "What does woman want?" Lacan stresses, on the contrary, that the true is "ex-centric to Truth" (p. 94) by responding to Freud's question: "She does not want to know anything about it." The true, like the woman, is not all, "because the truth is woman already from not being all, not all to be said [to speak herself] in any case."[19] The true, after Lacan, can only be *inter-dit*, located between words, between lines, providing an access to what is perhaps the most important discursive limit for Lacan: the Real.[20]

The Real—like feminine jouissance and like the true—is *im-prévisible*. Unseen and unforeseeable, it surges out of the unconscious, as terrifying as any God, no matter what name the latter carries. Is the unconscious, then, going to be gendered as being as feminine as the other limits of the

18. Heath, "Difference," pp. 51–55.
19. Lacan, *Télévision*, p. 64.
20. See the discussion of the Real in Chapter 6, above.

symbolic which it seems to hold in store for us?[21] Yes, the unconscious, like woman, is a locus of jouissance—and (the subject) doesn't want to know anything about it at all (p. 95). Woman as Other in the sexual relation is "with regard to what can be said of the unconscious, radically the Other, [. . .] that which has to do with this Other" (p. 75).

But if Man's unconscious is "woman," what about women's unconscious? Here we arrive inevitably at a question addressed first to Lacan by a feminist, Luce Irigaray's "scandalous question": yes, but *is* woman the unconscious or does she *have* one? Lacan will reply: "Both"—but only with regard to the male subject (e.g., p. 90). Irigaray will not be satisfied with that answer. But other women analysts will begin with this supposition in their attempt to define the "female subject"—at the coordinates of writing by men and feminine jouissance.

It is no accident that those analysts will confront that question through "literature." For is the modern question put to the literary text not the same as that asked about woman? Is literature our unconscious or does it have one? Lacan will again answer "both." It has one to the extent that it does not know what it is saying. It is our unconscious to the extent that it is the space of literariness itself: *lalangue*—as *"the cloud of language* [. . . which] *makes* [up] *writing"* (p. 109). Writing is that letter which escapes discourse as its "effect," just as lalangue is that which "is at the service of completely other things than communication" (p. 126). Like the unconscious, the written text is a *savoir faire* with lalangue (p. 127).

This succession of feminine spaces is enough to make the woman reader dizzy. Is writing then going to be gendered as being as feminine as "feminine jouissance," the "true," the "Real," and the "unconscious"? Here Lacan stops. Beyond the realm of intersubjectivity, for Lacan, there can be no understanding. Lacan will call a halt to his feminine metonymy when faced with literature itself—except to the extent that lalangue is necessarily maternal and that the "letter" always has what he calls a "feminizing effect."[22] In spite of Lacan's irritating paternalism we must not forget that he consistently shied away from going beyond his own early warning that "the images and symbols *within* and *by* (*chez*) woman can never be separated from the images and symbols *of* (*de*) woman."[23] If "woman" in his thought designates that which subverts the Subject, Representation, and

---

21. Freud obviously thought so, if only to the extent that "she" controls our destiny. See, for example, Freud, "The Theme of the Three Caskets," in *On Creativity and the Unconscious* (New York: Harper & Row, 1958), pp. 63–76.

22. Lacan, "Litturaterre," *Littérature*, no. 3 (1971).

23. Lacan, *Ecrits*, p. 728.

Truth, it is because "she" does so in the history of Western thought. To make such an assertion is perhaps to continue it uncritically. In any case, psychoanalysis alone can go no further than that recognition without rephenomenologizing its original conception. The next link in the feminine chain will be left to Lacan's Others.

One important group of those Others is no doubt what might be called the orthodox Lacanian women analysts. They are "orthodox," no matter what distance they may have taken from Lacan as a historical character, to the extent that they always begin where Lacan left off, without ever putting any of his hypotheses into question—and to the extent that they turn to literature for *exempla* of their theories. That is, they turn to literature as support for their theoretical systems, never as a questioning of those systems. While I cannot do justice to their work here, it is worth briefly following one or two chains of argument. That in itself is a difficult task for the feminist reader, because their chains of feminine signifiers, woman, women, feminine, femininity, are hopelessly entangled—in exactly the way Lacan warned they would be if men, women, and children became something other than "just signifiers."

One of Lacan's Others is Eugénie Lemoine-Luccioni. She begins with Lacan's barring of Universal Woman (~~the~~ woman): woman is not All. Woman is divided, partitioned, that is her specificity: "Rather than the anguish of castration, woman knows in this way the anguish of *partition*. She truly lives under the sign of abandonment: mother, father, children, husband, penis, the entire world deserts her."[24] Living under the sign of loss and partition, woman, for Lemoine-Luccioni, is that which has naturally to do with the double: doubled sexual organs (vagina and clitoris), daughter and mother, menstruation and childbirth, etc. Further, that this division-in-herself marks woman's specificity means that alienation is fundamental to her being-in-the-world (rather than merely fundamental to culture).[25] For Lemoine-Luccioni—and this is the core of her argument—it is only this intrinsic partitioning in and of woman that is capable of explaining what "has been known about women from the beginning of time." Even if "such declarations are not trying to define a status or an essence," nevertheless, "they put forward a current opinion, without ques-

---

24. Lemoine-Luccioni, *Partage des femmes*, p. 71. All further page references in text.

25. Orthodox Lacanian analysts will echo this in rapid succession. For example, "finally the woman finds her being not as woman but as phallus, which is the sense of the fundamental alienation of her being" (Moustapha Safouan, *La sexualité féminine* [Paris: Editions du Seuil, 1976], p. 137).

tioning the durability of that opinion, admitting the possibility that it will be found to be constant and general" (*Partage*, p. 10). Hers is an extreme Lacanian case of "The man will always . . . the woman will always . . ." (*Partage*, p. 9).[26] "Here is woman as we have described her: always divided, always deprived of half of herself, narcissistically divided between subject and object, an orphan in every way. In a word, narcissistic by structure and dedicated to a destiny of partition" (*Partage*, p. 100). For Lemoine-Luccioni, this partition would seem to explain woman's narcissism (*Partage*, p. 35); why she can't create ("even as a painter") (*Partage*, p. 165); why it is men who are the philosophers and poets ("We've known that since Dante"; *Partage*, p. 10). It would explain why woman is defined by her beauty (*Partage*, p. 151) or, if unattractive, by her career (*Partage*, p. 176). In fact, it explains everything—from woman's lack of talent for mathematics (*Partage*, p. 80) to her perennial modesty ("It is not in the nature of woman to expose herself"; *Partage*, p. 70).

In her second book, *Le rêve du cosmonaute*, Lemoine-Luccioni goes even further. There, she insists that women in fact incarnate Lacan's woman spaces. Women exist within his "feminine jouissance" (*Le rêve*, p. 49); they attain the Real "more surely" than men (*Le rêve*, p. 61). We must not change this state of things, according to Lemoine-Luccioni, for the Real must always come before the symbolic and the imaginary if we are to avoid "nothingness" (*Le rêve*, p. 89). For her, it is, above all, women who engender the lalangue upon which the symbolic order is founded and upon which it will always depend (*Le rêve*, p. 132).

Within this context, it comes as no surprise that feminism is denounced by Lemoine-Luccioni as a danger to the social contract itself.[27] For if "woman" were to disappear, "so too would the symptom of man, as Lacan says. And with no more symptom, no more language, and therefore no more man either" (*Partage*, p. 10). According to Lemoine-Luccioni, feminists, in their efforts to do away with the "stereotypes of the male imagination," play a dangerous game; seem indeed to be playing with the ultimate apocalypse; should "reflect before crying victory" (*Partage*, p. 99). For her, "the most inextricable ambiguity necessarily muddles up this politic which aims to restore to woman a look, the right to a look [. . .] This same

26. Stephen Heath, in "Difference," highlights the repetition of this syntagme by Lemoine-Luccioni.

27. Lemoine-Luccioni insists that woman's situation is universal—and that psychoanalysis can explain it whatever it may be: even feminism. For example, for Lemoine-Luccioni, if women are today demanding a right to abortion, it is because "the baby" has become unsymbolizable (*Partage*, p. 32)—representative of a new "default in objectivation" due to an extreme case of partition (*Partage*, p. 35).

look, poking holes right through the world, would ruin the symbolic order" (*Partage,* pp. 173–74). The only hope, therefore, is for women to claim their right, not to a discourse or to a look of their own, but rather to their difference-as-not-all.

What then would be women's place in the world? If women "incarnate" woman as the problem of identity, the discontinuity of the social contract, the symptom of Man, then "why not count on them to assume the irreducible difference that resists unification, since woman is there, and the sexual difference is there as well, and since woman alone can be the figure of division?" (*Le rêve,* p. 182). Lemoine-Luccioni would have us believe that only by stopping the struggle for autonomy and assuming our difference can women protect Man from the ultimate apocalypse. Saving the world would seem to be up to women . . .

Another woman analyst, Michèle Montrelay, while sharing the curious, logical mixture of pessimism and optimism apparent in Lemoine-Luccioni, is less dogmatically Lacanian.[28] Her analysis, while remaining strictly loyal to the Lacanian doxa, does not fall into the same anthropological commonplaces as does that of Lemoine-Luccioni. This is in part because she is not primarily writing about women, but about something called "femininity." But it is also because she is closer than Lemoine-Luccioni to the literary text. Montrelay would seem to want to render Lacan's "woman" incarnate in a different way. Her "woman" is not partitioned, divided, in the world, but rather the locus of a "primary imaginary" dedicated to "feminine jouissance." Women are not necessarily closer to this primary imaginary than men; in fact, "Women's books [only] speak of this 'feminine' imaginary which men—poets, among others—possess" (*L'ombre,* p. 155). Women may "pull toward" this femininity: a femininity which is unrepresentable, dark, outside of the symbolic economy, destructive of interpretation, and close to madness. But incarnated by a woman, it can only yield a monster, the Sphinx: "Does not the encounter with this enigmatic figure of femininity menace every subject? Isn't it this figure which is at the root of the ruin of representation?" (*L'ombre,* p. 66). That is, woman can incarnate this femininity, but only as "an effect of unconscious representation" (*L'ombre,* p. 66), for, according to Montrelay, it is the male poets, not women, who have provided us with an *access* to that imaginary—through writing.[29]

28. Montrelay, *L'ombre et le nom.* All page references in text.
29. There is, for example, the "jouissant substance of Roberte" in Pierre Klossowski's *Les lois de l'hospitalité* (Paris: Gallimard, 1965).

Here is where Montrelay completes Lacan's feminine metonymy more thoroughly than does Lemoine-Luccioni: "feminine jouissance can be understood as *writing* [. . .] this jouissance and the literary text (which is also written like an orgasm produced within discourse) are the effect of the same murder of the signifier [. . .] Is it not for this reason that, with Bataille, Jarry, Jabès, writing portrays itself as the jouissance of a woman?" (*L'ombre,* pp. 80–81).

The list of male writers continues throughout Montrelay's book. Women, writing, do not leave this "feminine substance" on the page, separated from their bodies—as men do. In any case, Montrelay finds it encouraging that women writers are gradually becoming "less feminist." For, ultimately, she shares the same apocalyptic sentiment as Lemoine-Luccioni. Somehow humanity must avoid the inevitable trauma of doing away with "woman" as Man's symptom—if we are to avoid bringing the social order, the order of language, crashing down.

Toward the Hysterical Body

For Montrelay, feminine jouissance as the space of the Other, and of writing, cannot be tied to referentially male and female bodies either as authors or as characters in fiction. She is not, of course, the first or only one to make this distinction, as we have already seen; the concept of "écriture féminine," for example, is firmly based on it. This hysteria of the textual body renders the task of feminist literary criticism most difficult.

For example, the novels of Marguerite Duras are the only writings by a woman consistently invoked by Lacanian analysts: Montrelay begins her book with a poetic reading of Duras's *The Ravishing of Lol Stein;*[30] Christiane Rabant reads the same novel as isomorphic to Lacan's writing;[31] and so forth. What is interesting is that these women analysts do little more than echo a very short text written by Lacan himself. Published in 1965, it is entitled "Hommage à Marguerite Duras"[32] and is nothing less than astonishing as an event. Lacan, in his vast culture, has a classical and highly Franco-centric taste in literature. But for a few references to such writers as

30. Marguerite Duras, *The Ravishing of Lol Stein,* trans. Richard Seaver (Ann Arbor, Mich.: reprinted for Grove Press by University Microfilms International, 1979, © 1964). All page references in text.

31. Christiane Rabant, "La bête chanteuse," *L'arc* 58 (1974).

32. Jacques Lacan, "Hommage à Marguerite Duras," *Cahiers Renaud-Barrault* (December 1965); reprinted in *Marguerite Duras* (Paris: Albatros, 1979), pp. 131–37. All page references in the text refer to the latter.

Borges, Gide, and Joyce, Lacan himself seems to draw the line at the end of the nineteenth century. Given the parameters of my inquiry, I searched extensively for writings by Lacan on a contemporary writer. And what do I find to be the only such instance? A text written by a woman and, what is more, by a woman who publicly presents herself as feminist. This is obviously the most difficult and yet the perfect place to start.

For Michèle Montrelay, the figure of Lol V. Stein in Duras's novels is the figure of femininity—not the representation of a woman. She is, for Montrelay, a figure of Lacan's Real: "There remains to S. Thala of Lol: two night-bird eyes destroyed by the light, dead from having nothing left to see. An uninhabited body, deserted, fallen to the ground like a stone, reduced to its matter: the Real" (*L'ombre*, p. 18). As figure, Lol is divided: "On one side is Lol's body. On the other, there is the head: thought, words, no matter which ones, which induce her and lead her where they will. The body, the words do not form a knot, do not make a heart" (*L'ombre*, p. 14). Lol is the perfect figure of that which is psychoanalyzable, lacking object (*L'ombre*, p. 22), lacking a look (*L'ombre*, p. 18). Lol is everywhere: she crosses from one space to the next—without *being* anywhere.

Montrelay is not totally unaware that in spite of the emptying-of-psychology prevalent in all of Duras's writing, the most visible remains there are sexed bodies in representation—men and women. But Montrelay never asks why it must be a woman's body that figures femininity, but rather only insists, with a sudden return to representation, on what Duras wants for her *men*: "To return them to a 'feminine' sort of jouissance from which they are exiled, to pull them there by placing them on the only road which leads to it, that of poverty [. . .] To bring them back to those countries where one drinks the milk of forgetting, where one falls into the delights, 'faded and sublime,' of empty memory [. . .] As if only a woman, by dint of being nothing, of 'remaining,' could open up love for them" (*L'ombre*, p. 21). For Montrelay, Lol is the positivized figure of that which must be saved in order for men to continue loving women: "Lol is that part of ourselves which remains on the side of the substance (*la chose*), thing, which lives in jouissance, in the Shadow, forever rejected outside, inhuman, crouched somewhere like an animal. Without her, the unconscious cannot exist. From now on, in order for lovers to love each other, the Lol-substance, the Lol-thing, mixed with the rye, must fix them with her wide-open pupils" (*L'ombre*, p. 23).

For Montrelay, fiction is a defense and illustration of a psychoanalytic theory which above all does not want to become a fiction.

But what of Jacques Lacan?

Lacan will not venture very far into Duras's novel. He is actually addressing a homage to the artist herself, as having always already "preceded the psychologist" (*Hommage,* p. 131).[33] That is, for Lacan, *Lol V. Stein,* as fiction, is a perfect *mise en scène* of that other scene which is psychoanalysis. It represents a perfect case of hysteria—with a perfect analyst caught in waves of transference. It is not that Lacan repsychologizes Duras's "characters"; on the contrary, Lol V. Stein is but the name of that which is lost: "paper wings, V, scissors, Stein, a stone, in the game of love [*la mourre*] you lose yourself" (*Hommage,* p. 131). She is that "part of ourselves" that must always drop out of the game of chance that is love. Ultimately, according to Lacan, it is not Lol (either as name or, much less, as woman character) that is put into balance by the narrative, but rather a male character, the "analyst"—Jacques Hold: "The least one can say is that the story puts someone in the balance here, and not only because M. Duras has made of him the voice of the narrative: the other partner of the couple. His name Jacques Hold" (*Hommage,* p. 132). Lol is presented by Lacan as only "the woman of the event," as "non-look" (*Hommage,* p. 134); she does not exist, rather "that which happens realizes her" (*Hommage,* p. 135). Lol may arrange the triangular dances forming her, but it is not she that is to be *comprehended:* "being understood does not suit Lol" (*Hommage,* p. 135). It is, rather, Jacques Hold who is to be *ap*prehended—Jacques Hold, the perfect analyst, the divided subject manifest (*Hommage,* p. 135). Hold is the only character in this novel for Lacan, a character with a centuries-old, impossible love for the lost figure of feminized, hystericized Lol (*Hommage,* p. 136). According to this reading, Jacques (Jacques Lacan? The name is never innocent) is the only possible (male) subject of this narrative, even if he is forever lost in his search for the indescribable (female) body.

No doubt, the homage is an ambiguous genre—especially as an act of courtesy and fervent pledge on the part of a man to a woman. Shall we in turn render homage to what remains an exemplary analysis on the part of Lacan? A difficult question, for the feminist reader cannot help but feel a bit lost here. For to the extent that one always reads, at least initially, through identification, the woman reader has most likely been identifying, not with either of the Jacques, but rather with two highly visible if improbable others: Lol and Marguerite Duras.

33. In this case, the artist has preceded Lacan only in that she has "understood" his theory without him. ("Hommage," p. 133.)

For the feminist reader, it is a question of this Lol who is prevented from being *there* (Lol-là), from being present; a question of this Lol who is separated from the *a* (the *petit objet a*, small object o, of Lacan's graph?) she would need to possess in order to exist as a subject—the *a* located in the surplus of T*a*-tia-n*a*, her sister-in-speculation. For the feminist reader, it is Lol V. Stein—the entire name—which forms the potential space of the text. What Lacan can perceive only as a "perfect case of clinical hysteria" is, for feminist readers, a clinic become the woman reader's world. Jacques Hold is not the one who possesses the look but is rather the name of Man at which Duras's narrative is looking. He is the analyst who always wants to appropriate, to make Lol's story his own—"I shall relate my own story of Lol Stein" (*The Ravishing*, p. 4)—but who fails miserably, reduced to silence by Lol's insistent look. The narrative is looking at a Jacques Hold, a Man, who, when Lol recovers her body for an instant at T Beach with a cry, will order the light of comprehension put out: "'Thank you, but that won't be necessary'" (*The Ravishing*, p. 171).

Jacques is the analyst who cannot understand the laughter and smiles Lol is subject to after that moment: "she laughs strangely, a laugh I have never heard" (*The Ravishing*, p. 175). Finally, Jacques is the fatalist who does not succeed in putting Lol *là*—there, where he wants her.

For the feminist reader, this book-written-by-a-feminist has only one subject: Lol V. Stein. Jacques is but the perverse figure who cannot "hold" Lol to accepting the answer that Oedipus gave to the Sphinx: Man.

This complex of woman-identification is increased if the female reader also reads *Duras* on Duras. A Duras who never fails to emphasize that her texts and films are, above all, *about* women: "It is all the same. All my women."[34] Even Lol V. Stein? "I think that many women are like that [. . .] They do their job as it is dictated by man."[35] For Marguerite Duras, her own novels and films are preeminently the space of an "intelligence of she"—"the written space of she."[36]

Feminist critics in France and the United States have reemphasized this Durassian insistence on the female character as the only space for a potentially new kind of subjecthood. Marcelle Marini finds Lacan's analysis predictable: "It's always man who is 'put in the balance' faced with woman and in that way attains the status of 'subject in its division.'" He cannot

34. Marguerite Duras and Xavière Gautier, *Les parleuses* (Paris: Editions de Minuit, 1974), p. 232.
35. Ibid., p. 20.
36. *Marguerite Duras,* p. 83.

possibly see, perhaps no body-coded-as-male can see, the ways in which this text lays painfully bare the impossibility for women to become subjects "except by becoming masculine—which is always covered over by being 'outside of sex,' 'sex-less.'"[37]

Another feminist critic, Christiane Makward, has echoed Duras in her insistence that her women characters are always militant, militant in their very silence. She points out that what male critics inevitably perceive as narcissistic regression is really the quiet "dream of a new life"; it is a *she* and not a *he* who will finally act: "Lol V. Stein awakens at the break of day, dawn makes her body rise. She has drawn into her anamnesis, into her regression to the original sea/mother two other human beings and henceforth it is she who *will act* because she has attained the capacity for an intelligence of life [. . .] The Birth of the day and the rendering of the text in the future tense with 'she' as the subject of verbs of action: this tableau is the opposite of morbid."[38]

How to account for these curiously disparate readings? It is obvious that the problem is not one of strict sexual identification. Michèle Montrelay's reading of *Lol V. Stein* corresponds for the most part to that of Lacan. Nor is it, at first glance, a question of "traditional" feminist versus "modern" nonfeminist readings. All of these readers valorize Lol as character in one way or another; all of them count very much on the fact that it is Duras-as-a-woman who has written the novel.[39] On second glance, however, it is evident that *the* irreducible difference in these readings concerns the possible representation of potential subjecthood. For the feminist critics—both nonanalysts even if in intense dialogue with psychoanalytic theory—the representation of Lol as a new kind of subject-in-the-world is categorical. For Lacan and Montrelay, as analysts, Lol is a trope; for them, subjecthood is that which can only be dissolved in this presentation of the Real as produced by the hysterical mechanism of the text.

What may be most important about this divergence in critical emphasis is not its polemics, but rather that the disagreement is produced where two machines of interpretation (feminist and psychoanalytic) have met up with a radically new kind of writing, a "postmodern" writing, above all, *about interpretation.* Duras's novel puts into action the entire analytic machine, complete with "hysterical female-body," "male-subject," and os-

---

37. Marini, *Territoires du féminin*, p. 32.

38. Christiane Makward, "Structures du silence/du délire: Marguerite Duras/Hélène Cixous," *Poétique* 35 (1978): 317.

39. Besides addressing his article to Duras, Lacan also establishes a link between Marguerite Duras and Marguerite d'Angoulême.

cillating name—Lol V. Stein. The resultant confusion is externalized for the analyst, for the reader, not to resolve or explicate, but to reinscribe immediately in the political: "the question posed by M. Duras concerns the possibility of an articulation of analytical discourse with its outside, which would be political discourse or, inversely, the possible articulation of political discourse with its analytical outside."[40] Fiction and theory, henceforth in a mimetic relationship to each other, spin round in interminable circles, creating new kinds of political questions that cannot be brushed aside. Our concerns here are with how those political questions are related to this strange process of gynesis. For the kind of political intervention that is to be made by any critic after Lacan will be entirely decided by whether the oscillating name is Lol or Lol-là, a body or a subject, woman or women.

Meanwhile, the unconscious body of that potential name lies waiting for a response: "Lol had preceded us. She was sleeping in the field of rye, worn out, worn out by our voyage."[41]

40. Philippe Sollers, "Détruire, dit-elle," *Revue ça/cinéma*, no. 1.
41. Duras, *The Ravishing of Lol Stein,* p. 181. My translation.

9

The Hysterical Text's Organs:
Angles on Jacques Derrida

> We are not denouncing, here, an incoherence of language or a contradiction in the system. We are wondering about the meaning of a necessity . . .
>
> Jacques Derrida, "Violence and Metaphysics"
>
> not knowing what . . . what she was—. . . what? . . . who? . . . no! . . . she! . . . SHE!
>
> Samuel Beckett, *NOT I*

It is essential to evoke, from the beginning, and for at least the second time, the difficulty one faces when writing to, with, for, or on Jacques Derrida. What is more, to move directly from Jacques Lacan to Derrida, between the covers of one book, is to experience most acutely an uncertainty of opposition. Some American commentators would seem to feel irritation with both of these writers—for me, however, it is not a question of the same irritation, if irritation there may sometimes be. For Derrida's politics of enunciation are of an entirely different color from those of Lacan—mostly because his work is on and about the politics of enunciation itself. That is always where Derrida's style lands first—on those places where people start showing their colors.

(For) Derrida is a philosopher of respect, of respecting the Other (Text). He gives respect and expects it in return—when not received, he can bite (although he rarely draws blood).

(For) Derrida is (also) a non-violent reader, a philosopher of non-violence. A philosopher of the gift and the inevitable ensuing debt,[1] his major problematic has continued to be: Is there a way to name without violence, to give (a name) without the appropriation of debt? "To inspect is to demand identification papers, an origin and a destination. It's pretending to recognize a proper name. How to name without inspecting? Is it possible?"[2] That is, is there a way to "persuade," "give reason," "approach," without the *technē* cutting through *physis* with a Name-Blade?

(For) Derrida, this concern with naming extends to his own name first of all—to his paternal name that *is*. Ejaculated throughout his writing, beginning with *Dissemination*, D-e-r-r-i-d-a *rit-de-là, ja-mais-da*. Cryptonomy as autobiography, Gayatri Spivak will suggest:[3] the name as Thing—like the mother, feminized at the very least. "DIONYSUS ERIGONE ERIPETALE RE-SEDA"—the stuttering constellation of that which, "physisized," feminized, might perhaps at least *resist* the blade.[4]

(For) that which remains unnamed, internamed and overnamed is that which is without *eigen*[5] and most especially of the mother—or at least of/in the maternal tongue—which is also/must become a "whorish language"[6] (if not a Tower of Babel). In order to liberate mimesis from its history, *we must* (both words problematic) allow *physis* a voice as remainder: "to re-elaborate, accounting for the remainder, a thought of *mimesis*: without imitation (of a represented, identifiable, preliminary and repeated object), without repetition (of a thing, an event, a referent, a signified), without signification (of a sense or a signifier). Logic of an uncanny stricture. . ."[7] Res(te) Derrida. A male mother if there ever was O-N-E.

(For) to represent Derrida in a book is, unequivocally, an act of violence, from the minute we respect the name Derrida as the only survivor of his own writing. The present text may be (a "viens") addressed to women readers, but it will, as feminist, inevitably do violence to the-male-text-in-question. (This study is *truly* apocalyptic). But I must dare to proceed—with Derrida as my *pli*/plea—(*Da*).

1. On the "gift" and "debt" see, for example, Derrida, *Glas*, pp. 270–72.
2. *Glas*, p. 13.
3. Gayatri Spivak, "Glas-Piece: A Compte Rendu," *Diacritics* 7:3 (Fall 1977): 22–43.
4. *Glas*, p. 129. For an explication of this encrypted signature, see G. Hartman, *Saving the Text*, p. 94.
5. On *eigen* as *le propre/le proche,* see, for example, Derrida, *Margins of Philosophy*, p. 64.
6. *Les fins de l'homme*, p. 207.
7. *Glas*, p. 169.

Derrida has become a philosopher of honorary American citizenship in some quarters; an alien presence to be resisted at all costs in others. What is most curious about this situation is that American Derrideanism only traces the paths of Derrida's ghost: for it consistently decorporalizes, and de-eroticizes, Derridean text-sex-uality. A few phrases like "mothers as Dionysian concern," "bringing womanly speech to light," and "woman and mothers as deconstructive levers" pass across the borders.[8] But the deeply political and sexual stakes of the Derridean pornosophical wink tend to get lost in translation.

Also "lost" in translation is what might be called Derrida's "philosophy of faith." His textual contextualizations have a curious theological ring; although, in my opinion, it is not here a case of negative theology.[9] In Derrida's work it is never a question of belief or lack thereof, but rather of a faith—in an almost ultra-protestant sense. The word "protestant" may seem misplaced here, given the overriding Derridean textual insistence on the Jew-as-that-which-resists-philosophy-as-both-Greek-and-Christian. Derrida sees the Greco-Christian Dialectic as unfailingly antisemitic, and in his guerrilla warfare with Truth as the ultimate product of any dialectic, Derrida's own texts come to resemble the Judaic Tabernacle itself: "Nothing behind the curtains [Rien derrière les rideaux (*Der-i-do*)]. This explains the ingenuous surprise of the non-Jew when he opens it, when they let him open it or when he violates the tabernacle, when he enters the dwelling-place or the temple and after so many ritual detours to gain access to this secret center, he discovers nothing—except nothingness."[10] For Derrida, the Jew is that for whom there can be no *pour soi,* that which is fundamentally alienated from itself.[11] But, at the same time, in the repetition of his insistence, Derrida's writing at times seems to be less inflecting an (older) Old Testament than reforming a (newer) New Testament—in its battle against any *katholikós,* in its tension between the "already" and the "not yet," and in its emphasis on that writing-as-son

---

8. Cf., e.g., G. Hartman, *Saving the Text:* "But the fair sex, by a deep joke, has become philosophy itself" (p. 30); "It would be a vulgar though affective simplification to say that Derrida is exhibiting in *Glas* the difficulty of bringing a truly womanly speech to light" (p. 82); or, in another register, the metamorphosis of Hugo's Michelle and Esmeralda into (nothing more than) *toc-seins*—"deconstructive writing machines"—so that (as only once mentioned by Mehlman) "The erotics eventually *affirmed* in the text posit a plurality of sexual differences in opposition to *the* difference between the sexes." Jeffrey Mehlman, *Revolution and Repetition* (Berkeley: Quantum, 1977), p. 105.

9. As suggested by, among others, Edward Said in "Two Problems of Textuality."

10. *Glas,* pp. 59–60.

11. *Glas,* pp. 60, 64; and "Edmond Jabès and the Question of the Book," in *Writing and Difference.*

which has been martyred by the carnal and spiritual circumcision practiced by all "false doctors" of whatever belief. Derrida doth *protest*—religiously—and asks the same of his followers.[12]

Finally, Derrida is a philosopher of the unrepresentable and, pausing at the threshold of any new question, he makes sure that he himself remains so. Few critics find the where-with-all to write *on* Derrida—one is forced to write for him or with him. This is in large part because of the way the Derridean text infects its reader, binding him or her in a contagious, mimetic relationship. (Traces here.) One never can be sure when or where it is Derrida speaking or writing. As he states in *Positions,* "I am constituted as the proprietor of what I analyze"; or, worse yet, "what I denounce is attributed to me, as if one were in less of a hurry to criticize or to discuss me, than first to put oneself in my place in order to do so."[13]

Where, then, might we place our feminist questions? In the text, of course, but less the text as written by the man named Derrida than as read by a new generation of women theorists in France. Derrida, after Lacan, has had the deepest influence on both feminist and antifeminist thinking in France, with the scales tending to tip in the direction of the latter the more orthodox the Derridean: Hélène Cixous and Sarah Kofman, for example, are the most skeptical with regard to feminism, while a writer like Luce Irigaray remains as unorthodoxly one (feminist) as the other (Derridean). For non-Derridean women theorists, Derrideanism is more of a vaguely sympathetic foil than an influence (Julia Kristeva), or else—increasingly among politicized feminist theorists—an outright enemy (for example, the group *Questions Féministes*).

The fact that the Derridean corpus has engendered such diversity on and among women should come as no surprise. For example, when closest to himself, Derrida's observations tend to strike a continuous, at least potentially feminist note. During a discussion of Giorgione's *La tempestà,* for instance, Derrida urges his male colleagues to change their ways of looking: "The woman is looking at me, concerns me, and it is beginning with her demand or this look that I re-interpret this painting and that I

---

12. A study on the relationship of Derrida's texts to Judaic thought is long overdue. It is often announced by his critics, but has not been forthcoming, although we are now fortunate to have Susan Handelman's *The Slayers of Moses,* in which Derrida's work plays an important role. The particular essays by Derrida that would be central to such a larger study would no doubt include those on Levinas, Jabès, and, more recently, Walter Benjamin. (The question needs to be asked in relationship to the work of Hélène Cixous and others, where there is emphasis on the woman as inevitable Jew.)

13. *Positions,* trans. Alan Bass, pp. 50, 53.

historically, politically displace the 'auto-interpretation' of the painting or its dominant dictation."[14] But Derrida's texts are no more homogeneous than those he deconstructs and, when further from himself, it becomes obvious that Derrideanism is much more than marginally anti- or post-feminist: "Phallocentric hierarchy is a feminism, it submits itself dialectically to Femininity and to Truth, both capitalized, making of man the *subject* of woman."[15] I attribute this statement to Derrida only to the extent that feminism is consistently denounced as phallogocentric by his most orthodox women disciples.[16]

This oscillation in attitude is not due only to the undecidability of Derridean texts, but also to the fact that, with Derrida, we are beyond the realm of intersubjectivity while remaining in dialogue with that most powerful of sciences in intersubjectivity: Lacanian psychoanalysis. Female sexuality—as resituated by Lacan—is the beginning question for this philosophy after Lacan, and Woman, therefore, is the primary deconstructive device for those facing the history of philosophy.[17]

This is because Derrideanism is a philosophy of the unnatural and, on occasion, of the supernatural; as a project, it is about the necessary culturalization of nature. To the extent that natural words and the natural world are at the foundations of all Hellenistic philosophies, Derrida denaturalizes both the word and the world according to a logic that can move in its range from pyramids to wells, sources to trees, circles to rectangles. Anything physical (and therefore coded as feminine or maternal) or metaphysical (classed as masculine and phallic) is susceptible to denaturalization through Derrida's logic of the between.[18] This inevitably brings about what Sarah Kofman has called a *"sexualization of the text* and *a textualization of sex."*[19] Swinging between the sexes, no longer opposed but heterogeneous, the object of speculation becomes strange as it moves toward that space of general equivalency so constantly devalued by our history. It opens onto a new dimension of *hetero*, sexual erotics "as the father's phallus works in the mother's hymen."[20]

---

14. *Les fins de l'homme,* pp. 343–44.

15. *Glas,* p. 130.

16. The least reductive way to present Derrida and feminism as a topic would be to let him take part: see Derrida and McDonald, "Choreographies."

17. Some Derridean women theorists start with this device without further explanation: see, for example, Sylviane Agacinski, "Le tout premier écart," in *Les fins de l'homme,* pp.117–32; e.g., "The aim was to make 'women' appear as a deconstructing motif in Aristotle's text" (p. 117).

18. See the discussion of "the between" in Chapter 6, above.

19. Kofman, "Ça cloche," in *Les fins de l'homme,* p. 107.

20. Spivak, "Glas-Piece," p. 23.

For Derrida, the questions of how women might accede to subjecthood, write surviving texts, or acquire a signature of their own, are the wrong questions—eminently phallogocentric questions.

Rather, it is *woman* that must be released from her metaphysical bondage and it is writing, as "feminine operation," that can and does subvert the history of that metaphysics. The attributes of writing are the attributes of "woman"—that which disturbs the Subject, Dialectic, and Truth is feminine in its essence.

Within those larger parameters, Derrida oscillates beyond the book coded as strictly philosophical, connecting it to "fictional" texts fascinated with woman, and women—Jabès, Mallarmé, Genet, Blanchot, Sollers. As has been pointed out by others, most of these texts are written by late nineteenth- or twentieth-century French men.[21] And, in all of them, woman is somehow that which cries out for response from within a babel of maternal tongues; woman is always, via Derrida, that which calls out to Man, that which puts him into question.

Derridean reading clearly does not respond to that call, placing woman and her parts into discursive circulation merely to titillate the male reader—although she undoubtedly remains more than quietly seductive to the male reader, since, among other things, "she," for Derrida, is that which does not name, that which does not do violence through naming.

But then (and here is perhaps the place for our difficult feminist questions), for the woman reader, and if naming is always violence, is the process of being un-named through a re-naming-in-parts any less violent?—even when born within a nonviolent, even at times feminist gesture?

The body-image with which women claim they have been saddled by a certain metaphysical logic here begins a strange disintegration into labyrinths of female voices, hymens, veils, vaginas, *tocseins,* traces, and texts. And it is from within those labyrinths that Derrida pulls on the feminine thread, unraveling the fabric of Western thought.

If there is a common measure to Derrida's texts, it is the inscription of the imperative within the act of spacing. As pointed out by Jean-Luc Nancy, "Within the register of meaning as well as within that of the subject, the imperative is and does nothing but space. The imperative *spaces* [. . .] The difference, the process of spacing, writing therefore, would in this way be the law of the law."[22]

21. Roger Laporte, "Nulle part séjournant," in *Les fins de l'homme*, p. 204.
22. Jean-Luc Nancy, "La voix libre de l'homme" in *Les fins de l'homme*, p. 180.

From his earliest texts, Derrida has insisted that our first imperative is to break down vulgar, metaphysical notions of the relationship between space and time: that is, the becoming time of space through the negation of the *Aufhebung*. For the metaphysician, time is space's only possible destiny, its only truth: "Time is the true, essential, past space, space as it will have been thought, that is, *relevé*. *What space will have meant is time*."[23] This notion of space and time—ultimately space as nature (as feminine) and time as culture (as masculine)—must be thought differently, even, for the moment, before their opposition. Derrida moves the metaphysical opposition over, off-center, respaces it, and emphasizes one of its derivative couples; for example, the "near" (*le proche*) and the "clean and proper" (*le propre*): "The near and the far are thought here, consequently, before the opposition of space and time, according to the opening of a spacing which *belongs* neither to time nor to space, and which dislocates, while producing it, any presence of the present."[24] This spacing is, for Derrida, the movement of writing, and he is at his clearest when reminding us that "spacing as writing is the becoming-absent and the becoming-unconscious of the subject";[25] that this spacing does not obey the laws of representation;[26] and, most important, that it ruins any claim of entitlement to meaning or truth.[27] Working through the "between" and the "what's more" (*en plus*) in a movement impossible to describe, it upsets all boundaries, inside, outside, up and down—those boundaries that define (male) subject and (female) object.[28] (To those critics who would criticize Derrida's "There is no outside-of-the-text," he might respond that "There is no inside-of-the-text either.") Writing is the "general space" that disrupts all presence and absence and therefore all metaphysical notions of limits (as well as the possibility of transgressing any one of those limits).[29] Writing has no master, author, or agent;[30] it is a positive, productive, and generative force. Writing as spacing is a new kind of philosophy and reading impatient with those who feel entitled merely to save Time: "Let us space. The art of this text is the air that it circulates among its partitions. The links are invisible, all appears improvised or juxtaposed. It induces by

23. Derrida, "The Pit and the Pyramid," in *Margins of Philosophy*, p. 89. Also see "*Ousia* and *Grammē*," pp. 40–46.
24. *Margins of Philosophy*, pp. 132–33.
25. *Of Grammatology*, p. 69.
26. *Writing and Difference*, p. 217.
27. See "The Double Session" in *Dissemination*, pp. 178–79.
28. Ibid., p. 252.
29. *Margins of Philosophy*, p. 327.
30. *Positions*, trans. Alan Bass, pp. 27–29.

agglutinating rather than by demonstrating, by placing things side by side or by prying them apart rather than by exhibiting the continuous, and analogous, teachy, suffocating necessity of discursive rhetoric."[31]

This new kind of philosophy, in its rewriting, that is respacing, of all traditional notions of space and time—the coordinates of our intellectual word and world—inevitably reinvents those coordinates, re-marks certain spatial figures in order to disrupt any of our too well formed conceptual habits.

For example, the overall disruption pursued by Derridean dissemination is characterized by the chiasma X ("thematic diagram of dissemination"):[32] the X-mark as non-identity, as question (*chi* in Greek or *qui* in French), the point where identity and difference coincide. It is the figure of four moving beyond all trinities in a double gesture (and double cross).[33] The agent of that disruption is de-marked by the figure of the signature in dissimilation—a spacing of the-name-of-the-father into a multiplicity of inauthenticity. For the Derridean, to "sign" is not necessarily to signify.[34]

From parergonal to encryptic logic, from labyrinths to writing machines, Jacques Derrida denaturalizes the world, explores the intrasymbolic borderlines of the spatial words and worlds we thought we knew.[35]

31. *Glas*, p. 88.

32. *Dissemination*, p. 44.

33. Alongside "chiasmatic conceptuality," certain "chiasmatic images" (as what Hartman calls "x factors") come to mind, some of which are occasionally, if obliquely, touched on in Derrida's texts. For example, the chiasmatic mark sometimes has something modest about it; Michelle Le Doeuff has called it a "fig leaf" applied so as to "deny a character (x) to an object or place which, according to common sense, actually possesses it; to attribute it on the other hand, to everything else" (Le Doeuff, *L'imaginaire philosophique*, p. 183). As image, the (x) is that which, doubled, *marks*, the female (xx) (as opposed to the male—xy); it is the mark of Cain (x) (the mother's favorite) as opposed to Christ (†) (the father's favorite); and so on. (On the conceptual leap from three to four, see especially "Dissemination.")

34. On the signature as textual dissemination, see, e.g., "Signature, Event, Context" and "Limited Inc." On the signature (proper name: Genet) that, as flower (in the lower case: genêt), "signifies no longer," see *Glas* (esp. pp. 39–52, right-hand column). A question we cannot go into here is that of the potential spaces of the woman writer's signature—especially after she has already displaced her father's name with that of her husband or her first name. For example, if the male signature cannot ever decide proprietorship once and for all, because of the always already "feminine dissimilation of the text," does that mean that a female signature renders the text even more female than female? (Maternal?) Does her signature (*seing; sein?*) *match* her text?

35. On the logic of the "parergon" see "Le parergon" in *Digraphe* 2 (1974); "Le sans de la coupure pure" ("Le Parergon II") in *Digraphe* 3 (1974); and *La vérité en peinture* (Paris: Flammarion, 1978). E.g.: "No 'theory,' no 'practice,' no 'theoretical practice' can effectively intervene in this field if it does not weigh (upon) the frame, the decisive structure at stake, at the limit invisible to (between) the interiority of meaning [. . .] *and* (to) all the empiricisms of the extrinsic which, not knowing how to see or read, miss the point of the question." ("Le parergon," p. 43.)

Within the spacing-which-is-writing, Derrida pries loose the structures of those words and worlds at their hinges, locating their oscillation at the place where the text folds, breaks, or turns at an angle.[36] What is most extraordinary is how, turning those angles, one inevitably comes upon the feminine gender. Writing, as the very locus of nonbeing, belonging to no-one, is where all resonance (without signification) has been forced by the Western logos into muteness. It is our *colpos,* the place where nothing and no one reigns: "In Greek, it is the breast of the mother but also that of the nurse, but also the fold of a garment, the fold of the sea between two waves, the valley that sinks into the bosom of the earth."[37] Writing is the locus of the "golden fleece," a tissue of veils, in-credibly modest, dis-similating in its feminine technique.[38] Because of this dissimilation, it is impossible to know, to see, to decide, what is or is not there: "One can therefore no longer decide, that's the whole *interest* of writing, whether or not there is a style under the fleece."[39]

The undecidability intrinsic to writing, captured in its folds, is not polysemy, nor ambiguity; it is neither what Freud calls the "narcissism of minor differences"[40] nor exactly a "double-bind"[41]—while all of these are in its favor. At once (not?) undeniable and uncastratable,[42] it is, above all, the oscillation between the potentialities of male and female. And, like Lacan's "feminine jouissance"—within a movement of the neither male nor female—it is located in a feminine place. For Derrida, the undecidable marks the impossibility of a relationship between the sexes of the text within and because of the latter's "feminine" dissimilation of jouissance.

On the logic of the "crypt," see "Fors," trans. Barbara Johnson, *Georgia Review* 31:1 (Spring 1977). "A very specific and peculiar place, highly circumscribed, to which access can nevertheless only be gained by following the routes of a different topography" (p. 66).

36. The Hinge (*La Brisure*) is one of Derrida's first words for that place in the text where meaning begins to implode or explode. See *Of Grammatology,* p. 65.

37. *Glas,* p. 83. (*Colpos* would be the second degree of Derrida's maternal connotations meshed with the text after his double reading of *seing* [sein].)

38. See, especially, *Glas,* pp. 79–82.

39. *Glas,* p. 82.

40. Freud, *The Complete Psychological Works,* vol. 7, p. 272.

41. On the "Double Bind," as a signal of modernity, see, e.g., Lyotard's *La condition postmoderne.*

42. See *Glas,* pp. 252; 56. ["L'indécidable n'est-il pas l'indéniable [. . .] L'indéniable est l' incastrable."] "This does not mean that there is no [qu'il n'y a pas de] castration but that this *there is* [il y a] does not take place. There is [il y a] that one cannot decide between the two contrary functions recognized in the fetish, anymore than between the thing itself and its supplement. Or even between the sexes."

It will come as no surprise that Derrida's pursuance of the logics of undecidability over the last twenty years has brought about what might be called a "sedimentary genderization" within his larger hetero erotic project. Any overall, chronological consideration of his work with reference to the accumulation of that sediment would certainly run into problems that Derrida has already foreseen: "early work" versus "mature work," the time lags of translation. But certain patterns have emerged, nevertheless, as his texts have settled, bringing about marked changes in both "style" and "fleece" according to a not wholly undecidable—or unpredictable—logic.[43]

For example, *Of Grammatology* is what some American scholars would call a straightforward exposition of Derrida's project. What we are calling "sedimentation of gender" is rare, but the "obligatory connotations" of what will later become deconstructive spaces are very much present. In the representational, and "feminist," scenes of that early work, Derrida showed how it is always the male anthropologist "who violates a virginal space so accurately connoted by the scene of a game and a game played by little girls";[44] how it is always the male philosopher who can go about his replacement of mothers in the way he does because, through his belief in Nature, and in the "natural image of woman," he is able to save "the virility of man and the masculinity of the male."[45]

The distinctions between Nature and Culture propagated by anthropology and philosophy can only "stand up" if the dissimilation of writing is ignored. Derrida's own style goes to work on the myth of the natural; for as myth of pure maternal presence, and voice as pure virginity before writing, it is a male myth.

In the other scene of that early text, we can also, however, begin to see the workings of other, later, more visible Derridean genders. Ridiculing Rousseau's "dangerous supplement" (masturbation), and dislocating any

---

43. The question of the "biographical" stubbornly arises here—especially in France, where the "revolution" of 1968 brought about, among other things, an urgent call for men "to get in touch with their femininity"—and at the same time brought about the feminist movement as such. But, again, in spite of its emphasis on certain "personalities," this study is not implicating their persons.

There does remain, of course, that ultimate in apocalyptic genres, the "public interview": "Were you asking me a personal question? I would love to write like (a) woman. I try . . ." (Transcription of discussion following Derrida's presentation of his paper, "La question du style," at the July 1972 Cerisy colloquium, published in *Nietzsche aujourd'hui?* [Paris: 10/18, 1973], p. 299.)

44. *Of Grammatology*, esp. p. 113.

45. Ibid., p. 175; see esp. pp. 165–268.

possible definition of literal virginity (*pucelage,* preservation of an un-broken hymen), Derrida posits his first key deconstructive word located on this side of meaning: the trace as the mark of difference: "*The (pure) trace is differance.* It does not depend on any sensible plenitude, audible or visible, phonic or graphic. It is, on the contrary, the condition of such a plenitude." The trace, nonexistent, invisible, and overwhelmingly passive,[46] marks the spot—of future feminine connotations.

All of the earliest Derridean texts (published before 1970) continue to follow "male logic" in its various incarnations, turning it inside out and upside down. But only once in this early work does the still somewhat strangely "feminist" voice of *Grammatology* break through—at the intersection of Emmanuel Levinas and James Joyce, in a footnote that could serve as matrix for all of the future Derridean explorations in gender: there we find already evoked what Joyce called "feminine logic"; the fact that the subject of philosophy is always man (*vir*); femininity as ontological category; and the essential virility of metaphysics, even when practiced by women.[47] Echoing *Grammatology* in its sorting out of "male logic" and "sexual identities in representation," this footnote announces, at the same time, a new turn toward the strategies-in-genderization to be pursued henceforth (whatever the "historical order" of writing these essays might have been).

Those strategies-in-genderization, as well as a certain sedimentation of gender categories, reached their full force in Derrida's two major collections of writing published in France after the *Grammatology*. With *Dissemination* and *Margins of Philosophy* (both published in French in 1972), the feminine-as-alternative-logic is everywhere visible. From the publication of these two texts in 1972 to the publication of *La carte postale* in 1980, through numerous oscillations in style and fleece, that logic as alternative to metaphysics never leaves its woman and her obligatory connotations behind. Whether one is sifting through the conceptual fates of individual words (the "frivolous," "adornment," etc.) or entire philosophical systems (Hegel, Austin and Searle, Nietzsche, etc.), hieroglyphs, paintings, or letters of fiction or love, "woman" serves as what Barthes might call the *punctum* of Derridean reading.[48]

---

46. Ibid., pp. 62–65, 167.

47. "Violence and Metaphysics," in *Writing and Difference*, pp. 320–21, n. 92.

48. On the Barthesian notion of *punctum*, see *La chambre claire*. (The emphasis on the mother as invisible *punctum* of Barthes's text could yield a striking reading with/of the maternal *toc-sein* of *Glas*.)

The essays in *Dissemination* deserve brief attention here, for they mark a kind of spatial transition from grammatological "feminism" to deconstructive "genderization." Dissemination, as an alternative logic to castration, is where female sexuality may perhaps finally find its matrix, between the preface (as female) and the book (as male).[49] For the "space of dissemination" is the undecidable *plus* (no longer/more), the process of simultaneously adding to and subtracting from infinity: "The space of dissemination does not merely place the *plural* in effervescence; it shakes up an endless contradiction, marked out by the undecidable syntax of *more*."[50] Dissemination is "l'au-delà-du-tout."[51] *En plus, pas tout*—extra, what is more, not All: with Derrida, we are perhaps not as far from the Lacanian "woman" as we thought.

In "Plato's Pharmacy,"[52] writing receives even further sets of still reticent but nonetheless obligatory genderizations from Greek philosophy. The truth of writing is the "non-true" (PP, p. 74); for all Greek thought, it serves as but the supplement of Truth, as the (feminine) moon supplements the (masculine) sun, or night the day (PP, p. 89–90). Writing is, in fact, the supplement in motion: liquid, inconsistent, im-proper, nonidentical to itself, it menaces all laws of purity. A kind of bastard son, it moves nonetheless beyond even the father-son opposition (PP, p. 146). "At the disposal of each and of all, available on the sidewalks" (PP, p. 144), writing (like Socrates) is the suppliant of the Father: a midwife when not a prostitute.

In "The Double Session"[53] we cross centuries to another pharmacy, that of Mallarmé, still, even after such a long time, in dialogue with Plato. It is here that Derrida elaborates on one of his most powerful deconstructive levers and completes his genderization of writing—as the place where male and female remain undecidable—as feminine. Here, the undecidable, like the *pharmakon* in Plato or the *supplement* in Rousseau, becomes, in fiction, (Mallarmé's) "hymen."

In "The Double Session," Derrida reads Mallarmé reading Paul Margueritte's writing of "Pierrot assassin de sa femme," a theatrical mime. Pierrot, a mime, mimes having murdered his wife—by tickling her feet

---

49. "Outwork, prefacing," in *Dissemination*, pp. 48–49, n. 47.
50. Ibid., p. 43.
51. Ibid., pp. 56–57.
52. "Plato's Pharmacy," in *Dissemination*. Hereafter referred to as PP. Page references in text.
53. "The Double Session," in *Dissemination*. Hereafter referred to as DS.

until she died laughing. In black and white, the mime alternates roles, back and forth, between assassin and victim until telling them apart becomes impossible, "both" having reached a painfully high pitch of hilarity. The "wife" dead, the "assassin" cannot stop laughing (i.e., cannot die)—until the wife reappears, laughing, in a portrait over his head, and so on and on.

What seems to fascinate Derrida about this uncanny scene of constant reversals is not only the way in which a "crime," as absolute laughter, can take place without taking place: "no violence, no stigmata, no traces" (DS, p. 201); but that it does so within a mounting undecidability of sexual identity, even after both "his" and "her" deaths.

It is finally this uncanny undecidability of sexual difference that is most impossible within Platonic conceptions of mimesis. Derrida therefore takes on the concept of mimesis—complete with its dialectics, truths, values, and icons—with sexual difference serving as privileged lever between fiction and (the) truth: mime versus mimesis. Derrida renders mimesis strange through endless mime; mime as the writing (outside) of the book: "The Mime ought only to write himself on the white page he is; he must *himself* inscribe *himself* through gestures and plays of facial expressions. At once page and quill, Pierrot is both passive and active, matter and form, the author, the means, and the raw material of his mimodrama" (DS, p. 198).

This Pierrot *is* writing, for (it, he/she) reflects no reality, remains inaccessible in a supreme spasm—writing as a "dramatization which *illustrates nothing*, which illustrates *the nothing*, lights up a space, re-marks a spacing as a nothing" (DS, p. 208).

That is, Pierrot is a *hymen*, a word designating both marriage and the membrane of the female vaginal tract. For Derrida, the hymen is the "absolute" in undecidability: there is hymen (virginity) when there is no hymen (marriage or copulation); there is no hymen (virginity) when there is hymen (copulation or marriage). The hymen is the locus of the abolition of the difference between difference and nondifference—the explosion of laughter and death which does no violence. "Beyond" this culturally determined puzzle, what interests Derrida is the "white marriage"—the *mariage blanc*, where what takes place takes (a) place without taking place. The place where, between the metaphorical (marriage) and the literal (the membrane), there can be no more distinction for the Father to judge.[54]

---

54. On the "white marriage" and its consequences for Judith and Holopherne as well as for any reading of Freud's "Taboo of Virginity" (*The Complete Psychological Works*, vol. 11), see Sarah Kofman, "Judith, ou la mise en scène du tabou de la virginité," *Littérature*, no. 3 (October 1971): 100–116; reprinted in her *Quatre romans analytiques* (Paris: Galilée, 1974).

Under Derrida's pen, the hymen—that which has always been "read" by the father in all the decidability of its presence or absence—becomes the father-less, always feminine paradigm of undecidability. Derrida emphasizes that the word "hymen" is not indispensable—as *syllepsis*—to either "his" or "Mallarmé's" text; like all previous words of undecidability, and some others, it merely designates in echo "a very singular relation to writing" (DS, p. 221).[55]

The hymen remains, however, the privileged figure for the second "scene" of Derrida's text, metamorphosing into multiple configurations before our very eyes. Folded, the hymen begins to float—becoming now the dance of a pen, now a woman dancer, the V of ballet: the text miming Mallarmé's "dancer" itself begins to dance, "[is] always, *in addition,* descriptions/inscriptions of the structure and movement of the literary textile, a 'hesitation' turning into writing. In folding it back upon itself, the text thus *parts* (with) reference, spreads it like a V, a gap that pivots on its point, a dancer, flower, or Idea" (DS, p. 239).

There is no question of a woman here, "but a metaphor" (DS, p. 242) designating that which dances across the secure territories of truth, unsettling them. Ultimately, the metaphysical V of the dialectical *versus* explodes into the Derridean wings (*ailes* [L's]) of the butterfly, the *angles* (L's) of the text: into the crisis of the (Mallarméan) book, leaving behind only the *elles,* "shes" of a now (eternally) feminine écriture . . .

Is there any room left here for our feminist questions? We could emphasize the narrative on which this entire (de?) construction nevertheless rests: a man murdering his wife. Or we could ask why Derrida silences the male homosexual potentialities for this Mallarméan/Derridean "double play": "the very mark of the feminine position with respect to the father, of homosexuality (the tearing of the anal 'hymen')."[56] Or we could emphasize the abundant stereotypes attaching to virginity (whiteness, etc.), or their "sources" in Freud.[57] Or we might even ask why Derrida did not operate a complete reversal—on the testicles, for example, as perfect parergon of any male text; why have they not received the same dramatic

---

55. Pressed (in another place, much later) to comment upon his use of the hymen with regard to women, Derrida writes of "re-sexualizing a philosophical or theoretical discourse which has been too 'neutralizing.'" Derrida and McDonald, "Choreographies," p. 75.

56. See Kristeva, *La révolution du langage poétique,* p. 603. Derrida's analysis of Mallarmé receives its symbolic place in this chapter, "A la recherche d'une souveraineté"—as pre-Oedipal. The two studies should be read together.

57. For example, see Wladimir Granoff, "Membranes, pellicules: l'hymen" and "Le jeu de la membrane dans le texte freudien," in *La pensée et le féminin.*

space as the hymen, given that the latter has been the object of male fantasy for centuries?[58]

But all I want to emphasize here is that Lacan's "feminine jouissance" ("not All," "extra," "everywhere," "invisible," "half-said"), as supplement, has finally openly re-entered its new hysterical body: the text as écriture.[59]

It is impossible, here, to follow the "sedimentation" of this new body among its numerous Derridean pages. I will therefore direct attention briefly and rather impatiently to the place of its most open and frank appearance: *Spurs*.[60]

With *Spurs*,[61] "woman" most visibly becomes (as becoming to) the unfolding of the hymen that is writing: in this case, the writing-in-Nietzsche so as, first, to loosen Nietzsche's texts from the grip of the "ortho-dontics" of moralistic judgment;[62] and second, to save *the* text as (Nietzsche's) "woman." Any attempt to summarize the Derridean "positions" as to "woman" in *Spurs* and Nietzsche would be doomed to failure. But assuming that risk, we can nevertheless follow, very metonymically, a certain string of attributes predicating "woman," that is, writing, in *Spurs*.

58. Only one short page in *Glas* (p. 129) is given to the subject. My thanks to Jane Gallop for pointing out this missing male part.

59. For another argument, the reader will want to refer to Suzanne Allen's 1972 Cerisy colloquium paper, "Hymne/Hymen," published in *Les fins de l'homme*, pp. 230–36. (The ensuing debate was not taped.)

60. But along the way, we must not forget:
—Derrida's "Dissemination": where the Father-Author finally disappears from writing-beyond-castration as echoed through . . .
—Derrida's "tympan": where the unfolding of the new body continues with added organs; where the ear as philosophical machine (and female sexual organ and matrix) is rendered strange, denaturalized in its passivity, taken, apart. The labyrinth of the ear-vagina is entered, slowly, eroticized, so that its tympan may be broken through, toward a different logic, as with . . .
—Derrida's "différance": where Lacan's wandering, feminine "small a" would seem to have finally lodged itself, if only temporarily, in the feminizing process: writing as physis in différance with itself, finally landing in . . .
—Derrida's "Glas": where "In order for castration to coincide with and confirm virginity, for the phallus to reverse itself into the vagina, for supposed opposites to equal and reflect one another, the flower must turn back upon itself like a glove and its style like a sheath" (*Glas*, p. 57). Or like an umbrella . . which we have not forgotten as/in . . .
—Derrida's "Spurs."

61. All page references are to the bilingual edition of *Spurs/Eperons*, trans. Barbara Harlow (Chicago: University of Chicago Press, 1979), hereafter referred to as *Spurs*. Also of interest is the discussion following Derrida's presentation of *Eperons* at the 1972 Cerisy colloquium, published in *Nietzsche aujourd'hui?* pp. 235–87.

62. "'How much conscience has had to chew on in the past! And what excellent teeth it had! And today—what is lacking?' A dentist's question." Nietzsche, "Twilight of the Idols," in *The Portable Nietzsche*, trans. W. Kaufmann (New York: Viking, 1968), p. 470.

For "woman" is Derrida's "subject" (*Spurs*, p. 37)—who, after all, will not have been his subject (*Spurs*, p. 121), to the extent that this short text might be seen as but an exegesis on Lacan's "*La* femme n'existe pas." There are as many "womans" as there are styles in Nietzsche and Derrida ("Nietzsche must have been familiar with all genres [genders]" [*Spurs*, p. 39]). If there is a point (spur) to Derrida's text, then, that is it, right there (in all of its decidability). But there is more.

"Distances" and "Veils"

From reading Nietzsche's "Women and their Action at a distance,"[63] we learn that "The value of dissimulation marked in this movement is not at all extraneous to the relation between art and woman" (*Spurs*, p. 47). Men must remain at a distance from women (*die Frauen*), according to Nietzsche, in order for seduction to operate.[64] Derrida's reading affirms Nietzsche's notion of *woman-in-distans* (even if, slightly and at the same time, he inserts a feminist note: "Such might also be the advice of one man to another: a sort of scheme for how to seduce without being seduced" [*Spurs*, p. 49]. But then, if one must stay at a distance from "the feminine operation" (*actio in distans*), perhaps it is because "woman" is *distance(ing) itself*: "Perhaps woman—a non-identity, a non-figure, a simulacrum—is distance's very chasm, the out-distancing of distance, the interval's cadence, distance itself, if we could still say such a thing, distance *itself*" (*Spurs*, p. 49). That is (if our narrator is trustworthy), "woman" can be neither "truth" nor the "nontruth of truth" for Nietzsche—and therefore is akin to the spacing which is writing for Derrida. "Because, indeed, if woman *is* truth, *she* at least knows that there is no truth, that truth has no place here and that no one has a place for truth. And she is woman precisely because she herself does not believe in truth itself, because she does not believe in what she is, in what she is believed to be, in what she thus is not" (*Spurs*, p. 53).

First attribute of "woman": "Woman" (in truth) is not to be found, taken; "that which will not be pinned down by truth is, in truth—*feminine*" (*Spurs*, p. 55).

---

63. Nietzsche, *The Gay Science*, trans. Walter Kaufmann (New York: Random House, 1974), Fragment 60, p. 123.

64. The alternations in Nietzsche's texts between *Frau* (which has noble, wifely connotations) and *Weib* (the "female"—at most, a prostitute) would need to be sorted out to untangle fully "woman" and "truth" in his texts.

"Truths"

"[T]his should not, however, be hastily mistaken for a woman's femininity, for female sexuality, or for any other of those essentializing fetishes [. . .]" (*Spurs*, p. 55). The (pre)inscription of truth, not the *Truth* or *Non-Truth* as substantive, is, then, the "feminine operation" (*Spurs*, p. 57): "Because woman is (her own) writing, style must return to her. In other words, it could be said that if style were a man (much as the penis, according to Freud is the 'normal prototype of fetishes'), then writing would be a woman" (*Spurs*, p. 57). Derrida posits (rather strangely) all of these Nietzschean theses as "feminist in appearance" and, at the same time, as being in congruence with Nietzsche's anti-feminist thesis. He says in fact that this is a "rigorously necessary" congruence (*Spurs*, p. 57): "Such, in any case, will be the thesis of the present communication" (*Spurs*, p. 57).

For woman as skepticism, dissimulation, and swirl of veils (as feminine operation) wants nothing to do with feminism (based in a belief in the truths of castration and of anti-castration). Truth-in-castration is "the masculine *concern*" (*Spurs*, p. 59).

> "Woman"—her name made epoch [as the pause of indecision]—no more believes in castration's exact opposite, anti-castration, than she does in castration itself. Much too clever for that (and we ourselves—who we?—might learn from her or in any case from her operation) she knows that such a reversal would only deprive her of her powers of simulation, that in truth, a reversal of that kind would, in the end, only amount to the same thing and force her just as surely into the same old apparatus. She knows that she would only find herself trapped once again in a phallocentrism . . . (*Spurs*, p. 61)

Second attribute of "woman": she is what does not believe in either castration or anti-castration, in Truth or its negative, even if, nonetheless, she needs their effects.

"Adornments"

Hence the extreme *"Skepsis des Weibes"* (*Spurs*, p. 63). Only Man ("l'homme") believes in the pros and contras of castration. Derrida adds with Nietzsche: "And in truth, they too are men, those women feminists so derided by Nietzsche. Feminism is nothing but the operation of a woman who aspires to be like a man. And in order to resemble the masculine dogmatic philosopher this woman lays claim—just as much claim as he—to truth, science, and objectivity in all their castrated delusions of virility" (*Spurs*, p. 65). For Nietzsche (and Derrida), the feminist wants nothing more than a *parure supplémentaire*, "new adornment for herself," whenever she seeks *une explication à son propre sujet*, "enlightenment about herself." For Nietzsche, feminists (male or female) "lack style," are "sterile old maids"—as opposed to Nietzsche who, Derrida adds, is, on the contrary, "the thinker of pregnancy" (*Spurs*, p. 65).

Third attribute of "woman," then: she is that which is not feminist (and who is therefore *with* style): "feminism too seeks to castrate. It wants a castrated woman. Gone the style" (*Spurs*, p. 65).

"Simulation"

The "feminine operation" is designated by the spacings in and by Nietzsche of "woman"—as *affirmative*: "she [woman] is twice model, at once lauded and condemned. Here, in a manner like to that of writing, surely and safely, she forces the proxy's argument to bend before a sort of *kettle logic*. [. . .] She plays at dissimulation, at ornamentation, deceit, artifice, at an artist's philosophy. Hers is an affirmative power" (*Spurs*, p. 67). Nietzsche, in his praise of dissimulation, ranks her with the Jews—both equally comedians.

Fourth attribute of "woman": *Das Weib ist so artistich*—and affirmatively so (*Spurs*, p. 69). "Woman" is not to be found through the Truths and Lies of concept and knowledge, "yet it is impossible to resist looking for her" (*Spurs*, p. 71).

"History of an error"

It would seem that Nietzsche wanted to substitute an "aesthetic of production" (connoted as masculine) for the traditional "aesthetic of consumers" (connoted as feminine) (*Spurs*, pp. 71–79). But as Heidegger pointed out, he also is "seeking something else" (*Spurs*, p. 79): not a simple inversion of the hierarchy, nor anarchy, but rather, the very transformation of the notion of hierarchy itself.

("Woman" is absent from this very philosophical interlude.)

But with "Feminina vita"

(Re) "entre la femme" (*Spurs*, p. 82). Because Derrida lays emphasis on the fact that Heidegger, in the wake of these remarks, in his "explication" of Nietzsche's "History of an Error," does not comment upon Nietzsche's reflection that "the idea becomes woman [*Weib*]" with Christianity. Not an innocent lapse, Derrida explains—for it signals not only a Heideggerian moment of metaphysical blindness, but also the inscription of "becoming-female" as a "process of the idea" (*Spurs*, p. 87). Woman and Truth have a history—and "woman as castrated" (Christianity) is only an epoch now long past.

Fifth attribute of "woman": she is something that Nietzsche, as opposed to Heidegger (and metaphysics), was attempting to think in (her) history.

"Positions"

Nietzsche's propositions on "woman" are therefore heterogeneous—and that is his merit as a great stylist, according to Derrida. "[His style] is manifest in the very heterogeneity of the text" (*Spurs*, p. 95). For outside of the positivities and negativities of the dialectic, "the reversal, if it is not accompanied by a discrete parody, a strategy of writing, or difference or deviation in quills, if there is no style, no grand style, this is finally but the same thing, nothing more than a clamorous declaration of the antithesis" (*Spurs*, p. 95).

Nietzsche's positions are, schematically, three, according to Derrida: 1) Woman is condemned as nontruth; 2) Woman is condemned as truth; 3) Woman is recognized, beyond this double negation, as affirmative and Dionysian. "And no longer is it man who affirms her. She affirms herself, in and of herself, in man" (*Spurs*, p. 97). (Castration and anti-castration have no place in this third position—nor do feminism and antifeminism). "Nietzsche might well be a little lost in the web of his text, lost much as a spider who finds he is unequal to the web he has spun. Much as a spider indeed, several spiders even. Nietzsche's spider. Lautréamont's, that of Mallarmé, those of Freud and Abraham" (*Spurs*, p. 101). What's more, Nietzsche was all of these women, "at once, simultaneously or successively, depending on the position of his body and the situation of his story" (*Spurs*, p. 101).

"The gaze of Oedipus"

"For just this reason then, there is no such thing either as the truth of Nietzsche, or of Nietzsche's text" (*Spurs*, p. 103). There is no *woman*, as truth or nontruth in itself. Derrida adds that all "feminists"—"Mme. Roland, Mme. de Staël, M. [Monsieur] Georges Sand [Nietzsche adds George Eliot]"—are "rightfully chastised" by Nietzsche for their "bad taste" (*Spurs*, p. 103).

It is the question of woman, not "the woman question," that suspends the opposition between truth and nontruth those women were attempting to isolate: "there is no truth in itself of the sexual difference in itself, of either man or woman in itself" (*Spurs*, p. 103) . . . and what that recognition unleashes for a modernity "beyond" metaphysics, therefore, is not a question of men and women, but rather "the question of style is immediately unloosed as a question of writing. The question posed by the spurring-operation (*opération éperonnante*) is more powerful than any content, thesis, or meaning" (*Spurs*, p. 107).

Le coup de don

"Man" and "Woman" change places infinitely, then, according to their "attributes"—for example, according to whether they "give themselves" (*en se donnant*) or "take themselves for" (*se donnant pour*)—a problematic that Derrida desires to think before the problem of being or identity. He warns that to ignore that necessity is to remain "[in] the onto-hermeneutic presupposition, [. . .] in its pre-critical relation to the signified"; it is to "return to the presence of the spoken word, to a natural language, to perception, visibility, in a word, to consciousness, and its phenomenological system" (*Spurs*, p. 113).

"Abysses of truth"

That is, "Perhaps truth's abyss as non-truth, propriation as appropriation/a-propriation, the declaration become parodying dissimulation, perhaps this is what Nietzsche is calling the style's form and the no-where of woman." And finally . . . "The gift, which is the essential predicate of woman, appeared in the undecidable oscillation of to give oneself/to give oneself for, give/take, let take/appropriate. Its value or price (*coût*) of a *pharmakon*" (*Spurs,* pp. 119–21). That is, of *writing*: woman as writing.

"*I have forgotten my umbrella*"

Even a piece of writing like "I have forgotten my umbrella" is "like a woman or like writing, [in that] it passes itself off for what it passes itself off for" (*Spurs,* p. 127). The umbrella, shown to be undecidable in its sexual genders (as opposed to its Freudian phallic symbolism), is nonetheless very decidable in its attributes and operations—they are feminine. In fact, the umbrella is like the texts signed by Nietzsche with Derrida, protecting (us)—as woman—from the illusion of one sexual difference (*Spurs,* p. 139).

Sixth and final attribute of "woman": Derrida and Nietzsche.

Spurs is a reading of Nietzsche that separates Nietzsche from himself, removing his texts from the sources of their own authority. The deconstructive lever to accomplish that separation is the word "woman," a word whose attributes, in synecdochic succession, slowly become intrinsic to the operation itself. For example, it is with the word "veil" that Nietzsche's styles are most consistently separated from themselves here. The text is a realm of sexual undecidability (*le viol, la viole, le voile, la voile*) where Truth is not to be decided, because "the text veils itself by itself unveiling itself"—like a woman.[65] The text is veiled—both open and closed, like a flower, like a woman. But it would be a mistake to think that something lies behind its veils. The text hides neither truth nor untruth, but operates an uncertainty of vision which is no longer anguished, an uncertainty as to castration and noncastration—a dissimulation that, in its effect, is female to the extent that it is affirmative (that is, not anguished).

Not to be "taken," believing in nothing, never negative, not to be found through concept or knowledge, affirmative, forever transitory, with style—writing, as woman, is that which philosophy and, indeed, the male philosopher must become if the boundaries of metaphysical thought are to be crossed.

---

65. *Glas,* pp. 159–62. The image of the veil is a Romantic one. Blake, Wordsworth, Coleridge, Emerson, and Shelley, for example, make extensive use of it as something to be "lifted" rather than to be "played with." Ideas for a doubled reading of Derrida's veils with those Romantic ones—and George Eliot's—might be gleaned from Gilbert and Gubar, *The Madwoman in the Attic,* esp. pp. 468–77.

For the Derridean, undecidability—first and foremost between male and female—is, then, at least temporarily, in favor of the "feminine." And wherever the "metaphysical writer's" text oscillates is where the "essential virility" of metaphysical discourse is shaken.

An orthodox Derridean, Sarah Kofman, follows Derrida in this conclusion—adopts his "woman," "veils," and "hymen" to read the male philosophical texts in a mode that seems feminist in inspiration. But Kofman is more openly antifeminist than her Derridean male colleagues; for her, feminism is a phallocentrism no matter what the sex of its speaker, and no matter what the context.[66] What interests her, as for Derrida, is "woman" and her attributes—those that subvert the structure of any text claiming to know, be that text "feminist" or "masculinist."

For example, she would seem to agree absolutely with Derrida's reading of Nietzsche: "Let us not hasten to 'decide' whether or not to declare Nietzsche 'misogynist.'"[67] For in his praise of the affirmative, Dionysian woman, Nietzsche passes beyond all theological arguments on woman and truth.[68]

Even Auguste Comte would have his "feminine side" from Kofman's point of view. In her book, *Aberrations: Le devenir femme d'Auguste Comte,* Kofman asks why Comte "wrote so badly": "Hypothesis: 'bad expression' is the price he must pay for having wanted to *conceive.* Having wanted to enjoy a forbidden jouissance like a woman [. . .] A bad style, scientific, masculine, if we accept Comte's word, would be—this is my hypothesis— a means of forbidding access to this impossible to admit secret."[69] But Comte did not always write in "a masculine vein." Due to a liaison with a woman named Clothilde, Comte "reconciled himself openly to his femininity."[70] Changing his sex, Comte necessarily changed his style: with his *Système,* Comte left behind the "scientific, virile style" of his *Cours,* and— "became a woman" (i.e., "became pleasing to his reader").[71]

Freud too, after Nietzsche, Comte, and, indeed, all male philosophers, has his "feminine moments." Kofman's *L'énigme de la femme: La femme dans les textes de Freud* is first a polemic against Luce Irigaray's "feminist

---

66. See, for example, her paper, "Ça cloche," in *Les fins de l'homme,* pp. 90–100. "Orthodox" is used here in the same way as in "orthodox Lacanians"—see Chapter 8, above.
67. Sarah Kofman, *Nietzsche et la scène philosophique* (Paris: 10/18, 1979), p. 270.
68. Most important, through his insistence on the figure of Baubô: see Kofman, *Nietzsche,* pp. 295–97.
69. Sarah Kofman, *Aberrations: Le devenir femme d'Auguste Comte* (Paris: Flammarion, 1978), p. 15.
70. Ibid., p. 241.
71. Ibid., pp. 29–30.

reading" of Freud, and only secondly a Derridean reading designed to divide Freud against himself. The text is devoted to the demonstration of woman's status as enigma in the text of Freud. On the one hand, there is Freud-the-phallocrat and his phallocentric science; on the other hand, there is another Freud—the one of "On Narcissism," where, according to Kofman, Freud meets with Nietzsche:

> That which would render woman enigmatic would no longer be some "native defectiveness," some lack, but on the contrary her narcissistic auto-sufficiency and her indifference; it is no longer she who will envy man for his penis, it is he who will envy her for her elusive libidinal position, for having known how to keep her narcissism in reserve, while he, the man—one must wonder why—has become impoverished, has depleted himself of this originary narcissism for the benefit of the loved object.[72]

Through his comparisons of this "self-sufficient woman" to children, cats, criminals, and humorists, Freud has described that woman whose model is Nietzsche's "affirmative woman."[73] Freud therefore cannot be dismissed simply as a metaphysician, for his insistence on the insolubility of the enigma that is woman could also be interpreted as a "Nietzschean gesture" in favor of woman and, therefore, in favor of writing, since, like Nietzsche, Freud refuses to define either.[74]

It is clear that taking "men" and "women" out of opposition, and thinking the "masculine" and the "feminine" as a kind of pre-logic disturbing the male theorist's text, allows a thinking of differences in surprisingly different ways. But, ultimately—and as Derrida has never ceased to point out—one cannot hope, at least for now, totally to escape metaphysical boundaries. They are always already there. And the genderization of writing as "feminine operation," and its inevitable valorization-in-a-new-hierarchy, is perhaps where those metaphysical boundaries have retaken their place in spite of complex Derridean avoidance strategies.

But, on the other hand, it is also clear that this genderization-beyond-opposition is not just a Derridean idiosyncrasy. It is, it would seem, somehow intrinsic to modernity as a "new vision." Beyond the universal

---

72. Kofman, *L'énigme,* p. 61.

73. Ibid., pp. 60–63. Kofman suggests that this is through the mediation of Lou Andreas-Salomé.

74. Kofman concludes, more or less, that Freud was more guilty of metaphysics than Nietzsche: for instead of crying out *Mulier taceat de Muliere,* he deviously addressed himself to women (contrary to what Irigaray sees as Freud's exclusion of them) in order to win their complicity. Ibid., pp. 123–24.

Subject, Dialectic, and Truth, things get "sticky"—*gl(u)a(nt)s*. As in fiction?

The Hysterical Text's Organs

Derrida working on and with "fiction" is rather different from Derrida on "philosophy."[75] With fiction, Derrida's woman-as-process and the fiction's women-in-narrative approach each other more often, if only to separate more definitively, in very precise ways that are of interest here.

"Living On/Borderlines," for instance, is ostensibly a reading of three texts: Shelley's poem "Triumph of Life" and two of Blanchot's "narratives": *La folie du jour* and *L'arrêt de mort* [*Death Sentence*].[76] I concentrate here on *Death Sentence,* both because it is the major focus of "Living On" and because Maurice Blanchot is Derrida's *palimpseste*—even his *crypte*. He enacts, as a fiction writer, writing-as-without-precedent in "images" that continually return to haunt Derrida's own texts. And all of those images have to do with the impossibility of deciding on a story—on a "narrative": "A narrative? No, no narrative, never again."[77]

Blanchot, in *L'entretien infini,* has distinguished between a "narrative voice" and a "narratorial voice." As Derrida puts it,

> The narrative voice [. . .] is "a neutral voice that utters [*dit*] the work from the placeless place where the work is silent." The placeless place where the work is silent [its *Glas*?]: a silent voice, then, withdrawn into its "voice-lessness" ["*aphonie*"]. This "voicelessness" distinguishes it from the "narratorial voice," the voice that literary criticism or poetics or narratology strives to locate in the system of the narrative, of the novel, or of the narration. The narratorial voice is the voice of a subject recounting something, remembering an event or a historical sequence, knowing who he is, where he is, and what he is talking about. It responds to some "police," a force of order or law ("What 'exactly' are you talking about?": the truth of equivalence). (LO, pp. 104–5)

At the price of acting-as-police, we ask what is the "narratorial voice" of *Death Sentence*?

75. Derrida's "Living On/Borderlines" was translated to be published first in the United States in *Deconstruction and Criticism,* pp. 75–176. Hereafter referred to as LO.

76. Percy B. Shelley, "The Triumph of Life," in *The Poetical Works of Percy Bysshe Shelley* (London: Fredrick Warne, 1928), pp. 478–91; Maurice Blanchot, *La folie du jour* (Paris: Fata Morgana, 1973); *Death Sentence* [a translation of *L'arrêt de mort*], trans. Lydia Davis (Tarrytown, N.Y.: Station Hill, 1978). Hereafter referred to as *AM.*

77. Blanchot, *La folie du jour,* p. 33.

An "I," distinctly coded as male, is going to tell a story of "certain events," "unbelievable" as they might be. These events took place "around 1938," and sometime around the beginning of World War II. This "I" will, however, in his/story, leave monumental-events-of-a-male-world behind, and dive into a world of "women" inhabiting a strange universe between life and death, impervious to "The Male Definitions of Death" around them. He will descend, not into a "world" of women exactly, but into a series of events linked together by women's names. These names provide the metonymy of the "narrative" that we are demanding from the text. This "narrative" is slim, meager, almost impossible, since the largest part of the text is absorbed in what has been traditionally called "interior monologue." It does, however, still operate. What is the story?

Of all the women, it is a woman named "J." whose presence (we are still pre-Derrida) permeates the first sixty pages of the book. To make a long story short, J. is dying [*elle se meurt*].[78] The narrator remains "distant" from J., connected to her only through a series of phone calls, writing, and brief visits, while her "imminent death" is constantly deferred. Finally, one morning, he "comes" too late, finding her "dead"—until he calls her by name. With a cry, she opens her eyes: "they opened abruptly and they opened to reveal something terrible which I will not talk about" (*AM,* p. 20). J. "lives" another "day"; but when her attacks begin again, she asks the narrator for a shot. He finally gives in; she dies from the shot, and the narrator can write no more.

Here there is a break in the text, and on the following page we read: "I will go on with this story, but now, I will take some precautions" (*AM,* p. 31). After several pages of "reflections," a new series of women engage the narrator, with N(athalie) dominating this "second narrative." A shadowy ballet between "I" and N(athalie) follows, culminating in a subway scene where the narrator and N(athalie) exchange "words" (marriage vows) in her maternal tongue (we are never told what it is) and, finally, in "his." After this scene, N(athalie) disappears. The narrator searches for her and finds her in one of his hotel rooms; a strange "mystical communion in coldness" takes place between the "he" and the "she." "He" goes to live with "her." N(athalie) announces that she is having a clay molding made of her head and hands (echoes of a "mortuary mask" in the "first nar-

78. There are many "narratives" by Blanchot focused on death—the death of an Other which slowly becomes the "I's" own death. Many of Blanchot's Others are "women"—for instance, Anne in *Thomas l'obscur* (Paris: NRF, 1950). No doubt Poe would approve: the death of a "beautiful woman" being the "most poetic topic in the world." "The Philosophy of Composition," in *The Complete Poems and Stories of Edgar Allan Poe, with Selections from His Critical Writings,* ed. A. H. Quinn (New York: Knopf, 1951), vol. 2, p. 982.

rative"). They speak in a "cryptic tongue" about this "project." The narrator "reflects" on these "events."

Even those who are totally unfamiliar with Blanchot's text will sense the violence done to it by this summary, this telling of the story. And, indeed, after a reading of *Death Sentence* with Derrida's "Living On/Borderlines," this kind of summary becomes impossible. It is not possible here to follow all of Derrida's reading directions as to why this is so. But I do want to touch on those places in Derrida's text where it becomes clear how our "summary," our "story," remains possible nonetheless: that is, on those places where the "feminine operation" disrupting this kind of "police reading" would itself be impossible without certain *representations of women*. "Woman" or her "hymen" cannot disrupt this text without its women.

If there is an overall accent in "Living On," it is on that of the undecidability of *limits,* beginning with the title "Survivre": living on, on living, afterlife, life after death, life after life, etc. ("Nomination is important, but it is constantly caught up in a process which it does not control" [LO, p. 81].) This undecidability extends even to the limits among "texts" themselves. Derrida shows, for example, how the three texts he is reading are themselves in transference: the boundaries among them are no clearer than are the boundaries "within" them. This is done by looking at how the three texts under consideration put into operation, "pre-logically," certain privileged signifiers, so as to "undo" a metaphysical opposition: in this case, life and death.

Derrida has often insisted before on the semantic chains tied to these two words; for example, in Hegel, where "Life is life, life is light, life is truth."[79] Metaphysics is a "philosophy of life,"[80] where "death" can only be life's opposite, its limit, its banal ending. To take life and death "out of opposition," out of "mutual exclusion," is to move toward "a place without passage, without a beyond, toward a *living* which is finally intransitive, which is worth 'perhaps even dying.' "[81] It is to think, with the poet, life's and death's attributes: force and weakness, light and dark, speech and writing (Thot was not only the god of writing but also a god of death), masculine and feminine, etc. It is to explore, gropingly, the shady areas between life and death: "the pre-logic of the crypt."[82]

79. Derrida, *Glas,* p.91.
80. Derrida, "Speech and Phenomena," pp. 10–11.
81. Derrida, "Pas," in *Gramma,* nos. 3–4 (1976): 138.
82. "Fors" is perhaps Derrida's most extensive reflection on the life and death opposition. There he mentions, because of its exemplarity, Blanchot's *Death Sentence,* "a truly cryptic story" (p. 104).

It is in Derrida's wandering through *La folie du jour* that we find the first indications that this opposition-in-narrative cannot be undone without taking gender into account. This is so on two levels: first, most obviously, because of the clear gender-in-pronouns of Blanchot's "narrative," where "a number of signs make it possible to recognize a man in the first-person speaker," as Derrida puts it (LO, p. 95). It is women (characters) who shake up men's (the narrator's) certainties about life and death.

But, second, this reading cannot be gender-neutral because the "narrative" is shaken up in its very structure, is, in Derrida's words, "invaginated": "By definition, there is no end to a discourse that would seek to describe the invaginated structure of *La folie du jour*. Invagination is the inward refolding of *la gaine* [sheath, girdle], the inverted reapplication of the outer edge to the inside of a form where the outside then opens a pocket" (LO, p. 97). This infolding of the "narrative" produces a structure *en abyme* which can no longer even be called a "narrative": the demand for narrative and its truth "is itself recounted and swept along in the endless process of invagination" (LO, p. 98). Women and "woman" here coincide to disrupt the authority of the text and its "vision," with the process of "double invagination" designating "the *narrative of deconstruction in deconstruction*" (LO, p. 100).

Before moving on, specifically, to *Death Sentence,* Derrida remarks that this "narrative in deconstruction," the process of invagination, is Blanchot's "narrative voice" (as opposed to the "narratorial voice" of our summary). There is no ego-centric voice in Blanchot's text; and Derrida only briefly stops over the question of why the reader does in fact recognize a man in the first person pronoun: "We might wonder—and this is one of the questions that will run through my reading of this fragment— why the neuter of the *il* that is not an 'I,' not an ego, is represented in French, according to Blanchot, by a pronoun that privileges the affinity or apparently fortuitous and external resemblance between the masculine *il* ['he'] and the neuter *il* ['it']" (LO, p. 105). Derrida never answers this question, even if it "runs through his reading." He insists only on the necessity of the neuter for a "narrative" that would be "borne beyond the system of philosophical oppositions" (LO, p. 106). The rest of the reading will be, in fact, more about showing that necessity than asking why it might be one.

With the title, *Death Sentence,* we arrive, already, at the first undecidability of the text (*arrêt de mort* as both death sentence and stay of death)—to be incarnated by the woman named J. in life and death with and through the lives and deaths of the narrator. Through an analysis of that undecidability, Derrida renders his "first conclusion": "It is thus not a question of *one* death, one dead woman, a person who is dead or living on, between life and death—not one dead woman, one death, that is decided or undecided in this *arrêt de mort,* but *death, la mort (personne de mort:* no dead person, the person of death)—*la Chose*—itself as *other"* (LO, p. 120). Death in its contagion leaves no *One* dead. Living-On is the progression "beyond" life and death, incarnated by J.: "'Living, living on' differs and defers, like 'differ*a*nce,' beyond identity and difference" (LO, p. 136).

For Derrida, it is not at all a question of the representation of a woman dying. Instead, J. incarnates the *process* that disrupts any narrative based in the philosophical opposition of life and death.

Derrida again wonders, briefly, about the necessary "maleness" of the narrator and "femaleness" of N(athalie) in the "second narrative" (which is not necessarily second, etc.), most specifically as in the hotel scene between "him" and "her":

"I" is addressing himself here not to the merely grammatically feminine, the feminine gender of "thought" or "speech," *la pensée* or *la parole,* or to a neuter (beyond sexual difference), but rather, *it seems,* in the present, indeed, to a woman. (True, this woman is no one: "I can say that by getting involved with Nathalie I was hardly getting involved with anyone: that is not meant to belittle her; on the contrary, it is the most serious thing I can say about a person") (LO, p. 147)

This is the last Derrida says of "what seems to be." He concentrates instead on the subway scene between the narrator and N(athalie), for the "words" they exchange there have to do with marriage—with hymen. The narrator does not disturb N(athalie) with his "proposal of marriage" when uttered in "her tongue," but only when he speaks it—those "unheard of new words"—in his own (French). N(athalie), in her confusion, is then swept away by the crowd; commitment cannot take place: "The essential irresponsibility of the promise or the response: this is the crime of the *hymen*" (LO, pp. 154–55).

With the word hymen, we reach the outer limits (or perhaps inner core) of Derrida's reading.

For N(athalie) wants to have a death-mask made of herself just as J. was to be embalmed in the "first narrative." This echo effect (only one among others) is again (one of) the place(s) where the text invaginates itself:

Two *récits* in one, one *récit* in two, synonymous, homonymous, anonymous. He (the narrator, whose identity is doubly problematic: he had no name, and there is no guarantee that he does not have two, from one half-*récit*—or half-mourning—to the other) loves them. He loves them . . . dead. He loves (by) seeing them. He loves (by) seeing them dead. [. . .] But each woman is also the double, death mask, cast, ghost, body at once living and dead, of the other. Separated: joined. [. . .] By the same double token [*coup*], himself by the same token double, "I" becomes two, absolutely foreign to himself, divided, partitioned in his crypt: he belongs to two different *récits,* two different vows; he has another, a woman, dictate to him what he says and tell him what has to be done—another, a woman, who *inspires.* (LO, pp. 163–64)

As always, man, faced with woman, becomes a divided subject. Here, the play of doubles indicates the hymenal structure—doubled invagination— of the text, not among identities, but of the text to and with itself. The narrator, who in his division cannot stand to "live" the hymen, preserves himself from it by letting one woman preserve him from the other in endless oscillation.

Next comes Derrida's (own) *coup:* "Nothing seems capable of surpassing this terrifying, triumphant affirmation [. . .] Unless there is something even worse—and thus more desirable, more madly terrifying—for the narrator: the *hymen* between the two women. What if the structure of the *récit,* the interruption between the two stories, guaranteed at first the non-meeting of J. and N.?" (LO, p. 169).

This is Derrida's "mad hypothesis," then: that the two women (J. and N.) love each other across the boundaries of the "two narratives" in and without hymen. "No normal category of readability, then, could give credence to the mad hypothesis according to which the double invagination that attracts us in this *récit* could make it possible to read [*donner à lire*] the unreadable *hymen* between the two women: one *with(out)* the other" (LO, p. 170). Another kind of reading is necessary: we need deconstruction, as strategy of reading, in order to understand that "in everything that happens, it's as if the narrator desired (in other words forbad)— from the moment he comes to say 'I' onward—one thing: that the two women should love one another, should meet, should be united in accordance with the *hymen. Not* [*pas*] *without him, and immediately without him*" (LO, p. 172).

Here, after a hundred pages of reading (with only two self-conscious remarks on the fact that the women's names do, in fact, "seem to" represent women)—we have arrived, abruptly, at a surprisingly *feminist* "conclusion." The "I" of the male pronoun and persona keeps women apart . . .

But we must remember that, at the same time, it is not a question of identities for Derrida—*that* is what the hundred pages have been "about." It is rather a question of texts. It is texts that are kept apart, not women— or rather, "like women." This is made clearest in "Borderlines," that other and yet same text that runs along, typographically, the lower edges of

"Living On," in dialogue with "Living On," "at a distance and without knowing each other, like the two 'women' in *L'arrêt de mort*" (LO, p. 80). To call "Living On" a feminist reading in its "conclusion" would be to impose "traditional limits" on the undecidability of the hymen. So too would it be if we were, from the beginning, to doubt the reading, as feminists. Derrida telegraphs this warning to us in "Borderlines," complaining of "the feminist leader, a prodigious reader of Blanchot, who realizes, after the fact, that it was hard for her to bear that a 'man' should have dared the 'mad hypothesis' of the *hymen* between the two women; she used the most academic criteriology against me, demanded 'proof,' and so on" (LO, pp. 166–67). Derrida tells us that feminist questions, demanding to know what is going on here, would arrest in the most traditional of ways that process which, only as process, can recognize "style in female hymen," that process in favor of woman. Echoes of Nietzsche: it is women, not men, who don't like women . . .

It is difficult not to save Derrida's text, just as he saves one man's text after the other, from the moment that we recognize sexual identity's foundations in process—for Derrida, in the feminine process of writing. But then, on the other hand, the genderization of that process and its locus as feminine would seem to be impossible without some very traditional, recognizable images and destinies of women.

Is this merely a question of a new ruse of reason, a kind of "seducing" of feminist discourse; an attempt to render feminist discourse seductive (to men)? Might there be a new kind of desire on the part of (Modern) Man to occupy all positions at once (among women, among texts?) Are we here only brushing up against a new version of an old male fantasy: that of escaping the laws of the fathers through the independent and at the same time dependent female? Are men projecting their own "divisions" onto their primordial interlocutors—women? Do they hope to find a way of depersonalizing sexual identity while maintaining the amorous relationship through women?

How can we emphasize the political stakes of those questions without betraying the necessity of asking them knowingly—even "academically"?

What turns feminist criticisms will take at the angles of these questions—and others—will depend on how we respond to contemporary thought—a thought where woman *is* the angle.

A thought where "the L (*Elle*) is illuminated only like a letter in a breviary"[83]—in a breviary, whether as summary or book of prayer . . .

---

83. G. Hartman, *Saving the Text*, p. 82.

10

Becoming a Body without Organs:
Gilles Deleuze and His Brothers

It is no longer possible to think in our day other than in the void left by man's disappearance. For this void does not create a deficiency; it does not constitute a lacuna that must be filled. It is nothing more, and nothing less, than the unfolding of a space in which it is once more possible to think.

Michel Foucault, *The Order of Things*

Physicists say: Holes are not the absence of particles, but particles going faster than light. Flying anuses, rapid vaginas, there is no castration.

Gilles Deleuze, Félix Guattari, *Mille plateaux*

The position held by Gilles Deleuze and Félix Guattari (D+G) in this study—as a kind of "third"—is a function both of the particular kinds of questions we are asking and of the chronological illusion created by the history of their own work.

It is a function of our questions because, first, Deleuze and Guattari, as opposed to Lacan and Derrida, have no, or very few, women disciples, and thus the connections between their variations on gynesis and feminism are less direct. In fact, as mentioned before, to date only one feminist in France, Rosi Braidotti, has made extensive use of their work, and even in that case only as "the lesser of the evils" within the context of contemporary French thought.[1] Second, the degree of obligatory feminine con-

---

1. Braidotti, "Féminisme et philosophie," p. 253. I have also allotted less room to D+G's work because of Braidotti's study: a thorough presentation of the possible interactions between the "philosophy of desire" and feminist thought.

notations in D+G's work somehow remains intangible. Psychoanalysis and theories of écriture have participated in gynesis through the interactions of tangible (whether human or textual) bodies; they have created "feminine spaces" overrunning traditional conceptual boundaries that are still localizable. The new spaces unfolded by D+G, on the other hand, are not only body-less, but less often explicitly genderized as well. From rhizomes to the hypersphere, the genderization process of gynesis works silently, culminating explicitly only in *le devenir femme*, "the becoming woman"—presented separately from D+G's multiple voyages through inner and outer space and yet absolutely dependent upon them.

The "chronological illusion" of D+G's work refers both to their work in itself and to its American time of reading. First, their work, since at least 1972, as science and fiction, has had a perhaps inevitable aura of futurity. It leaves behind not only the Family of psychoanalysis and the Printed Word of écriture, but Deleuze's own, earlier, academic philosophy as well. Sea animals, computers, volcanoes, birds, and planets are more likely to serve as models for their thought than the bourgeois family hearth and its books. Their extreme, cosmic version of empiricism renders even the most daring feminist critique, as fundamentally empiricist as it might be, rather terrestrial. Second, D+G's work has attracted a very specific kind of American reading: an active and politically pragmatic one. They were read actively in the United States before they were actively read in France, where they were perceived, for the most part, as re-acting to psychoanalytic and Marxist theory. This split-in-reading between France and the United States was, in effect, programmed by their own texts. For them, France is the old world, the sedentary one, where logic is arboreal, history directs the future (*l'avenir*), and transgression sacralizes or pornographizes, "pornologizes" sexuality. The United States is, on the contrary, the territory of rapid movement: movement(s) based in rhizomatic logic, where only geography can govern any possible becoming (*le devenir*), and where sexuality, far from sacred, is dissolving into mass and perverse confusion. At the same time, while taking the United States as their ideal, D+G's work remains overwhelmingly Francocentric in its philosophical teleology. Their voyages to the outer continents of reason are firmly directed from their homefront, where they are at war with their own European heritages—from Plato and Hegel to Sartre and Lacan. Impertinent, anarchical (without *archē*), philosophers of deterritorialized desire, D+G remain very much in the (European) tradition of the (male) *chevalier de la foi:* they are the faithful and vigilant keepers of the future.

For all of these reasons, I shall only outline here some of D+G's major spatial reconceptualizations so as to arrive more quickly at what has, from D+G's overall work, most interested French feminist thought and been most ignored by American readings: the imperative of *le devenir femme,* the imperative to become woman. For if Lacan and Derrida's "woman" is intrinsic to their minute analyses of the potentialities for the pre- and intersignifications of modernity, D+G's "woman" is endemic to an era of *post*-signification—an era, it would seem, that human subjects, their texts, and the world itself are rapidly approaching.

First of all, the theories of "desire" for which D+G are so notorious on both sides of the Atlantic should not be confused with those of want, need, pleasure, or any other intersubjective category. All of these words remain eminently anthropo-logical, whereas D+G insist on tracing a desire beyond the person or personality: "Desire is not [. . .] interior to any subject, nor does it tend toward an object: it is strictly immanent to a plane which it does not pre-exist, to a plane which must be constructed, where particles will emit themselves, where fluxes will combine."[2] Desire cannot be a question of "interior drives" (instinctual or otherwise), for to think of it in that way is to reestablish the realm of interiority common to Man. Desire is neither natural nor spontaneous, let alone human: *"there is only arranged, pre-arranged [machiné] desire"* (DLS, p. 115). According to Deleuze, the misconceptions of desire may be summarized as three: "it can be put in relationship with lack or the law [i.e., transgression]; with a natural or spontaneous reality [i.e., acceptance]; with pleasure or even and above all celebration [i.e., reversal]" (DLS, p. 125).

That desire is "mechanized" in modern culture rather than "personalized" or "naturalized" does not mean, however, that it is mechanical: "The machine is on the contrary an assemblage of 'proximities' among independent heterogeneous terms (the topological proximity is itself independent of distance or contiguity)" (DLS, p. 125). This *voisinage,* as proximity, is in a perpetual movement of decoding, what D+G call an *agencement,* the process of arranging, of configurating elements: "The minimal real unity is not the word, the idea, or the concept, nor the signifier, but the *arrangement,* the configuration. It is always an arrangement that produces utterances. [. . .] The utterance is a product of an arrangement, always collective, which puts into play, in us and outside of us, populations, multiplicities, territories, becomings, affects, events" (DLS, p. 65). This *agencement,* as arrangement, does not have anything to do with an organization, but rather with a consistency—as, for example, in contem-

2. *Dialogues,* p. 108. Hereafter cited in the text as *DLS.*

porary music, where "certain contemporary musicians have pushed to the limit the practical idea of an immanent plane that has no more hidden principles of organization, but where the process must be understood [heard] no less than what results from it, where forms are only kept in order to liberate the variations of speed among particles or sonoric molecules, where themes, motifs, and subjects are only kept in order to liberate floating affects" (DLS, p. 113). It might help to think of this kind of arrangement as a "screening" of a large urban city, all of its movements crossing and dispersing with no hidden order, intentionality, or goal in view. There is no panopticon from which to interpret, plan, or even map that movement in its lack of teleology—it is a pure event.

In order to develop a way of conceptualizing a consistency that has no organization or signification, D+G have developed a series of a- or parasignificant models. These models vary according to whether they are apposed to the natural or to the human sciences. In all cases, that with which they do away, first and above all, is any concept of the body. For example, the Saussurian Linguistic Sign as Corporeal is exploded into multiple series; the Book as Corpus is imploded and infolded through an analysis of its signifying registers—this by loosening its shape, undoing its binding, metamorphosing it into, for example, one instance of a particular mode of delirium: unsentimental, depersonalized passion. Along these lines, *Tristan and Ysolde* would belong to a signifying arrangement described as follows: "a small packet of signs, a small block of signs, running along an unlimited, straight line, marking upon it a succession of processes, of finished segments, each one having a beginning and an end [. . .] Tristan and Ysolde follow the passionate line of the boat carrying them along: Tristan, Ysolde, Ysolde, Tristan . . ."[3]

D+G want to denaturalize Bodies of all kinds—and especially the "human" one. To do that means denaturalizing sexuality and especially its polarized genders. This process began in *Anti-Oedipus* with the term "desiring machines."[4]

"Men" and "Women" are henceforth but *agencements machiniques,* mechanized, involuntary, automatic arrangements—configurations of the male and female: "neither is there anything in common between the two sexes, nor do they cease communicating with each other in a transverse mode where each subject possesses both of them, but with the two of them partitioned off, and where each subject communicates with *one sex or*

3. See *Dialogues,* pp. 127–31. Or, for an extensive example, see *Proust and Signs,* trans. Richard Howard (New York: G. Braziller, 1972).
4. Deleuze and Guattari, *Anti-Oedipus.* Hereafter referred to as *AO.*

the other in another subject" (*AO*, p. 60); "everywhere a microscopic transsexuality, resulting in the woman containing as many men as the man, and the man as many women, all capable of entering—men with women, women with men—into relations of production of desire that overturn the statistical order of the sexes" (*AO*, pp. 295–96). If, later, D+G renounced using this "metaphor," it was because it was too often taken as, precisely, a model—and especially as a model for woman (cf. *DLS*, p. 121):

> But the problem of the desiring machine, in its essentially erotic character, is not at all to know if a machine could ever give "the perfect illusion of woman." It is on the contrary: [to know] in which machine to put woman, in what machine a woman puts herself in order to become the non-oedipal object of desire, that is to say nonhuman sex? In all desiring machines, sexuality does not consist of an imaginary couple woman-machine as a substitute for Oedipus, but of the couple machine-desire as the real production of a girl born without a mother, of a non-oedipal woman (who would not be oedipal either for herself or for others).[5]

As opposed to insisting on desiring machines, therefore, D+G have increasingly preferred to denaturalize the human body through the constructions of a "Body-without-Organs" (BwO). The BwO is "what remains when everything has been removed. And what has been removed is precisely the fantasy, the ensemble of significations and subjectifications."[6] D+G's strategies for evacuating our prefabricated fantasies to make way for new kinds of process are radical. The BwO is the temporary site for that radicality—a body without an image, capable of including everything from death (*AO*, p. 329) to contemporary writing (*MP*, pp. 9–13). It is opposed to metaphysics (life or death), the body of psychoanalysis, and even theories of writing with their still human and corporeal, even if alternative or partial, organs.[7] In fact, the BwO does not really exist yet, but is always there, next to us, as a limit of desire (*MP*, p. 197).

Luce Irigaray has insisted on how both the "desiring machine" and the "Body-without-Organs" resemble, above all, beyond their obvious con-

5. Gilles Deleuze and Félix Guattari, "Appendice: Bilan-programme pour machines désirantes," in *L'anti-Oedipe* (Paris: Editions de Minuit, 1975), pp. 471–72.

6. "Comment se faire un corps sans organes?" in *Mille plateaux*, p. 188. Hereafter referred to as *MP*.

7. Derrida would seem to be addressing D+G when he writes in "Tympan": "But indefatigably at issue is the ear [. . .] It is an organ whose structure (and the suture that holds it to the throat) produces the pacifying lure of organic indifference. To forget it—and in so doing to take shelter in the most familial of dwellings—is to cry out for the end of organs, of others" (p. xvii).

ceptual links to the fragmented body of the *infans* or psychotic, the female body as imagined by men. In spite of D+G's refusal of any model, Irigaray has nonetheless asked: "And the desiring machine, does it not still take the place, in part, of woman and of the feminine? Isn't it a sort of metaphor that can be used by men? Notably in function of their relationship to the techno-cratic?" For Irigaray, the BwO is nothing other than the historical condition of woman:

> And does not one risk, once again, taking back from woman those/her as yet not territorialized spaces where her desire could come into its own? Women having been assigned at the same time to the care of the "material body" and to the "without organs," won't the "body without organs" come to occupy the place of their [women's] own schize? Of the emptying of their desire in their bodies? Of the still and forever "virginity" of their desire? In order to make of the "body without organs" a "cause" of jouissance, isn't it necessary to have had, with respect to language and sex—to organs?—a relationship which women have never had?[8]

All of Irigaray's questions seem particularly pertinent when we remember that the only approach to the BwO as limit is along what D+G have called *lignes de fuite*. These "escape lines" or "vanishing lines," as opposed to the "molar lines" (sedentary, binary stages) and "molecular lines" (lines more fluid, but still with definite frontiers) of Western culture,[9] are consistently connoted as "female"—partially through their connections with the unconscious (as opposed to the sedentary conscious and the in-between preconscious). They are the "way" toward thinking a new body and a new spatiality—a body and spatiality that are, among other things, *lisse,* smooth and sleek; a body and spatiality whose "archetypal model is the sea."[10] They are the way(s) toward thinking an a-signifiant, incorporeal "extra-being" as the locus of the production of thought.

It is not surprising that the potential for finding that way will depend, in essence, upon the potential for becoming woman.

When and how does one become a woman? After the first menstruation, says traditional culture; that is, at the point where a female human being is capable of bearing children. Or, a girl is said to become a woman

---

8. Irigaray, *Ce sexe,* pp. 138–39.

9. For a summary of these three "lines," as alternative logic to the dialectic, see *Dialogues,* pp. 151–62.

10. See "Le lisse et le strié," in *Mille plateaux,* p. 598. As primary illustration for their discussion of this new kind of spatiality, D+G propose the quilt, a traditional art of women.

when she is no longer a virgin—especially when that condition comes about through marriage.[11]

In psychoanalytic theory, a girl literally becomes a woman when she changes her object of desire from the mother to the father: "Till then there is no trace of the Oedipus complex, but now the girl gives up the desire for a penis and replaces it by the desire for a child (child = penis) and *to this end* she turns to her father. The mother is then set up as a rival, and the little girl has become a woman."[12] Or, more abstractly and more recently, psychoanalysis has told us that anyone may become a woman in order to have a privileged relationship to jouissance: "Everything happens as if 'to become a woman,' 'to be a woman,' opened access to a *jouissance* of the body as feminine *and/or* maternal,"[13] as, for instance, with the President Schreber, for whom

> . . . the sex change was therefore directly tied to the impossibility of taking the name after the father; and Schreber chose at that time to go back to the origin of names, that is, to he who by an act of spontaneous generation would have begot the first man, without going through the other, woman, copulation. From which Schreber succeeded in systematizing his delirium; he found the simple solution that consisted of letting himself be penetrated by God in order to beget a new race. For this, he had to become a woman. . . .[14]

Or, even more abstractly, there is the consensus among contemporary theorists of writing in France that the male poet must become a woman in order to write: "And sometimes I do find where to put the being-of-several-lives which I am. In the elsewheres opened by men capable of others, capable of becoming a woman [. . .] (Only poets, not novelists, who are in solidarity with representation. Poets because poetry is only to draw force from the unconscious and because the unconscious, the other country without limits, is the place where the repressed survive: women, or as Hoffmann would say, the fairies.)"[15]

With D+G, however, none of these reasonings about becoming woman hold sway. There are, of course, overlappings (as, for example, with "There is a becoming-woman in writing" [*DLS,* p. 55]), but they are few. For what is involved here is *le devenir femme de tout le monde,* the becoming

11. In the classical male plot, marriage (as the telos of comedy) not only signifies becoming a woman but signals the end of narrative as well.

12. See the "Introduction" to J. Chasseguet-Smirgel, *Female Sexuality: New Psychoanalytic Views* (Ann Arbor: University of Michigan Press, 1970), p. 8.

13. Montrelay, *L'ombre et le nom,* p. 69.

14. Lemoine-Luccioni, *Partage,* p. 132.

15. Hélène Cixous and Catherine Clément, *La jeune née,* pp. 181–82.

woman of everyone, everything, the whole world. With D+G, "to become woman" is less a metaphor for describing a certain social or textual
process than a true metamorphosis—one thinks of Kafka's Gregor Samsa
waking up as a bug.

This is mainly because D+G's imperative "to become woman" has very
little to do with *women*, at least not with women as D+G perceive them, as
caught up within a Western binary machine over which they cannot and
will never have control.

In order to understand why this is so, it is essential to remember that the
devenir, "becoming," for D+G, is a process, one which cannot be described or put into motion by any of our current conceptual machinery:
"To become is never to imitate, nor to conform oneself to a model,
whether it be of justice or of truth. There is no term from which one
departs, nor one to which one arrives or should arrive. Nor are there two
terms which are interchangeable. The question 'what's become of you?' is
particularly stupid. Because as someone becomes, what he becomes
changes as much as he does" (*DLS,* p. 8). With "becoming" there is no
past or future, and certainly no present—there is no linear history: "In
becoming, it is more a matter of involuting: this is neither regressing nor
progressing" (*DLS,* p. 37). "Becoming" is topological, geological, geo-
graphical, not historical (*DLS,* p. 48).

"Becoming," for D+G, means becoming caught up in a process of
osmosis (not metaphor) with de-anthropologized entities—for example,
women, infants, animals, foreigners, the insane—in order to resist the
dominant mode of representation presented by any majority: "People are
always thinking of a majority future (when I'm grown up, when I'm in
power . . .). When really the problem is one of a becoming-minority: not
to act like, not to do like or imitate the infant, fool, woman, animal,
stutterer, or foreigner, but to become all that, in order to invent new
forces or new weapons" (*DLS,* p. 11). This osmosis maintains no identities,
no images. For example, to be caught up in a "becoming animal" means
not that one will resemble either Man or the Animal, but, rather, that each
will "deterritorialize" the other. The final stage of "becoming" is to become "imperceptible"—beyond any *percipio* as historically required for
Man to master the world—or woman.

This does not mean, however, that all of these becomings are in a
relationship of equality one to the other. The need for one or the other in
fact changes according to the binary machine one is "escaping" from and,
in all cases, the "becoming woman" always has, over all the others, what
D+G call a "particular introductory power" (*MP,* p. 304), a status as "first

quantum" (*MP*, p. 342): "However, if all becomings are already molecular [as opposed to molar], including the *becoming-woman*, it should also be said that all becomings begin and pass through the becoming-woman. It's the key to the other becomings" (*MP*, p. 340).

Again, this is not to say that "becoming woman" has anything to do with women *per se*. D+G's becoming woman is one "which is not [to be] confused with women, their past or future, and it is necessary that women enter into this becoming in order to exit from their past, their future, their history" (*DLS*, p. 8). We are not talking about men and women here, because they can only exist in the Western binary machine. It is a question "not [of] man and [of] woman taken as sexual entities, held in a binary apparatus, but [of] a molecular becoming, the birth of a molecular woman in music, the birth of a molecular sonority in a woman," and so on (*DLS*, p. 122).

Why then do D+G privilege the word woman? First, as they explain through a series of unanalyzed stereotypes, because it is "sexuality itself" which is the ultimate, uncontrollable becoming, when it can manage to escape immediate Oedipalization. ("*Sexuality passes through the becoming-woman of* [*the*] *man and the becoming-animal of the human*" [*MP*, 341].) But also because, as "introductory power," "Woman" both is the closest to the category of "Man" as majority and yet remains a distinct minority.

D+G explain that the notions of majority and minority here should not be opposed in any purely quantitative way: "Let us suppose that the constant or standard is Man—any white-male-adult-city-dweller-speaking a standard language-European-heterosexual (the Ulysses of Joyce or of Ezra Pound). It is obvious that 'the man' has the majority, even if he is less numerous than the mosquitoes, children, Blacks, peasants, homosexuals . . ." (*MP*, p. 133). The problem is not to gain, or accede to, the majority but to become a minority; and this is particularly crucial for women if they desire to remain radical, creative, without simply becoming (a) Man: "The only becoming is a minority one. Women, regardless of their number, are a minority, definable as a state or sub-set; but they only create by rendering possible a becoming, of which they do not have the ownership, into which they themselves must enter, a becoming-woman which concerns all of mankind, men and women included" (*MP*, p. 134). The woman who does not enter into the "becoming woman" remains a Man, remains "molar," just like men:

Woman as a molar entity *must become woman*, so that man as well may become one or be able to become one. It is certainly indispensable that women engage in molar politics, in terms of a conquest they conduct from their own organism, from their own history, from their own subjectivity: "We as women . . ." then appears as the subject of the enunciation. But it is dangerous to fall back upon such a subject, which cannot function without drying up a source or stopping what is fluid. The song of life is often struck up by the driest women, animated by resentment, by the desire for power and by cold mothering. . . . (*MP*, p. 339)

That is, woman (with her obligatory connotations: "transparent force, innocence, speed," etc. [*MP*, p. 354]) is what Man (*both* men and women: "virility, gravity," etc. [*MP*, p. 354]) must become. There must be no "becoming man" because he is always already a majority. "In a certain way, it's always 'man' who is the subject of a becoming [. . .] A woman has to become woman, but in a becoming-woman of all of mankind" (*MP*, p. 357).

That is, Man is always the subject of any becoming, even if "he" is a woman. A woman who is not a "woman-become" is a Man—and a subject to that extent and to that extent only. Woman is never a subject but a limit—a border of and for Man; the "becoming woman" is *l'avenir de l'homme tout entier*—the future of all Mankind. For D+G, She is what the entire world must become in order for Man—men and women—to truly disappear.

But to the extent that women must "become woman" *first* (in order for men, in D+G's words, to "follow her example"), might that not mean that she must also be the *first* to disappear? Is it not possible that the process of "becoming woman" is but a new variation of an old allegory for the process of women becoming obsolete? There would remain only her simulacrum: a female figure caught in a whirling sea of male configurations. A silent, mutable, head-less, desire-less, spatial surface necessary only for *His* metamorphosis?

Becoming a Body without Organs

Most important theorists have a repertory of exemplary fictions; fictions that they call upon frequently to interact with their specific theories in creative if predictable ways.

Between the scene of Lacanian psychoanalysis and that of Lol V. Stein's ravishing, the privileged rapport is one of repetition: for Lacan, Marguerite Duras understood and repeated his teachings without him.

Between the invagination of Derrida's écriture and that of Blanchot's narrator, what is privileged is the process of mime: for Derrida, Blanchot understood his writings with him, inseparably.

D+G's exemplary fiction writers include Lewis Carroll, Kafka, Klossowski, and Michel Tournier—to mention only a few. What all of these writers' texts share with those of D+G is the surface quality of their figures: the privileged modality of relationship between the configurations of Deleuzian becoming and those of fiction is allegory. This is made most clear through Deleuze's essay on Tournier's 1967 novel *Vendredi, ou les limbes du Pacifique*.[16] There, it is no longer a question of whether Lol, as hysterical body, is or is not a subject of narrative; of whether J. and N., as organs of a hysterical text, are or are not simply new angles for modernity. For here, it is a case of a true Body-without-Organs: Speranza, a woman who is not *a* woman but a female figure (an island) to be molded into new configurations for the metamorphosis of Man.

In *Vendredi*, we first stumble across Robinson just after he has been shipwrecked on his island. Finding himself completely alone, the Only and perhaps Last Man on this island, he first succumbs to depression, evasion, infantile panic—leaving himself exposed, helpless. For Deleuze, this signals Man's first steps outside of intersubjectivity: "What happens when others are lacking in the structure of the world? There only reigns the brutal opposition of the sun and the earth, of an insupportable light and an obscure abyss . . ." (*LS*, p. 355).

To avoid loss of self, however, this twentieth-century Robinson first tries the old solutions. He creates for himself a task: he spends months, perhaps years, perhaps even decades—the length of time does not matter—building a new boat-structure in which he might escape. But once the vessel is completed, it is too large and too heavy for him to push to the sea toward freedom. Robinson succumbs, once again, to the deepest depression—and, indeed, abjection: "He kept eating, his nose to the ground, unspeakable things. He went underneath himself and rarely missed rolling in the soft warmth of his own excrement [. . .] He moved about less and less, and his brief movements always brought him back to the wallow. There he kept losing his body and delivering himself of its weight in the hot and humid surroundings of the mud, while the noxious emanations of the stagnating waters clouded his mind" (*VLP*, p. 38).

Haunted by his lost sister (who died young), his mother (sometimes

16. All references to Michel Tournier's *Vendredi ou les limbes du Pacifique* (hereafter referred to in the text as *VLP*) are taken from the Folio edition (Paris: Gallimard, 1972). Deleuze's essay on the novel appears in the appendix to *Logique du sens (LS)*, pp. 350–72.

cold but always self-sacrificing), his wife (left behind in old England), Robinson-the-Man has a brush with what Man calls insanity. And so, as a Man, Robinson decides that he must henceforth master both himself and the island if he is to survive. He sets about building a kingdom: he creates a calendar; he invents a way to write; he builds a house, cultivates the land. He names the island Speranza and realizes that, now, in time and mastery, she is his slave. Woman is, therefore, no longer absent from Man's adventures, even though he remains outside of intersubjectivity: "Besides, it seemed to him, when looking a certain way at the map of the island which he had sketched approximately, that it could represent the profile of a headless female body, a woman, yes, seated with her legs folded under her, in a posture within which it would have been impossible to sort out what there was of submission, of fear, or of simple abandonment. This idea crossed his mind, then it left him. It would come back" (*VLP*, p. 46).[17]

In spite of various humiliations, depressions, and disappointments, Robinson continues his mastery over Speranza. A decisive step is the introduction of time, a primitive clock, into this one-Man kingdom. In the "future," Robinson succumbs to his former states of abjection within the space of Speranza only when that clock of progress stops.

Slowly, however, and in spite of his frenzied, productive activity, Robinson realizes that his relationship with "himself" is changing. His "self," in fact, can no longer exist in a world without the Other. Robinson is ready to lose his Self, his Man-hood: "Who *I*? The question is far from being pointless. It isn't even insoluble. *Because if it's not him, it must be Speranza.* There is from here on a flying *I* which will sometimes alight on the man, sometimes on the island, and which makes of me, in turn, one or the other" (*VLP*, pp. 88–89).

Robinson's insight is this: in this new world, in this new time, the Other does not have to be human, indeed does not need to exist at all. In those moments when he is not caught up in mastering the elements, he begins to look to the sky and then back to Speranza, alternately, beginning to perceive another possible Speranza (*VLP*, p. 94) than the object he as subject has been so busy cultivating. The distinction between subject and object breaks down. Robinson becomes, in fact, what he calls "the living consciousness" of Speranza while she, in turn, becomes Robinson's body. From this point on, Robinson more and more frequently loses sight of his

17. When accused of writing nothing more than another male adventure novel, Tournier objects, "On the contrary, it's a great feminine cosmic novel [. . .] woman is the island, she's the sister, the wife, the mother, everything . . ." Statement by Tournier on the French radio broadcast France-Culture, August 1975.

terrestrial labors and, instead, as he attempts to escape their constraints, he looks to the sky—but without leaving the other Speranza behind.

Deleuze points out that by this stage, earth, air, sky, the island, Robinson, etc. are no longer representations of Nature and Man, but figures— configurations—potential new arrangements of the four elements: "But the earth is what encompasses and restrains them, it contains them in the depths of the body, while the sky, with light and the sun, carries them to the pure and free state, freed from their limits in order to form a cosmic energy of the surface, unified and nonetheless unique to each element." The earth and sky are in combat, and the island, Speranza-the-woman, is the new frontier for the ensuing battles: "That's why it's so important to know which side she'll turn toward, whether she's capable of pouring into the sky her fire, her earth, and her waters, and to herself become solar." That is, the "hero" of the novel, as Deleuze puts it, is as much Speranza as Robinson, or later Vendredi: "The island changes its configuration in the course of a series of doublings, no less than Robinson himself changes form in the course of a series of metamorphoses. The subjective series of Robinson is inseparable from the series of states of the island" (*LS*, p. 351).

Robinson has already begun to merge with Speranza. He enters another stage, a second life, a series of intimate encounters with her, this time as a "person": "Speranza was no longer a property to manage but a *person*, of an indisputably feminine nature, toward whom he was inclined as much by his philosophical speculations as by the new needs of his heart and his flesh" (*VLP*, pp. 101–102).

Robinson slips into Speranza's crevices, covering himself with her milk; he attentively watches as her plants and animals make love; both violently and erotically, he himself makes love to Speranza.

But, finally, even though he recognizes that through these encounters he is engaged in a positive process of dehumanization, he also knows that both ways he has taken thus far (the "Maternal Way" and the "Vegetable Way") for escaping his selfhood, his Man-hood, have been "fruitless," have not produced fruit. Robinson must accomplish true metamorphosis. He must merge completely with Speranza; he must "become" her; "exist" in her (*VLP*, p. 129); he must allow her to suspend him with her in limbo between heaven and hell; Speranza must be no longer either his incestuous mother (as in the caverns) or sister, or even his wife. Robinson leaves the Oedipal structure and its predictable objects of desire far behind: "When I was thrown on these banks, I was freeing myself from the moulds of society. The mechanism that detours the naturally geotropic vocation of sex in order to place it within the uterine circuit was already in place in my stomach. It was to be woman or nothing. But little by little solitude simplified me. The detour had no more object, the mechanism softly fell away" (*VLP,* p. 133).

Robinson begins a third life: he unites with Speranza in a cosmic orgy of love and death. Where his sperm falls, a strange new flower-child grows, "the white fleshy roots [of which], curiously bifurcated, indisputably represented the body of a young girl" (*VLP,* p. 137).

The fruits of this perversion, of this union, are valorized by both Tournier and Deleuze:

> The thesis, the Robinson-hypothesis, has a great advantage: it presents to us as due to the circumstances of the deserted island the progressive effacement of the structure of the Other [. . .] Moreover, is not this progressive yet irreversible dissolving of the structure what the pervert achieves by other means, on his own interior "island"? To talk like Lacan, the "foreclosure" of the other has as its result that others are no longer perceived as others, because the structure is lacking which could give them this place and this function. But then isn't it as well our entire perceived world which collapses? To the advantage of something new? . . . (*LS,* pp. 359–60)

The fruits of perversion are, indeed, positivized. The "pervert" is not some-one who desires rightly or wrongly, but who introduces desire into a completely different kind of system; who launches desire on a completely new path. "The pervert is no more an ego which desires than the Other is for him a desired object endowed with a real existence." Tournier's novel is not *on* or *about* perversion. It *is* perversion; it lays bare the mechanism of perversion, as liberating: "This is not a thesis novel. Nor a novel of characters, since there are no others. Nor a novel of interior analysis, [since] Robinson has so little interiority. It's a surprising novel of comic adventures, and a cosmic novel of avatars. Instead of a thesis on perversion, it's a novel that develops the very thesis of Robinson: the man without others on his island" (*LS,* pp. 353–54).

But even this is a story that has already been told. Perversion is not enough; Otherness must be more radically refigured. And so arrives Vendredi—an Indian whom Robinson has unwittingly helped to escape from his tribe (where he had just been condemned to death by "a witch"). He and Robinson quickly become brothers, "lone brothers" who "form the ideal, sterile, eternal couple; other couples are only satellites; they live in the midst of vicissitudes."[18]

18. Statement by Tournier, quoted in Lemoine-Luccioni, *Partage,* p. 104.

Robinson at first tries, of course, to master this "savage" just as he had tried to master Speranza. But Vendredi operates according to another logic completely. He tries to obey his master, to whom he thinks he owes his life, but, whenever possible, laughs, sings, plays, dances. He even tries to follow his master through the mechanics of Robinson's prior metamorphosis: he too inseminates Speranza, slips deep into her caves. But Vendredi is not to be tamed, and Robinson gradually becomes fascinated by this uncontrollable new element; he is ready to enter still another phase beyond his Man-hood, a "fourth life": "The speech that is in him [Robinson] and that had never deceived him mumbles to him in half-words that he is at a turning-point of his history, that the era of the island-wife—which succeeded that of the island-mother, itself posterior to the administrated island—has in turn just come to an end, and that the time is near for the arrival of absolutely new, unheard of, and unforeseeable things" (*VLP,* p. 180).

Robinson begins to perceive "another Vendredi" just as he had perceived "another Speranza"; and it is this new Vendredi who accidentally explodes all of Robinson's all too human constructions to heaven for good.

Thus begins a new apprenticeship for Robinson: "toward something else" (*VLP,* p. 189). He follows Vendredi's example. They become, together, twins: "Sun, deliver me from gravity. . . . Sun, make me like Vendredi" (*VLP,* p. 217). Vendredi-the-boy-brother replaces Speranza-the-woman as crucial to Robinson's metamorphosis. Vendredi and Robinson, too light for earth, become elementary themselves. Vendredi—the day of Venus, the day of Christ's death—lifts Robinson from his terrestrial bondage. Not that they are in love. Robinson and Vendredi are too elemental, too near the sun, for earthly sexuality; sexual difference and sameness have long since been left behind. Even Speranza's primary configuration—the feminine—has been left behind as well: "If it were necessary to translate into human terms this solar coitus, it would be best to define me in feminine terms, as the wife of the sky. But this anthropomorphism is a misunderstanding. In truth, at the supreme degree which we have attained, Vendredi and myself, the sexual difference has been surpassed, and Vendredi can identify himself with Venus just as one can say in human language that I open myself up to the fertilization of the Aster Major" (*VLP,* p. 230).

Deleuze reminds us that Vendredi is not, here, a rediscovered Other, but a completely other-than-Other. The structure of same and other, subject and object, has been surpassed.

Surpassed, that is, until a ship pulls into Speranza's harbor. It has been twenty-eight years since Robinson has seen a Man, and after exchanging words with the captain of the boat and watching the sailors-as-mere-men master Speranza, he decides to stay with her and with Vendredi. But the next morning, and near the end of the text, Robinson awakes only to realize that Vendredi has abandoned him, has left with the captain and his Men. Fear of solitude again overtakes Robinson, until he discovers that a galley-boy-child has jumped ship and stayed on the island to replace Vendredi.

A child, ultimate fruit of Robinson's perversion, has finally descended from the sky, not grown from the earth, or in woman. Robinson names him Jeudi: "It's Jupiter's day, the sky god. It's also the Sunday of children" (*VLP*, p. 254). Created from a union between Robinson and the sky, Jeudi, son of Jupiter, is a solar miracle (echoes of Schreber); he is the *apotheosis* of Robinson's own metamorphosis.

In this extended allegory of the disappearance of Man, Speranza was the space, the BwO, that allowed Robinson to explore his psyche in a way that had been impossible until he found her. But he is beyond her now: "Speranza disengaged herself from the veils of fog, virgin and intact" (*VLP*, p. 254). Speranza: Virgin Gynema in a new world of brotherhood . . . without any women at all.

It would seem that the most radical promises offered by D+G's theory, as exemplified in Tournier's fiction, are not to be kept—at least for now. For when enacted, when performed, they are promises to be kept only between bodies gendered male. There is no room for new becomings of women's bodies and their other desires in these creatively limited, mono-sexual, brotherly machines.

Does that mean that D+G's work holds no promise for those of us who have been left in silence by it, left in limbo? No, for as with the other male writers in this study, their work represents the efforts of new kinds of male bodies attempting, if not always successfully, to invent new kinds of subjectivities. If these men were to accept the challenge of their own work, they would see that it is up to them to requestion their assumptions about Desire (capital D); to re-explore their seemingly unmeasurable fear of a desire that has not preexisted any of us, has not been prearranged—has not been allowed even to appear—in patriarchal culture. It is, of course, up to women not to disappear from that space of exploration.

GYNESIS IV

INTERFERENCES

An interaction of elements in a system which modifies
the natural effect.

II

Borderline Disputes: Oedipus, Orestes, et al.

> . . . it is not at all certain that literature and modernity are in any way compatible concepts.
>
> Paul de Man, *Blindness and Insight*

The theoretical fictions we have been exploring, those attempting to think modernity as both concept and practice, are, as we have seen, in step with a certain fiction that, if not coded as "literature" by those theories, is not coded by them as "theory" either. This distinction between contemporary fiction and the institution of literature is an important one for the writers I have privileged in this study: they see the contemporary fictional text, as opposed to canonized literature, as both their pre-text and inter-text, as the passionate source and receptacle of their own discourse; and yet, at the same time, they continue to emphasize its discursive otherness even when dislocated by their own. "The literary substance," as Shoshana Felman names it—that which resists interpretation—may be found in all texts, but it would seem to be more operative in what we habitually call fiction than in theory, and most operative in the fictions of modernity, in certain kinds of contemporary fiction.

Given this, I have tried to avoid two of the most pernicious clichés of contemporary criticism: the stand-off between, on one hand, the "traditional" attitude maintaining that the theoretical and fictional text are separate (the latter being the object of the former); and, on the other, the more "modern" one affirming that they are the same (neither having an "object"). Thus far, in order to do that, I have tried to renegotiate the borderlines between fiction and theory, emphasizing instead "modernity" (or, rather, what is diagnosed as modernity) as an epistemological *topos,* both fictional and theoretical, as related to another *topos,* another process: gynesis. I have stressed both modernity and gynesis as conceptualized in texts coded as theoretical and, to a lesser degree, as read in fictional texts by that theory, fiction and theory echoing and informing each other in a perhaps unanalyzable fashion.[1]

But there are other borderlines to be negotiated here, more briefly and in a somewhat different fashion. This involves repositioning somewhat our heretofore oblique and often tacit "comparativism." Rather than addressing (Anglo)American feminist questions to primarily French theoretical texts, I should now like to consider the borderlines between French and American texts coded as fiction, not theory. This repositioning involves a somewhat more direct "comparativism," but it is not a parallel one. It is not a question of looking now, in mechanical fashion, at "American theoretical texts" and their readings of "American fiction." That, at the very least, would be to ignore the most basic dangers of classical comparative thinking.[2] My interest is neither in distinguishing "theory" from "fiction" nor in positing some kind of metaphysical "French" or "American" essence or identity. Nor is my interest in suggesting that the French are thinking modernity while the Americans are somehow practicing it— or vice versa. It is, rather, in looking at the ways in which modernity and gynesis, as they have been thought and written in France, operate, and in sketching the problems that operation poses for (Anglo)American feminist thought. By privileging writing coded as fiction rather than theory at this point, I am in fact privileging *the* space of modernity as posited in France. In turn, however, and with a twist, by emphasizing *both* American and French fictional texts, I am testing the borderlines of both that "French" theory and our "(Anglo)American" feminist questions to the extent that they are inevitably caught in cross-currents of cultural specificity. That is, looking at the ways in which French and American contemporary fiction, written by men, are or are not participating in modernity— and the process of gynesis—as mapped thus far, may help us better to situate all of our questions about modernity, gynesis, and feminism—for future research.

To consider the questions, How American (or French) are our feminist

---

1. This project has no doubt been rendered easier by looking primarily at contemporary writing *in France,* where the institution of the intellectual is so separate from the academic institution which is intent on preserving generic categories of thought: the "intellectual" in France can be a fiction writer, psychoanalyst, semiotician, philosopher, or self-ordained cultural critic—or some, all, or none of the above—both within and without the university.
2. See "Preliminaries," above.

questions? and How French (or American) are modernity and gynesis? is not to try to impose artificially national borderlines, but to insist rather on their simultaneous solidity and fragility. Such developments as the Europeanization of world culture and the Americanization of Europe are increasingly rendering such questions hopelessly complex, and perhaps useless.[3] But, at the same time, if both modernity and feminism are to play a radical role in renegotiating the epistemological borderlines yet to come, it is necessary first to understand that the strategies available for use against the symbolic function—the relationship to the name, law, body, and so on—necessarily operate according to different economies in different cultures, even within the hegemony of Western culture, thus affecting *perceived* limits of representation. One only has to listen to the (rare) dialogue between an American Marxist and a French deconstructionist, a French theorist of the feminine and an American feminist, or an American behavioral psychologist and a French Lacanian to realize that they are not at all perceiving the same world—or texts.

In this last section, then, we will be referring to several specific fictions roughly contemporary with the other male writers we have been looking at in this study—those having written their most important fictions since 1945. They are all writers whose imaginative strategies are bound to gynesis and to the possibility or impossibility of writing itself—*the topos* of modernity. They are writers whose fictions are searching for their own fictions, through a self-referential magnification of language, this time, within the form of the novel, as it is playing itself out and wearing itself down at the end of the twentieth century.[4] Needless to say, still at stake are the limits and potentials of gynesis as process, no matter how unrecognizable that process might become.

> The "immanence" of Americans is undeniable (their being is in themselves and not beyond).
>
> Georges Bataille

The task of modernity, as it has been programmed in France, is to "kill the father" in all of his disguises, whatever his function or form. Because it

---

3. Also see Chapter 4, above. For brevity, in the pages to come I leave aside completely the future and necessary deconstruction of the term "Anglo-American," while concentrating on the U.S.A.

4. For insights into why the novel might be—or should be—breaking down as a generic form, see, for example, Kristeva, *Le texte du roman*, or her shorter article, "The Bounded Text," trans. in *Desire in Language*.

is preeminently narrative whose function is to assure communication between two or more paternally conceived egos, narrative is seen as that which must be disturbed first so that the creation of new breathing spaces in language may be affirmed and valorized. Along with narrative, those systems that support it—from the linguistic sign to the image, from the Cartesian subject to Truth—must also be dismantled if modernity is to accomplish its parallel task: to name the unnameable. The male authors of modernity have, in their collective murder of the father, detached the phallus from the father's body, and brought about such a *banalization* of castration that in fact, at least theoretically, it would seem impossible ever to name again. But, as we have seen, those new spaces and even that which cannot be named have, nonetheless, been consistently renamed—as "woman."

When one turns to contemporary American fiction, however, the first thing that strikes the imagination, if one has been thinking a great deal about the death of the father and its consequences, is that there would seem to be no father to kill—at least not "in" the narrative. The father as figure, or as character if you like, is already dead, seems to be absent from most contemporary American fiction, or else is only there as pre-text: to be explained, ridiculed, parodied, or ignored by the son.[5] In any case, he is certainly not there to be sacredly feared or adored; nor is his word there to be transgressed. For example, perhaps only an American writer could produce a fiction such as Donald Barthelme's *The Dead Father*.[6] Here the father is presented as exuberantly real rather than as imaginary or symbolic. He is a giant and clown—the beginning and end of Man's ridiculousness. He thinks he is on a serious quest for the Golden Fleece; but, of course, the fleece is only that which covers the hole in which the father must inevitably be buried, always already dead-alive. Intertextual authority and irony, a ridiculing of our meta-textual fathers, provide the rest in this textual plea for us not to take the myth of the father, or any myth, too seriously. After all, why go on killing the father if he is already dead? In fact, *The Dead Father* might serve as a prototype of the contemporary American novel in its desire not to take anything too seriously—not even itself.[7]

Even though it is dangerous to indulge in such generalities, one cannot

5. My intuitions about this absence of the father have been confirmed by two critics of American fiction: see Tony Tanner, *City of Words* (London: Jonathan Cape, 1971); and Fetterley, *The Resisting Reader*.

6. Donald Barthelme, *The Dead Father* (New York: Pocket Books, 1975).

7. A variant on this structure is John Barth's *The Floating Opera* (New York: Bantam,

help but be struck, in fact, by the enormous disparity between contemporary male textual experiments in France and the United States. And, on reflection, it slowly becomes evident that that disparity has to do, indeed, with different postures toward the father—or, more precisely, toward the paternal function as we have seen it defined up to this point.

To analyze how and why this might be so would require another entire study. Differences between the historical, political, religious, linguistic, and literary traditions, especially those of modernism, in Europe and those in the United States, the American impulse to launch its own traditions free from European ones, and so on, would have to be thoroughly analyzed. I will therefore point out only some of the most important factors that would have to be taken into consideration in such a study: the ways in which those traditions interfere, at the symbolic level, in the process of gynesis.

First, needless to say, such a study would involve two different histories. The history of France is the history of monarchy—the determination of alliance and filiation through the father within the Judeo-Christian tradition at a very symbolic level. Any disruption of the symbolic chain within that tradition involves the law (both human and divine) and the very fabric of social structure. It is filiation and history, through the divine right of the (Catholic) king, which has, for centuries, formed the matrix of substitution in French culture.[8]

The history of the United States, while obviously rooted in that of Europe, has a very different symbolic matrix: that of Protestantism and democracy. The differences between Catholicism and Protestantism—as symbolic traditions—are numerous, of course, but one of them is of particular interest with regard to the process of gynesis: the absence of the Virgin Mother as sacred object within the Protestant tradition. For example, in an essay on Samuel Beckett, "The Father, Love and Banishment," Julia Kristeva suggests that, for the Protestant son, the Father's death can serve only as a pre-text for his narrative—a narrative that, predicated upon the Father's death, at the same time represses and refuses the potentially

---

1956) where the Death-of-the-Father again serves as pre-text, propelling the American son into a series of Inquiries-on-Life as a supreme comedy and absolutely arbitrary narrative of events.

8. Here we are obviously limiting ourselves to a consideration of monarchy as France's *symbolic* matrix, not its historical one. For a detailed discussion of how France's entry into "democracy" shook apart that matrix without dismantling it symbolically, see, in particular, the second part of Kristeva's *La révolution du langage poétique*.

joyful incest with the mother as in Catholicism: "Beckett doesn't oblige them [the Latins] to experience the explosion of a nativity whose incestuous jouissance they celebrated."[9] The Protestant son searches for meaning in the absence of the Father, turning not to the Mother's body as compensation for that absence, but rather to a wasted object, "an undifferentiated woman, tenacious and silent, a prostitute to be sure, her singing voice out of tune in any case."[10]

This difference would seem to be accentuated and echoed by a primary distinction between monarchy and democracy. As Marx and Engels consistently pointed out, the state, not the father, is the focus of power in a democracy, even if there is only a "form" of a state, as is the case with the United States. In a democracy, the sons all resemble one another; any question of resemblance to their father becomes moot. And when the notion of resemblance is displaced from the father to society, identity is confronted with its own negation. If all of the children resemble one another, structures of narcissism and desire are no longer caught in the Oedipal triangle, but within society as a whole. The son's identity is acquired not by killing the father, but by killing his *semblables*—the copies of "his self."

And what of the "mother" within the democratic economy? Curiously enough, several theorists have seen another parallel shift, this time in terms of gender, from monarchy to democracy: it is not the father as king or Priest and the mother as sacred incestuous object that are primary in the democratic symbolic economy, but rather the maternal function as replacement for the father, as the central locus of (phallic) power within the nuclear family.[11]

The notion of the American form of democracy as a matriarchy has long enjoyed a certain popularity among contemporary male American writers—for example, William Burroughs, Norman Mailer, and Henry Miller; at least the fear (rather than the adoration) of the power of the "great mother" has been more pronounced here than in predominantly Catholic countries. That is, there seems to be, on the part of male American writers, an abiding fear of fusion, of nondifferentiation. On the one hand, the

9. Julia Kristeva, "Le père, l'amour, l'exile," in *Polylogue;* trans. in *Desire in Language,* p. 157.

10. Ibid., p. 149. Is it not possible that feminism has a longer and more vocal tradition in Anglo-Saxon countries because the Virgin Mother is not taken into account within the dominant symbolic economy of Protestantism? See Julia Kristeva, "Héréthique de l'amour," *Tel Quel* 74 (Winter 1977).

11. See Donzelot, *The Policing of Families.* In another vein, one might want to look again at Ann Douglas's *The Feminization of American Culture* (New York: Avon, 1977).

artist is confronted with the negation of his identity in mass culture. On the other, there is a fear of the Mother as central to the family. On the one hand, the writer fears his identity is being controlled or nullified by the invisible forces of society. On the other, he obsessively fears disintegration into the incestuous nondifference of the maternal space. The American male writer would seem to be caught between the state (Uncle Sam, Big Brother, bureaucracy, mass culture) and the Mother (almost always evil, cancerous, viscous, chaotic, uncontrollable, essentially monstrous phallic power)—with no father-identity to cling to. In American culture, it would seem not only that the father is dead, but that his name is completely missing. The Oedipal myth makes no sense to the American son—he reinforces his identity in an entirely different way.[12]

That way is, of course, just as mythical as Oedipus. For the myth of the weak or missing father is central not only to American culture, but also to *the* Oedipal antidote: Orestes and his successor, Nero. The apocalyptic vision of the matriarchy brings about, not the son's murder of the father, but his punishing of the mother for his father's death.

In the Oedipus myth adopted as psychoanalytic paradigm, the father is killed so that an erotic relationship with the mother can be enjoyed. Total fusion with the maternal is not dangerous as long as the identity conferred upon the son through his own symbolic actions may be retained.

In the Orestes or Neronic myth, it is the killing of the mother, or flight from her deathly sexuality, that confers the imaginary stamp on filial identity. And when this myth becomes central to an entire culture, we know that Oedipus has truly departed for Colonus.[13]

What is being proposed obviously is not a theory or even a system, but a hypothesis to account for the major factor differentiating contemporary male French and American writing. In the French writing, one finds an erotic merging and withdrawal across and through those spaces internal to signification, spaces that have been gendered as feminine. In the American writing, there is a total evasion of those internal spaces, an avoidance strategy mediated by technique. The "self" (a current American obsession) may be caught in a network of uncontrollable forces (both social and

12. For instance, Walter Abish's short story, "Crossing the Great Void" (see Chapter 2, above), may be seen as a parody of the Oedipus myth: the mother is not married but fled, and the father is not killed, even by accident, for he is nowhere to be found among the simulacra of his previous existence.

13. On Colonus as a "democracy," see Jean-Pierre Vernant, *Myth and Society in Ancient Greece*, trans. Janet Lloyd (Atlantic Highlands, N.J.: Humanities Press, 1980) or his *Origins of Greek Thought* (Ithaca: Cornell University Press, 1982).

maternal), but it can avoid fusion with those forces through a sustained cognitive control of and mastery over the signifier: a technical mastery protecting the self from the dangerous power of the signifier.

One of the more obvious examples of this function of technique is the writing of William Burroughs. There, the fear of fusion is, among other things, a fear of association. By attempting to avoid association or merging, the modern obsessional neurotic heeds a fundamental injunction not to touch—touching is, in fact, taboo. What Freud calls the "quantum effect," resulting from an original trauma, is displaced onto another representation, which is then repeated infinitely. The refusal of association does not lead to an exploration of the signifier and its internal spaces; it does not lead to transposition, but to the technique of the cut-up, a rearrangement of the textual surface according to a logic that is purely one of semantic isolation.[14] With Burroughs's writing, we are not beyond the sign, we are its masters. The "nodal points" of the text are separated, reconnected, repeated, left out, added, plugged in and out of one giant nightmare machine. The forces (cancerous and diseased) controlling the individual are ultimately seen as technological and programmatic. And Burroughs declares war on them with ever more advanced technology.

This is not to say that the writing strategies intrinsic to the modernity we have explored are not operative in the contemporary male American novel: narrative is untrustworthy and broken apart; truth is nowhere to be found; the image is decentered; the speaking subject is dislocated; the object of the discourse remains elusive. But the process in which these strategies are grounded is qualitatively different from those one finds in the contemporary male French text: it is an *external* process, manipulating language and exploding the semantic spaces of the *referent,* rather than an *internal* one, imploding the *signifier* itself.

That is to say, what might be called "scriptural audacity" is at a minimum in contemporary male American fiction. Syntax is for the most part normative (especially in the more "popular" writers like Mailer and Saul Bellow); the narrative is metonymically sound even if "cut-up" (as in Henry Miller or, on another wavelength, Richard Brautigan). The "text, quest, and sentence," as Roland Barthes might put it, are maintained intact. The "voice-over" of the text may be arbitrary, but it is an arbitrariness that is taken as an ideology itself: the unconditional freedom and originality of the author-self (especially in John Barth and Donald Barthelme). That "author" seems to want to avoid, at all costs, the relin-

14. See, in particular, William Burroughs, *The Naked Lunch* (New York: Grove, 1959).

quishing of control over his material: he remains sovereign, never putting the authority of his own discourse into question in any radical way. And that sovereign subject then participates in what Tony Tanner has called a "frolicsome evasion of social constructions"[15] rather than their excavation. For to dig deeper into the conceptual foundations of those constructions would necessitate digging into the American conception of the self itself.

A belief in the total freedom of the self—beyond adversity—goes to the very core of American ideology and its traditions (pragmatics, empiricism, pluralism, etc.); and, most important, it has engendered an approach to interpretation—perhaps *the* problem for modernity—increasingly incompatible with that of contemporary thought in France.

Two images might help to clarify those approaches. The contemporary American approach to interpretation might be compared to the process of painting: only one painter, always facing his painting, adds more and more material to his palette to create a "complete picture." The contemporary American writer adds more and more images, more narrative, more "characters," more words—however random—to cover up the emptiness at the foundations of his construction—an emptiness he fears. The contemporary French approach to interpretation might, on the other hand, be compared to sculpture: there may still be but one sculptor-subject, but he constantly moves around the material to be formed, never staying in one position very long, removing more and more material in order to create a shape. The contemporary French writer is participating in an extreme *emptying out* of images, narrative, characters, and words, in order to reach their silent but solidly significant core—an erotic core that he can then embrace. As the reader may have immediately recognized, the latter image is the one Freud applied to the process of analysis—a process he long regretted having brought to America where "ça ne parle pas . . ."[16]

And what of gynesis?

All of these qualitative differences between contemporary male French and American texts obviously have important implications for the process of gynesis. For gynesis is rooted in attempts to elaborate a new conceptualization and hence a new mode for and stance toward the problem of interpretation in modernity. Where the mode of interpretation and its relationship to the symbolic is fundamentally different—and where conceptualization as process has not been excavated but evacuated through

15. Tanner, *City of Words*, p. 416.
16. For Freud's distinction between suggestive and analytic technique, see "On Psychotherapy," in *The Complete Psychological Works*, vol. 7, pp. 260–61.

technique—gynesis must also operate differently. Indeed, can we say that it operates at all?

It could be argued that there is in the contemporary male American text a refusal, even a violent refusal, of the maternal; a refusal to explore the fragile infrasymbolic spaces of language as they have been excavated in France. The American interpretive response to twentieth-century crises in legitimation has not been one of exploding paternal identity, concepts, and narrative to get at their feminine core, through a rearrangement of *technē* and *physis,* a radical rearrangement of gender. The contemporary male text in the United States does not seem to have been acutely touched, at least in terms of its own textual gender(s), by gynesis as abstract, conceptual process. The writing subject and his sentence both remain integral unto themselves—and very male—by shoring up textual barriers against the "Nature" that threatens them (Burroughs's "virus") or by deriding and dismembering that body, which, if explored, would disturb their satire as technique (Barthelme's Mother and Julie).

And yet this avoidance strategy itself may participate in a form of "gynesis" that would seem to be operative in the American male contemporary text—albeit in a way strategically different from that in France. Gynesis—the putting into discourse of "woman" or the "feminine" as problematic—seems to exist here only at the level of *representation.* It has, in a sense, been externalized rather than internalized, and thematized rather than practiced, as the primary problem for any "narrative" or "subject-in-narrative"—without necessarily problematizing either one.[17]

Let us now move our more direct comparativism back into the margins and look at some novels individually, while keeping all of these different symbolic borderlines in mind.

17. In some ways, the American version of gynesis is more prevalent in "popular culture" than it is in "high theory"—especially in film.

12

The Fault of the Pronouns; Or, Perhaps the Century's Master Cabal

> "You are a storyteller," a friend said to me one day.
> "How can I be when words and images always cut in and want to be heard with their own aura, when the story is built out of bits of counter-stories, and when silence lies in wait for the world?"
>
> Edmond Jabès, *Yaël*

The interrogative return to the sources of our knowledge in the West has involved an obligatory return to the mother's body—a female body, no matter how unrecognizable; no matter how hysterical, textual, inanimate, or actual. And that return is just as much of a *topos* in contemporary male fiction in America as it is in the French texts we have examined thus far. —Except that in the American text, that female body remains traditionally *in representation* no matter how unrepresentable it might at first seem to be; it remains an image in representation unquestioned by the feminine and maternal as process, as internal to the workings of signification. The return to the mother's body, its destruction or phantasmatic dismantlement, is there narrated, not "constituted," as Barthes might say. The subject of enunciation is not put into question; it is not disturbed through an erotic merging with maternal boundaries, but strengthened through its technical evacuation of the mother's body from language itself. Is it possible, then, to speak of gynesis in contemporary male American fiction? Before further addressing that question, let us reclarify its boundaries by looking briefly at one last fiction of modernity in France: that of Philippe Sollers, a writer whose work has often been held to be synonymous with modernity in French intellectual circles.[1]

If we take into account a concise definition of what is specific to modernity, Sollers's exemplarity (however he might view it) becomes clear. Julia Kristeva defined that specificity some time ago:

> Literature was, perhaps until Freudian literature, something which, all the while playing on a code of the unconscious, by displacing in a minimal fashion what the social code imposed, nevertheless remained subordinate to and a tacit accomplice of this ideology [. . .] until the moment when the text itself, the "author" if you prefer, becomes conscious of the operation it is in the process of undertaking and makes explicit by means of precise theoretical references, or its own psychoanalysis, the action it is in the process of accomplishing, and therefore, in a certain way designates the limits of its proceeding and invests it in an ideological or social order; this has been happening for a very short time.[2]

The acute attention to the ways in which letters and words follow one another on the page to produce signification, rather than to the manner in which sentences add up to a "story" or "narrative," is that which accounts for many of the attributes of modernity we have already explored, such as the radical questioning of alterity, the impossibility of narrative and its representations, and the radical exploration of the internal logic of language (disruption of the subject-verb-object order). "It is as if literature had exhausted or overflowed the resources of its representative mode, and wanted to fold back into the indefinite murmur of its own discourse."[3]

Philippe Sollers's texts have not always actively participated in this self-conscious scrambling of representational codes. His first two novel-length texts, *Une curieuse solitude* and *Le parc,*[4] remain "traditional" in their representations. Since then, however, his writing has taken an increasingly complex path, culminating in his *Paradis* on the one hand—a text that, in its visible sabotage of readerly communication, is the culmination of his

---

1. His texts have been presented as exemplary of the spirit of modernity by Roland Barthes, Jacques Derrida, and Julia Kristeva, among others; beyond or rather in spite of the changing tides of Parisian intellectual and political allegiances. See Julia Kristeva, "L'engendrement de la formule," in *Recherches pour une sémanalyse* (Paris: Editions du Seuil, 1969), and "Polylogue," in *Polylogue;* Jacques Derrida, "Dissemination," in *Dissemination;* and Roland Barthes, *Sollers écrivain.*

2. Julia Kristeva, "The Subject in Signifying Practice," *Semiotext(e)* 1:3 (1975): 32.

3. Gérard Genette, "Frontiers of Narrative," in *Figures of Literary Discourse,* trans. Alan Sheridan (New York: Columbia University Press, 1982), p. 143.

4. Philippe Sollers, *Une curieuse solitude* (Paris: Editions du Seuil, 1958) and *Le parc* (Paris: Editions du Seuil, 1961). Sollers has disowned *Une curieuse solitude.*

own kind of spiraling "scriptural audacity"; and in *Femmes* on the other hand—a text that, in its visible return to readerly fantasy, is the culmination of his spiraling obsession with woman.[5]

Between those extremes is *Drame*.[6] Sollers considers *Drame*, published in 1965, as his first important book. It is, in fact, the "fundamental experience and experiment" of *Drame*, and Roland Barthes's reading of it, that have led to Sollers's exemplary position in terms of modernity—and, as we shall see, in terms of gynesis.[7]

Acting It Out

> . . . it's the fault of the pronouns . . .
> Samuel Beckett, *The Unnamable*

"Exactly as a drama performs itself, one can imagine that a novel writes itself before the eyes of the reader." This first statement on the back cover of *Drame* indicates why it would be impossible to summarize a story of *Drame* for readers who have not seen it performed on the page. Its overall movement, however, can be more or less described: there is a flow of words which at times seems to be attributed to the pronoun "he" (*il*) and at other times to the pronoun "I" (*je*). "I" seems to be writing what both "I" and "he" utter, but even that remains unclear as the sections with "he writes" and the cited sections containing the pronoun "I" fade in and out of one another in syncopated alternation.

Drame is a performance, neither "novel" nor "poem," without "story," without "characters," without "beginning" or "end." And yet it is clear that Sollers does not innocently retain the label "novel" under the title of *Drame*. For *Drame* does contain a quest.

Barthes describes this quest in the following way: "A man madly searches there for something, at times distanced, at times brought near this desired object by forces whose game-plan is prearranged, like in every novel. Who is this man? What is the object of his desire? What sustains him? resists him?" (DPR, p. 18).

5. Philippe Sollers, *Paradis* (Paris: Editions du Seuil, 1981) and *Femmes* (Paris: Gallimard, 1983).

6. Philippe Sollers, *Drame* (Paris: Editions du Seuil, 1965). All references in text are to this edition.

7. All citations of Barthes are from his "Drame, poème, roman" in *Sollers écrivain*, pp. 11–45 (originally published in 1965 in *Critique*). Hereafter referred to as DPR in the text.

Barthes answers his own questions at length in what remains an inimitable discussion of what is at stake in all of Sollers's work: the possibility and impossibility of, today, "telling a story":

> In this respect, Sollers's project is radical: he intends to lift at least once [. . .] the bad faith attached to any personal narration: of the two traditional halves, the actor and the narrator, united under an equivocal *I,* Sollers makes literally only a single person who acts [*actant*]: his narrator is entirely absorbed in a single action, which is to narrate; transparent in the impersonal novel, ambiguous in the personal novel, the narration here becomes opaque, visible, it fills the scene. [. . .] The consequence of this is that narration, the fundamental act of the subject, cannot be naïvely taken charge of by any personal pronoun: it is Narration which speaks, it is its own mouth and the language it emits is original; the voice here is not the instrument, even depersonalized, of a *secret*: the *id/it* [*ça*] which is reached is not that of a person, it's that of literature. (DPR, pp. 20–21)

As Barthes is well aware, "The depersonalization of the subject is common to many modern works." Nevertheless, there is a difference. "What is characteristic of *Drame* is that it is not *recounted* (reported), but *constituted* (so to speak) by the very action of the narrative" (DPR, p. 21, note 3).

Sollers's work explores alterity not through a narration, but through an act of "pure narrativity." This act of pure narrativity is accomplished through a formal alternation of the pronouns "I" and "he": "*he* is each time the one who is going to write *I*; *I* is each time the one who, beginning to write, will nevertheless reenter into the pre-creature who gave birth to him" (DPR, pp. 22–23).

"The man searching for something" in this novel is not *a* man but a textual assemblage of pronouns spinning around an empty space which is to be filled with—no One.

What is this "pure narrator" looking for? *L'histoire véritable* (the *real story*) is what the text indicates, and "we understand right away that the *real story* is none other than the search which is told to us" (DPR, p. 25). The "story" in *Drame* is the *desire* for a story with little overt concern for what the story is "about," or where it might lead. "Sollers follows very closely the fundamental myth of the writer: Orpheus cannot turn around, he must go forward and sing [about] what he desires without considering it" (DPR, p. 29).

A pure narrator is here constituting pure narrativity: the narration of pure desire itself, without a consideration of its object. And yet, Eurydice has not abandoned Orpheus. She is still there, but behind him.

Barthes suggests, in a note very early in his text, that *Drame,* while neither poem nor novel, might be read like a poem: as "the indistinct celebration of language and of the beloved woman, of their path toward one another, like the *Vita Nova* of Dante was in its time: isn't *Drame* the infinite metaphor for 'I love you,' which is the unique transformation of all poetry?" (DPR, p. 13).

The beloved woman? Yes, *Drame* is not only a formal, modern project in depersonalization, an emptying of the pronouns "I" and "he," but an old-fashioned heterosexual love story of sorts. For there are two other pronouns in *Drame,* which are never explicitly mentioned by either Sollers or Barthes: "you" and "she." Pronouns we have seen before.

> Ph.S.: "But, in order to limit ourselves to a general observation, let us just say that my interest in women, wouldn't you say, is certainly the motif, in the pictorial sense, which has provided the impulse for my writing, without any doubt."
>
> D.H.: "From the beginning?"
>
> Ph.S.: "Oh yes, it's visible."
>
> Sollers, *Vision à New York*

Sollers's first full-length novel, the one that brought him his first acclaim but that he has since rejected as too traditional, is the story of a young boy's parallel initiation into love and writing. *Une curieuse solitude* "tells the story" of that young boy's seduction by the mysterious, foreign, and older Concha; her abandonment of him; his initiation into writing necessarily concurrent with her absence; his rediscovery of Concha (and of her homosexuality); and finally his abandonment by her, leaving him alone to himself—and to the writing whose coming into existence would have been impossible without her.

Sollers's second novel, *Le parc,* is a succession of "still lifes"; shadowy images of women in various poses, coming and going silently through the rooms of a man's imagination as it slowly places itself before his notebook and ink: "the orange-covered notebook patiently filled, overflowing with writing, evenly driven to this page, this sentence, this period, by the old pen often and mechanically dipped in the bluish-black ink."[8]

8. *Le parc,* p. 155.

In *Drame,* the performance we participate in as reader, the link between "she" and "writing" will be maintained, but without plot, character, shadow, or image. The "you" who allows "I" to write, to whom "I" writes, and the "she" who allows "he" to speak of "I" are nothing more than the interlocutive spaces allowing the two masculine coded pronouns "I" and "he" to circulate, merge, separate, and come together again.

Within this circulation, it is not always certain that "you" is female; for example, it occasionally appears that "he" and "I" are addressing each other, the narrator of "he" addressing "you" ("You have the choice and more than the choice. The answer will tell you if you invented it. No more delays. To you." [*Drame,* p. 14]) just before the appearance of the first "he writes" in the text, and long before the first appearnce of "she." This "she," too, may not always apply to the shadowy woman in the next room (reminiscent of the "women" in *Le parc*); sometimes "she" explicitly designates the process of textual metamorphosis itself, sliding into the words as, nude, into a dress (*Drame,* pp. 33–34). Within a singular metamorphosis of pronouns, "she" may be the earth (*la terre*), the sea (*la mer*), language (*la langue*), or even *l'histoire véritable.* But in all cases, "you/she" is *coded* as feminine, as the space needed for the image to take form within and through the words, as they flow one after another on the page. "You/she" is the mediating, almost mathematical function needed for the time of narrative to continue projecting itself into space: "You now belong to the incessant depth which we envelope and which carries us: you have become space, and for the first time space responds" (*Drame,* p. 141).

"You/she" is a female body. Like the other female, hystericized bodies we have encountered—Lol, N., J., Speranza—she is a dismembered and fragmented body (legs and closed eyes)—indicating, alternately, the text's ultimate freedom and its absolute limits:

> She, for her part, becomes the joyous negation of these movements, indicating at that moment a liberty without limits, inaccessible, seen from bottom to top, her legs especially . . . Her naked legs and her standing laughing, without seeing anything . . . It's in this way that he most often sees her, rising up suddenly beyond a screen of broken signs, coming back and brutally putting an end to the situation, affirming her presence—or again thrown back on the sheets with her eyes open and not seeing anything. (*Drame,* pp. 45–46)

"You/she" is the movement of the text, its place of slippage, that which cannot be captured by the sign: "the sign that announces you disappears, you are withdrawn with respect to this sign as I am with respect to you" (*Drame,* p. 66).

"You/she" has no look or discourse of her own; she sees everything and nothing, for she is not a psychological persona, but the rhythm—the textual jouissance—allowing the "I/he" to lose their "selves" within "the margin of the void" (*Drame*, p. 64) necessary for writing:

> And often, when she is on the verge of breaking, and of falling (of coming), she appears to touch this center of time—her eyes become clear, more and more fixed, she says "look at me" and no longer sees anything. (*Drame*, p. 122)

> —and it's there that we bring each other with curiosity, and suddenly your face lying on the sheet tenses, comes undone, buries itself, while your other face returns on a counter-current, and it is through it that you want to follow in my eyes the same ascending fall (symmetrical, inverse), dilation of the pupils, pallor, brief stiffening . . . Words are then dispersed, destroyed . . . (*Drame*, pp. 134–35)

> He would like to set it all working, to put it to the test, to not lose contact with the close and distant rhythm that does not cease to grow larger and to filter in starting from here. (*Drame*, p. 90)

"You/she"—as female jouissance, the becoming rhythm, the écriture of the text—is that which allows the words to continue, one after the other, on the page. If "he" stands for a bow and "I" for an arrow (*Drame*, p. 133), "you/she" is the intersection of the two, the gap and friction of their meeting, that which allows the textual apparatus of pronouns to work—and the text to continue.

Sollers's radical explorations of alterity, like those of the writers we looked at earlier, involve a putting into discourse of the feminine—feminine pronouns in this case—as that which makes possible the displacement of the monological and mono-vocal structures of representation. The erotic merging with the Other (sex) is that which allows the male subject of enunciation enough distance from his "self" to explore language as performance, as act, as text, as writing itself.

What the fate of this gynesis will be remains to be seen. It appears, however, that this particular form of gynesis, taken to its extremes through an ever increasing emphasis on the pronouns "you" and "she" by male writers, leads for the most part to one of two limits: either to an overwhelming poetical, mystical, or religious celebration of "woman" (a valorization of "woman" unseen since the Renaissance) or to the eventual reappearance of women as psychological entities in the text, now caught up in a textual whirlpool of sexual hatred.

In the first case, that which is the "object" of discourse itself (not the narrative) is gendered as female and is valorized as both desirable and, at the same time, unattainable. For example, "woman" becomes the Book itself in the writing of Edmond Jabès.[9] Mathieu Bénézet describes Jabès's work in terms by now familiar to us: "Jabesian speech occupies the space left vacant after history, after the story—after the catastrophe. Speech of the ultralanguage, of catachresis. [. . .] Identity entrusted to the outside, to alterity. Strange history, strange story of being pushed aside by property, the name, the proper name. Except that what is our own is that of which we have been dispossessed and that which is lacking."[10] In Jabès's texts, we are led through an anagrammatical succession of feminine improper names, deduced one from another—in "monstrous filiation": Aely, Yaël, Elya . . . Letters spin around a central gap emptied of identity, a gap that makes the-writing-of-the-Book possible.

> A woman and a word.
> A woman turning
> around a word turning
> slowly, faster,
> unbelievably fast
> till they are but
> one circle in the space that spawned them
> pursuing a smaller
> and even smaller
> grotesquely tiny circle.
> A hole. An empty socket.[11]

"She" is still the body, the corpus, the Book, its source, its impossible limits—the very page upon which it is written:

Body outlined—every page like a foggy beach, O words still grey, not yet black; every page like a blaze of morning; all shape washed out by the white

---

9. The cryptic texts of Edmond Jabès deserve more than exemplary attention; I invoke his writing here primarily because of its extensive valorization in contemporary French thought. See *The Book of Questions: Yaël, Elya, Aely,* trans. Rosemarie Waldrop (Middletown, Conn.: Wesleyan University Press, 1983); *The Book of Yukel, Return to the Book,* trans. Rosemarie Waldrop (Middletown, Conn.: Wesleyan University Press, 1977); and *El, ou le dernier livre* (Paris: Gallimard, 1973).

10. Mathieu Bénézet, *Le roman de la langue* (Paris: 10/18, 1977). The reader might also want to look at his *La fin de l'homme* (Paris: Flammarion, 1979): "But I am also a woman—everybody today knows it" announces this text of maternal dialogue.

11. Jabès, *The Book of Questions: Yaël, Elya, Aely,* p. 11.

of the page, her body nearly white, barely sketched in by the wrinkles on the water surface, the reflections of the glass, the imagination of the cloud.

Yaël is in the book and already in the winter of the book.

The word is a word of distance, around death.[12]

"Woman" is what the "subject" and the "Book" must become in order to experience the pure jouissance of language. Only as woman ("those who enjoy the use of the signifier [. . .], those who are comforted by their entrance into the language which constitutes for them a place of jouissance and of speech")[13]—can man write.

In the second case, and in contrast, it is no longer primarily a question of "woman" as that space and process opening language to jouissance, but rather of *women* as opposed to men, a problem contemplated by a dislocated but still male subject of enunciation. In the case of Sollers, this second path has led to the two texts *Femmes* and *Paradis*—one the intertext of the other. In both cases, woman is no longer the silent, shadowy, nonseeing, nonspeaking feminine figure, or space of slippage, allowing the textual mechanism to bare itself in its nudity. "She" re-becomes instead the woman who incarnates sexuality, the woman who brings about Man's perpetual fall into language.

In *Paradis,* "she" remains textual—still very connected to the questions of modernity depending upon "her" for an answer. In *Paradis,* "woman" is that unrepresentable something, that "other God" that has brought about Man's demise, and "she" has now become the object of seemingly uncontrollable sex-textual rage. In what at times seems to be an exemplary text of male paranoia, "woman" becomes the "evil spirit," the demonic force that must inevitably bring about Man's fall, indeed, the apocalypse. The feminist reader is struck, in particular, by passages scattered throughout *Paradis* where women's "revindications of their rights" are explained away by the Oedipal machine in which we are all caught: "they [women] can't help it they must incarnate the law in order to complain of being neglected by it and you and we and they in there boring unconscious victims and you and all of us and all [women] . . ."[14] Or, at other times, one stops over passages where, in a self-conscious Rabelaisian whirlwind of superlatives, women are denounced as being at the source of all the faults of Man:

12. Ibid., pp. 26–27.

13. Bénézet, *Le roman de la langue,* p. 181. Also see Jean Daive, *Le jeu des séries scéniques* (Paris: Flammarion, 1976): "One night, I became a woman and my hand began to write, to ritualize the memory of my voice" (presentation of text, signed Jean Daive).

14. Sollers, *Paradis,* p. 72.

. . . if I could discover in myself what comes to me from woman for there is no vicious tendency in man which I affirm doesn't come from her is it a lie well then it comes from woman flattery from her and again perfidy from her simulation of lasciviousness from her from her rancor from her ambitions capricious cupidities vanities contempt fond desires scandelmongering inconstancy all the faults one can name or even that hell knows all come from her or almost all of them no I said all of them because even in vice they [women] are not constant constantly they leave one minute-old vice for one half as old I want to write against them [women] to hate them slander them . . .[15]

Sollers's *Femmes* is, in a sense, the "key" to his *Paradis;* there, "woman" and women alternate, less connected to modernity and its text. It is almost as if the "blueprint" for *Paradis* (as "fundamental experiment") had to be published elsewhere, in a more or less traditional, representational novel like *Femmes.* In *Femmes,* what is seen as the master formula of our contemporary culture is explicitly revealed: "the truth, finally, about the secret-women, about the secret that transpires through women and dissolves the belief that there is a world and a necessity for this world . . ."[16]

There is also, however, and sometimes incredibly so, a textual insistence in *Paradis* and *Femmes* that these texts are not engaged in some kind of "misogynist project" on the part of the "male author" but, rather, that it is once again "the structure of things" that is to blame: "what we are trying to mark here is simply the mounting the way in which this makes a collage the puzzle the weaving."[17] For Sollers and for the writers working in France whom I have privileged in this study, the problem of woman would seem to be one neither of "idealization" nor of "misogyny" in their texts, but of understanding why and how "she" has become so central to modernity, to the world and its texts in the late tewentieth century.

The "she" haunting much of the most important contemporary writing by men in France is at times angelic, at times monstrous. But "she" is always seen, above all, as that which must be explored through an erotic merging at the interior of language, through a radical dismemberment of the textual body, a female body. *Women,* as identity, may eventually reappear within the boundaries of that exploration, but never for long, usually separated from it, and always with duplicity. It would seem to be only "woman" that can serve as imaginative strategy for exploring the breakdown of the paternal metaphor within the epistemological laboratory of the late twentieth century.

15. Ibid., p. 115.
16. Sollers, *Femmes,* p. 306.
17. Sollers, *Paradis,* p. 248.

I Can Get along without You Mother

> . . . his quarry fitted in with the Big One, the century's master cabal. . . .
>
> Thomas Pynchon, *V.*

Christmas Eve, 1955, Benny Profane, wearing black levis, suede jacket, sneakers and big cowboy hat, happened to pass through Norfolk, Virginia.[18]

From the very first sentence of what has not failed to be recognized as one of the most important contemporary American novels, readers find themselves in a textual universe different from the one we have been exploring thus far. "Time," "place," and "character" remain unself-consciously intact. How can we possibly talk about gynesis?

And yet, Thomas Pynchon's *V.* is a perfect example of the thematization rather than constitution of gynesis in contemporary male American writing. *V.* is a novel *about* interpretation, *about* the possibilities and impossibilities of "making sense," of "making plots." And it is *a* woman who is at the source of those (im)possibilities. *V.* is about how a woman is narrative's problem, about how a woman is the object of the subject-in-narrative's quest. This woman is not, however, a "character" in the novel. Rachel Owlglass, Paola Maijstral, Charisma, and Esther pose only traditional problems for now traditional antiheroes. The woman who serves as matrix for this novel about interpretation may or may not exist; does and does not exist; must and yet cannot exist if narrative is to continue.

Around that woman, two psychologized male characters—Benny Profane and Herbert Stencil—revolve. The critics have seen Benny as "twentieth-century man"—he has no plot.[19] He is a "schlemihl," a "yo-yo," without goal, identity, object, or proper place. Benny wanders through plots that clearly are not his own. Benny's is a very profane metonymy.

Herbert, on the other hand, is "historical man." His life is nothing more than the series of analogous plots he has made up, lived, and dreamed. Forcibly dislocating his personality, Stencil refers to himself in the third person (p. 51); "Stencil" sees and lives plots everywhere, and we, as readers, follow those plots—even when "Stencil" is absent—through a series of third person narratives. Stencil is a master of metaphor, and his analo-

18. Thomas Pynchon, *V.* (New York: Bantam, 1961), p. 1. All page references in text are to this edition.

19. See, for example, Tony Tanner, "Caries and Cabals," in *City of Words*, pp. 153–80.

gical mode is the source of Profane's—and the reader's—metonymic paths.

Stencil's father is of course dead—long dead. He died on the Island of Malta, "where Herbert had never been and [about which he] knew nothing at all [. . .] because something there kept him off, because it frightened him" (p. 51). All he knows for sure is that his father was involved with someone, or something, called V., and Herbert's life quest is to find out who or what "she" is or was, what she had to do with his father's death, how his father, V., and Malta are connected. He of course rejects the notion that V. might be the mother he never "knew" . . . Stencil: "You'll ask next if he believes her to be his mother. The question is ridiculous" (p. 43).

V. is the *locus* of past, present, and future in this novel. "She" remains unrepresentable throughout a vertiginous series of representations. As unrepresentable factor, she nonetheless "represents" rather than constitutes the space of slippage, the spaces of nonresemblance, within the sign, among the signifier, signified, and referent. A "mysterious woman," she is a kind of "spirit" that can inhabit names, places, and images. The reader enters with "Stencil" and his endless identities, with "Profane" and his object-less stumblings across our readerly if stencilized paths, into an epistemological woman-hunt where V. may be, or be analogically linked to, one of numerous V-functions.[20]

"Vheissu" is one of the most important of these V-functions because it is a privileged "symptom," like V.: "Call Vheissu a symptom. Symptoms like that are always alive, somewhere in the world" (p. 445). Vheissu is also, like V., a legacy of several stencilized fathers; like the sewer stories Profane has heard, it does not matter whether it is real or not: "Truth or falsity don't apply" (p. 108). Vheissu, like Speranza in Tournier's novel,[21] is the twentieth-century son's bedtime story—a fantastic place of spider monkeys, rivers of rainbows and colors, volcanoes with cities inside them—as seen through "a madman's kaleidoscope" (p. 155). A dark continent, deep in the imagination, handed down from Father to Son, Vheissu is also feminine, a "woman":

> "But as if the place were, were a woman you had found somewhere out there, a dark woman tatooed from head to toes. And somehow you had got separated from the garrison and found yourself unable to get back, so that you had to be with her, close to her, day in and day out. . ."

20. The list of V-functions is long: it includes names of people—Virginia, Violet, Viola, Vera, etc.—and places—V-note Café, Vesuvius, Venezuela, Valetta.
21. See Chapter 10, above.

"And you would be in love with her."

"At first. But soon that skin, the gawdy, god-awful riot of pattern and color, would begin to get between you and whatever it was in her that you thought you loved." (p. 156)

For under "V.",'s skin, there is no soul, "like a woman. I hope I don't offend" (p. 155). In fact, under Vheissu's skin, there is but a terrifying nothingness: "Nothing [. . .] It was Nothing I saw" (p. 188). It may be that V. is nothing more than a luxury, an "indulgence" (p. 230) that the twentieth century can no longer afford—but then what about the void; how can we satisfy our need for her? (p. 230). Perhaps by eliminating her from our quest. We were wrong: V. is not V. but U. (V-is-u)—or "you," that pronoun of alterity absent from this text, beside the point, no longer needed.

So perhaps if V. is not Vheissu (which is you), perhaps she is nothing more than an image, a concept, "like a woman": "half of something there are usually two sides to" (p. 10). V. is not an X-factor, a chiasmus, or even a symbol marking the presence or absence of something, but only $1/2$ (V, Λ), in mirror image, of that which might allow us to make sense of what we see, or imagine.

Or perhaps we are already overinterpreting. Perhaps V. is simply: V. for victory; V. for the Mons Veneris; V. as the mark of the horizon to the East beyond which Western Man cannot see, "where it's dark and there are no more bars" (p. 2); V. as the stain that won't go away, even while remaining "hardly visible" (p. 78): "V. ambiguously a beast of venery, chased like the hart, hind or hare, chased like an obsolete, or bizarre, or forbidden form of sexual delight. And clownish Stencil capering along behind her, bells ajingle, waving a wooden, toy oxgoad. For no one's amusement but his own" (p. 50).

And the reader's; for by this time, V. is "a remarkably scattered concept" (p. 364) and cannot help but throw into overactivity the reader's own interpretive machine, pulling us endlessly into an endless joke on Signification.

As for Stencil, he as "subject" will never coincide with V. as his "object." He would not want to, for then his life and the text we are reading would end—with, perhaps, more than unsettling results: "'There is more behind and inside V. than any of us had suspected. Not who, but what: what is she. God grant that I may never be called upon to write the answer, either here or in any official report'" (p. 43). Then "why" (that child's question, the hermeneutic question) pursue her? "'Why not?' said Stencil" (p. 361). Stencil is forever claiming that "why" (y) is the wrong question—an outdated question, too old for the twentieth century. Perhaps his search for V. is nothing more than "an adventure of the mind" (p. 50). In any case, "why" is not important for Stencil. He must not be seen as anything other than "He Who Looks For V." (p. 210). Quite simply put: "He doesn't know who she is, nor what she is. He's trying to find out. As a legacy from his father" (p. 140).

Of course, V. is not Stencil's only legacy from his Dead Father. Throughout the text named *V.,* we find that V.'s major function is to undermine the entirety of Stencil's inheritance: Human Identity, Truth, Reason, History. The specificity of the twentieth century is that it has thrown all of those concepts into confusion. In the twentieth century, we need "eyes clear enough to see past the fiction of continuity, the fiction of cause and effect, the fiction of a humanized history endowed with 'reason'" (p. 286). "Truth" must be conceived with "no metaphysics" (p. 297). "History" can explain nothing.

One of the things "Stencil" and his others have consistently encountered through the "ominous logic" of the twentieth century (p. 423) is an uncanny falling away from the human, a progressive dehumanizing tendency, as appalling and frightening as it is beyond human control.

Throughout *V.,* certain "inanimate objects" or parts of them turn up in seemingly unrelated places and ways. Most have to do with the clock, our illusion of passing time. Many are mechanical. And some are a bizarre mixture of mechanical and human; that is, fetishes.

Slowly the reader begins to realize that V. herself is nothing more than a "fetish-construction"—an "inanimate object of desire" "beyond" the merely human. She is what Man will always search for, without ever knowing why. Stencil himself realizes this: "Stencil sketched the entire history of V. that night and strengthened a long suspicion. That it did add up only to the recurrence of an initial and a few dead objects" (p. 419). V. is nothing more than an assemblage of a few dead objects—and it is when Profane and Stencil finally leave for Malta that those inanimate objects slowly come alive, die, and perhaps live again—as V.

Malta: an island at the center of the Mediterranean, a true "cradle of civilization" to the extent that it has served over the centuries as a pawn in the battles of every major Western civilization. Its exposure to the Carthaginians, the Romans, the actors in the Second World War, and others is without parallel in any mainland empire or state.

But throughout the interminable battles over this exemplary inanimate object of desire, Malta has remained constant, unchanging; a Mother, unyielding, always ready to accept whatever new children come her way: "Malta is a noun feminine and proper [. . .] She lies on her back in the sea, sullen; an immemorial woman. Spread to the explosive orgasms of Mussolini's bombs. But her soul hasn't been touched; cannot be [. . .] as the Ark was to Noah so is the inviolable womb of our Maltese rock to her children" (p. 298). Malta is a matriarchal island (p. 301), the home of "Mara" (Maltese for woman), who is the spirit of womankind. Mara lives on the peninsula whose tip is Valetta—a peninsula shaped like the Mons Veneris (p. 438). And it is there, in Valetta, that the most probable of V.'s several hypothetical existences will materialize through Fausto's story of the Bad Priest.

The Bad Priest appears in the narrative of *V.* as an assemblage of the dead objects that have helped to hold together the narrative thus far; "he" is nothing more than the fragments of the text's "others" and their parts. Once literarily assembled, "he" must be literally disassembled—by the children of Malta:

> The Bad Priest. Wedged under a fallen beam. Face—what could be seen— impassive.
> "Is he dead," one asked. Others were picking already at the black rags.
> "Speak to us, Father," they called, mocking. "What is your sermon for today?"
> "Funny hat," giggled a little girl. She reached out and tugged off the hat. A long coil of white hair came loose and fell into the plaster-dust [. . .]
> "It's a lady," said the girl. (p. 320)

It's a lady and she comes apart. Hat, hair, combs, shoes—an artificial foot. Robes, cufflinks, trousers. "At her navel was a star sapphire. The boy with the knife picked at the stone" (p. 321).

It's a lady—and she comes apart just as does any machine of desire: false teeth, joints, a glass eye in the shape of a clock:

> I wondered if the disassembly of the Bad Priest might not go on, and on, into the evening. Surely her arms and breasts could be detached; the skin of her legs be peeled away to reveal some intricate understructure of silver openwork. Perhaps the trunk itself contained other wonders: intestines of parti-coloured silk, gay balloon-lungs, a rococo heart [. .] I lay prone under a hostile sky looking down for moments more at what the children had left; suffering Christ foreshortened on the bare skull, one eye and one socket, staring up at me: a dark hole for the mouth, stumps at the bottoms of the legs. And the blood which had formed a black sash across the waist, flowing down both sides from the navel. (p. 322)

Of course, the reader is never sure at any point that the Bad Priest is actually the V. that Stencil, and with him the reader, have been pursuing. For example, in the very last chapter of the text, the reader may recognize the horrid face and body of the woman who waves good-bye to Stencil's father—just before he disappears into the sea off the coast of Malta in 1919. But the coincidence of features between that woman and the Bad Priest may do nothing more than set the reader off on his or her own hopeless interpretive chase through the novel *V.* for clues to this analogy.

For V., as object, is never to be found—not by historical man, twentieth-century man, or the reader. Stencil disappears into the next to last chapter of *V.*; Profane into the Maltese night; the reader into the circular interpretive machine of his or her own invention.

V., this mother-fetish, is not meant to be found, but only deconstructed into her component parts, never adding up to a whole. A true body-without-organs, V. is the purely female desiring machine holding *V.* or any narrative together. V. is the very substance of the Other sex. The search for V., who is a bit like Godot except that she is female, will lead you only to interpretive Nothingness.

In *V.,* the guilty mother's body has been punished for the death of the American son's father; all zones of her inhuman body have been explored; "she" has been exiled to the matriarchal rock. Beyond that, neither the stencilized nor the profane man of the twentieth century has any more stories to tell. The twentieth-century reader is left with but the fragmented body of a *representation of* the unrepresentable, with the disjointed maternal body of the infantile or psychotic's fantasy—the novel entitled *V.*

> The words of his mother had come to him on the tongue of this woman.
>
> John Hawkes, *The Passion Artist*

The fictions of another American writer, John Hawkes, participate in the thematization of gynesis in a somewhat different way than does *V.* In these texts, the sons in fact "merge" with the mother—but only in narrative. They find their mothers, but only to leave or lose them according to the plot, a plot that remains paradigmatically androcentric. Two of Hawkes's novels in particular, *The Lime Twig* and *The Passion Artist,* clearly represent how the maternal body is both the beginning and the end of the son's *narrative,* both the source and receptacle of his *desire*—without problematizing either one.[22]

It is in the first twenty-eight pages of *The Lime Twig,* before Chapter 1, that the mother of William Hencher dies. These pages are also the pre-textual space out of which will be generated the third person narrative of the bulk of the fiction.

There, William Hencher is reminiscing about his mother. (His father is never mentioned; presumably he is dead.) Through an alternation of the pronouns "I" (Hencher) and "you" (the reader), the dream-like landscape of his existence as son is uncovered. It is wartime. A shell hits near the lodging where he and his mother live. His mother falls victim to the ensuing fire: "On hands and knees she was trying to crawl back to me, hot sparks from the fire kept settling on her arms and on the thin silk of her gown. One strap was burned through suddenly, fell away, and then a handful of tissue in the bosom caught and, secured by the edging of charred lace, puffed at its luminous peak as if a small forced fire, stoked inside her flesh, had burst a hole through the tender dry surface of my mother's breast" (p. 15).

Hencher's mother dies; and ten years later, he comes back to the same boarding house where a naïve and innocent couple, Michael Banks and his wife, Margaret, now live. He has come back to draw them from the house where his mother died into the nightmare of the fantasy structuring the narrative. As he draws the red circles around his white eyes, he swears into the mirror, "I can get along without you, Mother" (p. 28). *That* is where the American son's story seems to begin.

The third person narrative of *The Lime Twig* follows as a rewriting of the traditional crime thriller. The narrative is concerned with Michael and Margaret Banks's deepening involvement in the fantasy bequeathed to them by a soon dead Hencher: an involvement with and victimization by a band of criminals actualizing Hencher's ambitious dream of winning a horse race. Michael's involvement in the fantasy is primarily a sexual one—from his adoration and fear of the great white racehorse to his orgies with "Larry's women." By the time he realizes that he has become a victim of his own and Hencher's merged fantasies, Margaret has been captured and beaten, Michael is afraid for his life, and Larry, the prototypical fascist male in this novel of violence, is in control of everyone's fantasy.

22. John Hawkes, *The Lime Twig* (New York: New Directions, 1961) and *The Passion Artist* (New York: Harper Colophon, 1978). All page references in text refer to these editions.

Most interesting for our purposes here, however, is the fact that in this book "about" the death of innocence in the face of the inevitable violence of sexual fantasy out of control, the bare outline of the burning maternal breast is the most frequent haunting image in the nightmare enveloping Michael, Margaret, and the reader. It is the bare outline of color—the red nipple and white breast caught in red and white flames—that punctuates the text to its heroic son's end. Red and white are, in fact, the only two colors marking the narrative path of Michael and Margaret's phantasmatic destiny. From white horses, fog, bellies, and pearls to red blood, burning cities, lips and wine, the white and red of the maternal breast add the only color to this otherwise gray narrative of Michael and Margaret Banks's fall into evil.

The end of the narrative is the event of the Golden Bowl—the horse race where Michael's horse is to run illegally. Not surprisingly, the race track itself is oval and white with, in its center, a garden of roses. Michael Banks, in a last possible act of heroism, runs unexpectedly straight toward that oval and the smoke of the horses' hooves, straight into the path of the horse that was to fulfill his dream. The narrative ends with the image of Banks, horses, and riders crashing together in an exploding cloud of smoke. Michael Banks-the-husband inherited and ended Hencher-the-son's dream—and his nightmare. The image of the white oval track and its bed of roses, now covered in smoke, repeats the image with which this narrative of filial self-destruction began. It echoes the destiny of Hippolytus, killed because of his step-mother's treachery.

In *The Passion Artist,* the act of willed self-degradation and destruction on the part of the son is even more directly linked to the mother's body—in this case to a mother who literally murdered his father, and is in prison for that act.

The Passion Artist is a complex, allegorical exploration of the denied or embraced erotic union between son and mother and its potential consequences for the son-as-artist. At first, that union is denied. Konrad Vost lives an austere life in the town where his mother is imprisoned. The only women in his life are fictions—his dead wife, his daughter whom he does not know (he finds she's a prostitute), and his mother whom he never visits and from whom he was "denied any maternal love."

Suddenly, the women's prison is in revolt. The women want liberation—and the men of the town are ready to fight. Konrad Vost is among those men—and it is upon his entrance into the prison for women that he begins his descent into "him-self." Injured in the first battle at the interior of *La Violaine,* Konrad Vost descends into his "interior being," into his "psychic pit"—a "bed of stars," "a bed of coals." Through a series of dream sequences, he re-experiences the dark landscapes of his life-long sexual mutilation as a man: the world submits to metamorphosis, *simulacra* overwhelm representations. Through the exploration of interior and exterior "psychological functions," past and present, dream and reality intertwine within the psychic landscapes of the now castrated American son. As Konrad Vost first explores the psychological prison of his own sexuality, the boundaries between male and female remain strikingly clear: "whatever his own previous misconceptions, nonetheless age never obliterates entirely the streaks and smears of masculine or feminine definition. Never" (p. 91). But as his "psychological landscapes" become more complex, something new emerges:

> Konrad Vost found himself exactly where he had always wished to be without knowing it: in the world of women and in the world of the prison, where the more dangerous rudiments of common knowledge are unavoidable and where he would receive the punishment he deserved and desired, in confinement, for his acts of innocence as well as for his ultimate inability to be always right, always correct [. . .] But did his theories of the psychological function apply to women? Could such a person as himself ever be brought to even rudimentary knowledge of submission, domination, the question of woman? (pp. 120–21)

Captive in a small room at the women's prison with nothing but women's writings on the walls, Konrad Vost is visited by two women. One is his mother, the other the woman who had "castrated" him when he entered *La Violaine*. As his mother begins telling him her story, the second woman makes love to him; as his mother tells of his almost aborted birth, of the cruel men—the husbands and doctors—in her life, the other woman crushes him beneath the weight of her body: "It was then that he heard the silence in the prison room, realized that the vision of the village birth was gone, and realized that throughout his mother's narrative the large warm mouth of the tall woman had in fact been pressed to his own. All the while she had in fact been kissing him. The words of his mother had come to him on the tongue of this woman" (p. 133).

Alternating with phantasmatic images of his first sexual encounters, Konrad Vost the son's narrative is forced to take into account "the fierce spirit invested in all forms of female life" (p. 144). And finally, in a burst of self-revelation, he comprehends the analogy between "the woman question" and himself: "In no other way [. . .] can a woman so reveal her eroticism as by an act of the will" (p. 180). And touched by that will, loving that unknown woman, his mother's voice rocking his now helpless, infantile body, Konrad Vost is finally free to become a woman, to become an artist: "Konrad Vost knew at last the transports of that singular experience which makes every man an artist: the experience, that is, of the willed erotic union" (p. 181).

Konrad Vost is eventually allowed to leave *La Violaine*. As he returns to the light of day, however, he is killed by one of the men who chose not to enter the world of women. The willed erotic union with woman leads the artist to his only possible destiny: a deep "knowledge of himself," his hatred and rejection by other men, and the discovery of "what it was to be nothing":

> "Poor Gagnon . . . They may destroy me, they may devour me. But I am who I am."
>
> With this remark Konrad Vost achieved his final irony, for as he spoke he was already smiling and rolling over to discover for himself what it was to be nothing. (p. 184)

In these two novels, the American son returns to the mother's-body-in-narrative in order to find himself through an act of heroism and will—one directly leading to his death. In Pynchon's *V.,* the son makes that return almost in spite of "himself," but still in narrative, in an effort to understand the fictions that make up his life. In all cases, the maternal figure is guilty of something—a crime of some sort, even her own death—as imagined by the artist-son. Further, it is only the maternal figure who knows the story—the true story to be told—that might allow for the son's redemption.

The American son as artist *portrays* the "woman," and hence the mother, as something that must be known. He expresses rather than constitutes woman as modernity's problem without making her his own.

The American son-artist's seeming reluctance to let loose of the third person function within representation is not a result simply of what Blanchot called the "narratorial voice"—the voice-over of the text.[23] As Harold Bloom has suggested, exemplary American texts will most likely always prove resistant to "deconstruction" or "analytic association," because writing "in the American grain" affirms "the self over language."[24]

23. See the discussion of Blanchot's "narratorial" versus "narrative" voices in Chapter 9, above.
24. Harold Bloom, quoted in the *New York Times,* Book Review Section, January 31, 1982, p. 8.

In the American texts we have looked at here—subject in their exemplarity to exceptions as much as to rules, of course—the themes of gynesis are all present. The Cartesian subject is denounced as impossible (and occasionally as male); representations do not necessarily conform to "reality"; truth is a fiction. But these three pillars of humanist thought are thematically attacked, not scripturally subverted.

These are novels *about* interpretation; *about* the possibility or impossibility of narrative; *about* dehumanization; *about* sexuality as that which escapes the human; *about* loss of mastery. In them we find the man who descends into a "feminine world"; hallucinations of the female body; bodies-without-organs; the necessity of becoming woman to arrive at any kind of truth about art.

But as I have tried to indicate briefly, this is a thematization of gynesis very different from the conceptual, textual, constitutive process of gynesis inherent to modernity as diagnosed in France. The "woman-in-effect" in American male fiction, throughout its thematization of gynesis, is as far from the most radical tenets of modernity as it is close to the conceptual foundations of, among other things, (Anglo)American feminist thought itself.

It would seem that the late twentieth-century (Anglo)American feminist theorist is awkwardly positioned on a complex and changing epistemological and political field of battle. On the one hand, there is a "French version" of our modernity (and gynesis) whose inflationary discursive dependence on "woman" and the "feminine" challenges what she knows; and, on the other, a very different "American version" of our modernity (and gynesis) whose fundamental conceptual assumptions in fact underwrite and reinforce her own most comfortable ways of knowing.

One might conceivably object that feminism need not concern itself with either version of modernity—certainly not with the process of gynesis. According to this argument, modernity is seen as just one more "male concept," participated in and theorized and fictionalized by men, for men.

To come to such a conclusion, however, would be unfortunate—for reasons that I hope have begun to surface in this study. To ignore or dismiss modernity as conceptualized and fictionalized in both France and the United States over the past several decades would be a fatal mistake on the part of feminist thought: not only because this would increase the dangers of anachronism evoked early in this study, but also because it would ignore the possibilities for developing radically new fields of conceptuality essential to feminist theory and practice today.

Are there not ways in which feminism, as concept and practice, might be productively redefined in light of the new conceptual paths cleared by the texts of modernity? Do those paths not offer new directions with which women can link up with other minorities within and against the dominant Western conceptual systems?[25] Does not the refusal to ask where, why, and how those directions should be explored invite a new era of silence for women?

The potentials for modernity and feminism to unite in their efforts are strong and exciting primarily because, as many feminists have perceived, the theories and practices of modernity, *when taken up by female voices,* become strangely and irresistibly subversive, promising new questions and answers unburdened by the repetition forced on to traditional feminist discourse by the dominant ideology in the West. In particular, they shed new light on the increasingly dark caverns of male paranoia . . .

At the same time, and in the meantime, the questions of how the very form of our (Anglo)American feminist questions are culturally, historically, and conceptually limited, and of how women writers in France are or are not complicitous with "a uniquely male concept," need to be explored together—by women, productively rather than polemically. For instance, in the United States, what has been celebrated as the contemporary woman writer's feminist participation in a "New Realism" does not deviate in any major way from the fundamental conceptual foundations of the American men's novels we have so briefly looked at—no matter how "positive" the "role models" or "destinies" of female characters might become. It is more than likely that contemporary American women writers and feminist theorists are themselves thematizing gynesis, writing about women, most often with feminist inspiration, as those who disturb the male story. In France, on the other hand, many of the most important women writers, like the women theorists, are participating in the conceptual reworking of "male" and "female," in the process of gynesis, as much as the men. They too have embraced "the feminine," and are writing woman in what they see as an effort to radically change, from their very conceptual foundations, the male stories women—and men— have been forced to live. The question is: are they, in fact, writing "woman" differently? and if so, how?

25. I use the word "minorities" here in the Deleuzian sense—i.e., those who are fighting for their very survival under the majority rule of the Western-white-male-heterosexual-adult.

This book has been but an introduction to the potentialities of such questions—to the theoretical and political stakes involved in asking those questions today. Before closing, let us return briefly to the concrete context from which those questions were generated, so that they may be more readily asked again, elsewhere, by others, for others.

Afterwords

To be radical? It's the power to criticize even when it's not the
right moment.

Marcelle Marini

Before beginning this book, I spent several years working on
the texts of women writers and theorists in France—in particular, those of
Hélène Cixous, Luce Irigaray, and Julia Kristeva. Convinced of their importance, numbed by their complexity, and, at the same time, distrustful
of their rapid, uncritical assimilation in the United States as feminist (or
antifeminist) by feminists as well as their depoliticized recuperation by the
critical establishment—I went to France. There I encountered the problems of text and context evoked in the Preliminaries: problems larger than,
while not separate from, polemics, personalities, and group politics—
problems most often having to do with the articulation between theory
and praxis.

In fact, what I perceived was a series of impasses between theory and
praxis: theories of woman or the feminine and their insistence on the
(always) potentially subversive power of the feminine in patriarchal
culture had produced either no possibility for social and political praxis or
had resulted in a praxis that I perceived as being reactionary for women.
At the same time, those who had chosen to reject or ignore the major
theorists and texts of modernity, those who had chosen to remain deaf to
contemporary conceptual reworkings of the "male" and "female," most
often produced no theory at all, and, in any case—in their refusal to listen
to their own discourse—their praxis was often more reactionary than that
of their more feminine-minded sisters.

From within the clouds of rhetoric surrounding the interpretations of what these women were "really" writing, doing, or prescribing, at a distance from the contagious enthusiasm stirred by their discovery in the United States, I made what I saw then (and still do) as a decision of political urgency: to undertake a series of rigorous readings, not of the texts of those women, but of those men who have been important, indeed essential, to the women's texts—especially to the extent that those women have taken up the gynesis we have seen at work and have rendered it intrinsic to their own conceptual systems. As mentioned in the Preliminaries, the work of Cixous, Irigaray, and Kristeva has not been absent here, but has served as palimpsest—as those who know their work well will have already discovered.

As such, the writing of this book has been attended with both disappointment and exhilaration. Disappointment, because as I explored more closely the configurations of woman in the "male-written" and "female-written" texts of modernity, I slowly uncovered the usually troubling genealogies of the women's key arguments and words in "the men," often purely transcribed: genealogies of "the feminine," "the maternal," "difference," "dialectics," "truth," and so on. Exhilaration, because I discovered that the differences between the male-written and female-written texts of modernity were not, after all, in their so-called "content," but in their *enunciation:* in their modes of discourse ("sentimental," ironic, scientific, etc.); in their twisting of female obligatory connotations, of inherited genealogies of the feminine; in their haste or refusal to use the pronouns "I" or "we"; in their degree of willingness to gender those pronouns as female; in their adherence to or dissidence from feminism as a movement; in the tension between their desire to remain radical and their desire to be taken seriously as theorists and writers in what remains a male intellectual community; in the extent of their desire to prescribe what posture women should adopt toward the new configurations of woman in modernity; in the intensity of their desire to privilege *women* as proto-postmodernists.

At one point, I considered including Hélène Cixous in the category of "orthodox women Derrideans" discussed in Chapter 9. But there is nothing orthodox about Cixous's theory, fiction, or political praxis. It is no secret that Cixous's "primary text" is Derrida, nor that her primary theoretical weapon is "deconstruction." Her vocabulary and the philosophical, psychoanalytic, and literary texts from which she has taken that vocabulary are, almost without exception, part of what might be called "the Derridean corpus." She works on Nietzsche, Heidegger, Blanchot, and so on, stopping over many of the problematics now familiar to us: among them, masculine/feminine, *propre/proche,* sameness/difference, the un-decidable, the signature. But Cixous has gone a step farther than Derrida could or would have wanted to go: she has incarnated Derrida's "feminine operation" by and in women. She has named Derrida's "writing-as-femi-nine-locus": "feminine writing." And she has gone on to posit that if feminine writing does not require the signature of *a* woman, women nonetheless, today (after psychoanalysis and Derrida), do have a privileged access to it. The attributes of Derridean écriture have become those of a potentially new kind of women's writing. For Cixous, women today would in fact seem to be, almost intrinsically, proto-postmodernists.

Luce Irigaray's battles with the masculine libidinal economy of our metaphysical inheritance and her prescribed itineraries for the feminine are very different from those of Cixous. While her "primary text" is also Derrida, she has laid emphasis not on feminine writing, or even on wom-en's writing, but wholly on the same male-written texts taken on by Der-rida: those of Plato, Hegel, Nietzsche, Lacan, et al. Unlike Cixous, Irigaray has been less tempted by group politics—hers has remained a solitary and ironic voice of dissent, primarily from the Parisian analytic community and its texts. She limits her deconstructive strategies to dissec-tions of the "male text," interspersed with lyrical invitations to women to join with her in desacralizing male theory and liberating while valorizing the feminine repressed in male texts. Even though it is ultimately unclear in Irigaray's writing what women's relationship to the female spaces of modernity should be, it is clear that she sees those spaces as intrinsically related to women's bodies, and she insists, therefore, that women must allow their bodies to speak through and with those spaces.

Julia Kristeva has no "primary text"—in any case, it is certainly not Derrida. Along with Cixous and Irigaray—if very differently from both—she has concentrated on "the feminine" as that which has held our pa-triarchal history and its conceptual systems together. She has minutely analyzed the ways in which that feminine has been sublimated, fetishized, exalted, or liberated by male writers. She has emphasized how it is inex-orably linked to both the Mother and mothers within the classic Western Oedipal structure. At the same time, Kristeva has refused to definitively untangle the "woman subject" from "the feminine." She breaks with both Cixous and Irigaray when it comes to prescribing what women's rela-tionship to this feminine should be, or, at least, always approaches that topic with extreme caution. She has consistently rejected the notion that women should rejoin with or valorize this feminine whose function in Western patriarchal culture must continue to be analyzed. If Kristeva does have a primary text, it is Freud: for her, the moments when women deny culture and its texts, reject theory as masculine, exalt the female body, and so on are moments when they risk crossing over the cultural borderline into hysteria. While recognizing hysteria as a historical form of contestation, she also relentlessly emphasizes its very real limits: the fantasy of the phallic, all-powerful mother through which women reconnect with the very Law they had set out to fight. To embrace the feminine spaces bequeathed to us, even by the thinkers of modernity, would be to ignore the history of that modernity—its promises and limits.

To continue unraveling the threads binding together modernity, gynesis, and feminism entails submitting these women's texts—as well as those of other women tuned in to modernity—to the same kinds of questions we have asked of the men's texts. One would have to return to their texts in terms of the genealogies of the feminine spaces traced in this book. For example, exactly where, how, and to what end are the words "woman," "feminine," "femininity," "maternal," "women," and "feminism" used by them—both conceptually and in praxis? Which words and conceptual systems do they borrow more or less uncritically from the men, and which would seem to be their own—or at least where are their own accent and emphasis? That is, where exactly are their entries and departures from the male-written texts, in what contexts, in which texts, for what audience? Where are the borderlines between *their* conceptualizations of modernity and woman?

And what of the differences among the women participating in gynesis? For instance, Cixous, Irigaray, and Kristeva have all recognized that modernity entails a re-engendering, a reordering, and finally a certain valorization of woman; they all direct attention to the ways in which the mother and the maternal have been silenced and indeed mutilated in order for Western culture to thrive, and to the need for the maternal to be henceforth signified in new ways. They have all exposed the complex links joining the male and female libidinal economies to the outworn Occidental molds and habits of our minds. And yet the paths they have taken are very different indeed.

Finally, if—as has been more than suggested in this book—gynesis at work in the male text is rooted in male paranoia, what happens when women take over this discourse in the name of woman? Must we then necessarily speak of the symptoms of female paranoia? Or are there other symptomatic links to be found among gynesis, feminism, and contemporary theory and fiction when practiced by women?

I see this book as the necessary first step to reading and rereading the most important women theorists and fiction writers in France today. To miss that first step is to stumble past, without stopping at, what I see as their work's essential promise: a mapping of possible *new* configurations of woman and modernity.

The most important work by feminist theorists convinced of modernity's importance thus remains yet to be undertaken. It is henceforth in the dialogue between these texts by women in France and those by feminists in the United States that the future of gynesis might begin to be decided—for women.

SELECTED BIBLIOGRAPHY

The following listing contains only those works cited or referred to in the text and other works that are of the most immediate relevance to the topic. Both French and English editions are indicated where that is helpful. For texts originally published in German, French or English editions (occasionally both) are cited.

Abish, Walter. "Crossing the Great Void." In *In the Future Perfect*. New York: New Directions, 1977.

Abraham, Nicolas, and Maria Torok. *Cryptonymie: Le verbier de l'homme aux loups*. Paris: Aubier-Flammarion, 1976.

———. *L'écorce et le noyau*. Paris: Flammarion, 1978.

Agacinski, Sylviane. "Le tout premier écart." In *Les fins de l'homme*, ed. Philippe Lacoue-Labarthe and Jean-Luc Nancy. Paris: Galilée, 1981.

Albistur, Maïté, and Daniel Armogathe. *Histoire du féminisme français*. Paris: des Femmes, 1977.

Allen, Suzanne. "Hymne/Hymen." In *Les fins de l'homme*, ed. Philippe Lacoue-Labarthe and Jean-Luc Nancy. Paris: Galilée, 1981.

Althusser, Louis. *For Marx*. Trans. Ben Brewster. New York: Pantheon, 1969. *Pour Marx*. Paris: Maspero, 1965.

———. *Lenin and Philosophy*. New York: Monthly Review, 1971. *Lénine et la philosophie*. Paris: Maspero, 1969.

Arnold, Matthew. *Culture and Anarchy*. Cambridge: Cambridge University Press, 1950.

Assoun, Paul-Laurent. "Freud et la mystique." *Nouvelle revue de la psychanalyse* 22 (Autumn 1980).

Auerbach, Erich. *Mimesis*. Trans. Willard R. Trask. Princeton: Princeton University Press, 1953.

Barth, John. *The Floating Opera*. New York: Bantam, 1956.

———. "The Literature of Replenishment." *Atlantic Monthly*, January 1980.

Barthelme, Donald. *The Dead Father*. New York: Pocket Books, 1975.

Barthes, Roland. "L'ancienne rhétorique." *Communications* 16 (1970).

———. *La chambre claire*. Paris: Editions du Seuil, 1980.

———. *Critique et vérité*. Paris: Editions du Seuil, 1966.

———. "The Rhetoric of the Image." In *Image-Music-Text*. Trans. Richard Howard. London: Hill & Wang, 1977.

———. *Roland Barthes*. Paris: Editions du Seuil, 1975.

———. *Sollers écrivain*. Paris: Editions du Seuil, 1979.

———. *S/Z*. Trans. Richard Miller. New York: Hill & Wang, 1974. *S/Z*. Paris: Editions du Seuil, 1970.

Bataille, Georges. *L'expérience intérieure*. Paris: Gallimard, 1970–73.

Baudrillard, Jean. *De la séduction*. Paris: Galilée, 1979.

Beckett, Samuel. *Molloy, Malone Dies, The Unnamable*. London: John Calder, 1959.

Bénézet, Mathieu. *La fin de l'homme*. Paris: Flammarion, 1979.

———. *Le roman de la langue*. Paris: 10/18, 1977.

Benjamin, Jessica. "Authority and the Family Revisited." *New German Critique* 13 (1977).

Benjamin, Walter. *Charles Baudelaire: A Lyric Poet in the Era of High Capitalism*. London: NLB, 1973.

———. "On Language as Such and on the Language of Man." In *One Way Street*, trans. Edmund Jephcott and Kingsley Shorter. London: NLB, 1979. "Sur le langage." In *Mythe et violence*. Paris: Denoël, 1971.

———. "La photographie." In *Poésie et révolution*. Paris: Denoël, 1971.

———. "Theses on the Philosophy of History." in *Illuminations,* ed. Hannah Arendt. New York: Schocken, 1969. "Thèses d'histoire de la philosophie." In *Poésie et révolution*. Paris: Denoël, 1971.

Bergstrom, Janet. "Alternation, Segmentation, Hypnosis: Interview with Raymond Bellour." *Camera Obscura: A Journal of Feminism and Film Theory* 3–4 (Summer 1979).

Blanchot, Maurice. *Death Sentence*. Trans. Lydia Davis. Barrytown, N.Y.: Station Hill Press, 1978. *L'arrêt de mort*. Paris: Gallimard, 1948.

———. *L'entretien infini*. Paris: Gallimard, 1969.

———. *La folie du jour*. Paris: Fata Morgana, 1973.

———. *The Space of Literature: A Translation of "L'Espace Littéraire."* Trans. Ann Smock. Lincoln: University of Nebraska Press, 1982. *L'espace littéraire*. Paris: Gallimard, 1955.

——— *Thomas l'obscur*. Paris: NRF, 1950.

Bloom, Harold. "The Breaking of Form." In *Deconstruction and Criticism*. New York: Seabury, 1979.

Bovenschen, Silvia. "Is There a Feminine Aesthetic?" *New German Critique,* no. 10 (Winter 1977).

Braidotti, Rosi. "Féminisme et philosophie." Dissertation, University of Paris I, 1981.

Brooks, Peter. "Freud's Masterplot." *Yale French Studies* 55/56 (1977).

Burke, Carolyn. "Rethinking the Maternal." In *The Future of Difference,* ed. Hester Eisenstein and Alice Jardine. Boston: G. K. Hall, 1980.

Burroughs, William. *The Naked Lunch*. New York: Grove Press Inc., 1959.

Certeau, Michel de. "L'énonciation mystique." *Recherches de science religieuse* 64 (1976).

——. "Folie du nom et mystique du sujet: Surin." In *La folle vérité*, ed. Julia Kristeva. Paris: Editions du Seuil, 1979.

——. *La possession de Loudun*. Paris: Julliard-Gallimard, Collection Archives, 1970.

Chalier, Catherine. *Figures du féminin: Lecture d'Emmanuel Levinas*. Paris: La Nuit Surveillée, 1982.

Chasseguet-Smirgel, Janine. *Female Sexuality: New Psychoanalytic Views*. Ann Arbor: University of Michigan Press, 1970. *La sexualité féminine*. Paris: Payot, 1964.

Cixous, Hélène. "L'approche de Clarice Lispector." *Poétique* 40 (November 1979).

——"The Laugh of the Medusa." Trans. Keith Cohen and Paula Cohen. *Signs* 1:4 (1976).

——. "Le sexe ou la tête." *Cahiers du GRIF* 13 (October 1976).

Cixous, Hélène, and Catherine Clément. *La jeune née*. Paris: 10/18, 1975.

Cixous, Hélène, and Michel Foucault. "A propos de Marguerite Duras." *Cahiers Renaud Barrault*, no. 89.

Clément, Catherine. "Post-face 1980: De *l'Anti-Oedipe aux Mille plateaux*." *L'arc* 49 (1980).

——. *Vies et légendes de Jacques Lacan*. Paris: Bernard Grasset, 1981.

Cohen, Alain. "Proust and the President Schreber." "Graphesis," *Yale French Studies* 52 (1975).

Collin, Françoise. *Maurice Blanchot et la question de l'écriture*. Paris: Gallimard, 1971.

Cornillon, Susan Kopelman, ed. *Images of Women in Fiction*. Bowling Green: Bowling Green State University Press, 1972.

Culler, Jonathan. "The Turns of Metaphor." In *The Pursuit of Signs*. Ithaca: Cornell University Press, 1981.

Daive, Jean. *Le jeu des séries scéniques*. Paris: Flammarion, 1976.

Daly, Mary. *Beyond God the Father: Toward a Philosophy of Women's Liberation*. Boston: Beacon, 1973.

Danahy, Michael. "Le roman est-il chose femelle?" *Poétique* 25 (1976).

Dardigna, Anne-Marie. *Les châteaux d'éros*. Paris: Maspero, 1981.

Deconstruction and Criticism. New York: Seabury, 1979.

"Deleuze." *L'arc* 49 (1972; reissued 1980).

Deleuze, Gilles. *Différence et répétition*. Paris: PUF, 1969.

——. *Empirisme et subjectivité*. Paris: PUF, 1953.

——. "I Having Nothing to Admit." *Semiotext(e)* 2:3 (1977).

——. *Logique du sens*. Paris: Editions de Minuit, 1969.

——. *Nietzsche et la philosophie*. Paris: PUF, 1962.

——. *Présentation de Sacher Masoch*. Paris: Editions de Minuit, 1967.

——. *Proust and Signs*. Trans. Richard Howard. New York: G. Braziller, 1972. *Marcel Proust et les signes*. Paris: PUF, 1970.

Deleuze, Gilles, and Félix Guattari. *Anti-Oedipus: Capitalism and Schizophrenia*. Trans. Robert Hurley, Mark Seem, and Helen R. Lane. New York: Viking, 1977. *L'anti-Oedipe*. Paris: Editions de Minuit, 1972.

_____. *Mille plateaux*. Paris: Editions de Minuit, 1980.

Deleuze, Gilles, and Claire Parnet. *Dialogues*. Paris: Flammarion, 1977.

de Man, Paul. *Blindness and Insight*. New York: Oxford University Press, 1971.

"Derrida." *L'arc* 54 (1966).

"Derrida." *Derrida, + R (pardessus le marché)*. Paris: Galilée, 1975.

"Derrida." *Les fins de l'homme: A partir du travail de Jacques Derrida*, ed. Philippe Lacoue-Labarthe and Jean-Luc Nancy. Paris: Galilée, 1981.

Derrida, Jacques. "L'âge de Hegel"; "La philosophie et ses classes"; "Réponses à la Nouvelle Critique." in *Qui a peur de la philosophie?* GREPH (Groupe de Recherche sur l'Enseignement Philosophique). Paris: Flammarion, 1977.

_____. *La carte postale*. Paris: Flammarion, 1980.

_____. *Dissemination*. Trans. Barbara Johnson. Chicago: University of Chicago Press, 1981. *La Dissémination*. Paris: Editions du Seuil, 1972.

_____. "Fors." Trans. Barbara Johnson. *The Georgia Review* 31:1 (Spring 1977). Preface to Nicholas Abraham and Maria Torok, *Cryptonymie: Le verbier de l'homme aux loups*. Paris: Aubier-Flammarion, 1976.

_____. *Glas*. Paris: Galilée, 1974.

_____. "Ja ou le faux-bond." *Digraphe* 11 (April 1977).

_____. "Limited Inc." *Glyph* II (Fall 1977). Also published separately. Baltimore: Johns Hopkins University Press, 1977.

_____. "Living On/Borderlines." In *Deconstruction and Criticism*. New York: Seabury, 1979.

_____. *Margins of Philosophy*. Trans. Alan Bass. Brighton, Sussex: Harvester, 1982. *Marges de la philosophie*. Paris: Editions de Minuit, 1972.

_____. *Of Grammatology*. Trans. Gayatri Spivak. Baltimore: Johns Hopkins University Press, 1976. *De la grammatologie*. Paris: Editions de Minuit, 1967.

_____. "Où commence et comment finit un corps enseignant." In *Politiques de la philosophie*. Paris: Grasset, 1976.

_____. "Le parergon." *Digraphe* 2 (1974).

_____. "Pas." *Gramma*, nos. 3–4 (1976).

_____. *Positions*. Trans. Alan Bass. Chicago: University of Chicago Press, 1981. *Positions*. Paris: Editions de Minuit, 1972.

_____. "The Purveyor of Truth." *Yale French Studies* 52 (1975). "Le facteur de la vérité." In *La carte postale*. Paris: Flammarion, 1980.

_____. "Le sans de la coupure pure." ("Parergon II.") *Digraphe* 3 (1974).

_____. "Scribble." Preface to Warburton, *Essai sur les hiéroglyphes*. Paris: Aubier-Flammarion, 1978.

_____. "Signature, Event, Context." In *Margins of Philosophy*. Brighton, Sussex: Harvester, 1982. "Signature, évenement, contexte." In *Marges*. Paris: Editions de Minuit, 1972. Trans. in *Glyph* I (1977).

_____. *Speech and Phenomena, and Other Essays on Husserl's Theory of Signs*. Trans. David B. Allison. Evanston, Ill.: Northwestern University Press, 1973. *La voix et le phénomène*. Paris: PUF, 1967.

_____. *Spurs/Eperons*. Trans. Barbara Harlow. Chicago: University of Chicago Press, 1979. *Eperons: Les styles de Nietzsche*. Venice: Corbo e Fiore Editori, 1976. *Eperons*. Paris: Flammarion, 1978.

———. *La vérité en peinture*. Paris: Flammarion, 1978.

———. *Writing and Difference*. Trans. Alan Bass. Chicago: University of Chicago Press, 1978. *L'écriture et la différence*. Paris: Editions du Seuil, 1967.

Derrida, Jacques, and Christie V. McDonald. "Choreographies." *Diacritics* 12 (Summer 1982).

Descombes, Vincent. *Modern French Philosophy*. Cambridge: Cambridge University Press, 1980. *Le même et l'autre: Quarante-cinq ans de philosophie française*. Paris: Editions de Minuit, 1979.

Donovan, Josephine. "Feminist Style Criticism." In *Images of Women in Fiction: Feminist Perspectives,* ed. Susan Koppelman Cornillon. Bowling Green: Bowling Green State University, 1972.

Donzelot, Jacques. *The Policing of Families*. Trans. Robert Hurley. New York: Pantheon, 1979. *La police des familles*. Paris: Editions de Minuit, 1977.

Douglas, Ann. *The Feminization of American Culture*. New York: Avon, 1977.

Duras, Marguerite. *The Ravishing of Lol Stein*. Trans. Richard Seaver. Ann Arbor, Mich.: reprinted for Grove Press by University Microfilms International, 1979, © 1964. *Le ravissement de Lol V. Stein*. Paris: Gallimard, 1964.

Duras, Marguerite, and Xavière Gautier. *Les parleuses*. Paris: Editions de Minuit, 1974.

Eco, Umberto. "L'analyse des images." *Communications* 15 (1970).

———. *L'oeuvre ouverte*. Trans. Roux. Paris: Editions du Seuil, 1965.

Eisenstein, Hester, and Alice Jardine, eds. *The Future of Difference*. Boston: G. K. Hall, 1980. Forthcoming in paperback from Rutgers University Press in 1985.

Felman, Shoshana. *La folie et la chose littéraire*. Paris: Editions du Seuil, 1978.

———. "Women and Madness: The Critical Phallacy." *Diacritics* 5:4 (Winter 1975).

Fetterley, Judith. *The Resisting Reader*. Bloomington: Indiana University Press, 1978.

Firestone, Shulamith. *The Dialectic of Sex*. New York: Bantam, 1970.

Foster, Hal, ed. *The Anti-Aesthetic: Essays on Postmodern Culture*. Washington: Bay, 1983.

Foucault, Michel. *The Archeology of Knowledge*. Trans. S. Smith. New York: Harper & Row, 1976. *L'archéologie du savoir*. Paris: Gallimard, 1969.

———. "Les intellectuels et le pouvoir: Entretien M. Foucault–G. Deleuze." *L'arc* 49 (1972/80).

———. *Madness and Civilization*. Trans. Richard Howard. New York: Mentor Books, 1967. *Folie et déraison, histoire de la folie à l'âge classique*. Paris: Plon, 1961.

———. "Nietzsche, Freud, Marx." In *Cahiers de Royaumont*. Paris: Editions de Minuit, 1967.

———. *The Order of Things*. New York: Random House, 1970. *Les mots et les choses*. Paris: Gallimard, 1966.

———. "Theatrum Philosophicum." *Critique* 282 (1970).

———. "What Is an Author?" Trans. Josué Harari. In *Textual Strategies*. London: Methuen, 1980.

Freud, Sigmund. *The Complete Psychological Works of Sigmund Freud*. Trans. James Strachey. 24 volumes. London: Hogarth, 1955. (Hereafter referred to as the Standard Edition.)

_____. "Leonardo Da Vinci." The Standard Edition, vol. 11.

_____. *Moses and Monotheism*. Trans. James Strachey. London: Hogarth, 1974.

_____. "On Narcissism." The Standard Edition, vol. 4.

_____. "On Psychotherapy." The Standard Edition, vol. 7.

_____. "Psychoanalytic Notes on an Autobiographical Account of a Case of Paranoia." The Standard Edition, vol. 12.

_____. "Some Psychical Consequences of the Anatomical Distinction between the Sexes." The Standard Edition, vol. 19.

_____. "Taboo of Virginity." The Standard Edition, vol. 11.

_____. "The Theme of the Three Caskets." In *On Creativity and the Unconscious*. New York: Harper & Row, 1958.

_____. *Totem and Taboo*. The Standard Edition, vol. 13.

_____. "Die Verneinung (Negation)." The Standard Edition, vol. 19.

Gallop, Jane. "The Ghost of Lacan." *Diacritics* 5:4 (Winter 1975). Reprinted in *The Daughter's Seduction*. Ithaca: Cornell University Press, 1982.

_____. "*Quand nos lèvres s'écrivent:* Irigaray's Body Politic." *Romanic Review* 74:1 (January 1983).

_____. "Snatches of Conversation." In *Women and Language in Literature and Society,* ed. Sally McConnell-Ginet, Ruth Borker, and Nelly Furman. New York: Praeger, 1980.

Gautier, Xavière. *Surréalisme et sexualité*. Paris: Gallimard, 1971.

Genette, Gérard. "Frontiers of Narrative." In *Figures of Literary Discourse,* trans. Alan Sheridan. New York: Columbia University Press, 1982. *Figures II*. Paris: Editions du Seuil, 1969.

Gibbs, Anna, et al. "Round and Round the Looking Glass: Responses to [. . .] *New French Feminisms.*" *Hecate* 6:2 (1980).

Gilbert, Sandra. "What Do Feminist Critics Want? or, A Postcard from the Volcano." *ADE Bulletin,* no. 66 (Winter 1980).

Gilbert, Sandra M., and Susan Gubar. *The Madwoman in the Attic*. New Haven: Yale University Press, 1979.

Gilligan, Carol. *In a Different Voice*. Cambridge, Mass: Harvard University Press, 1982.

Girard, René. *Violence and the Sacred*. Trans. Patrick Gregory. Baltimore: Johns Hopkins University Press, 1977. *La violence et le sacré*. Paris: Grasset, 1972.

Goux, Jean-Joseph. *Economie et symbolique*. Paris: Editions du Seuil, 1973.

_____. *Les iconoclastes*. Paris: Editions du Seuil, 1978.

Granoff, Wladimir. *La pensée et le féminin*. Paris: Editions de Minuit, 1976.

Granoff, Wladimir, and François Perrier. *Le désir et le féminin*. Paris: Aubier-Montagne, 1979.

Groddeck, Georg. *Le livre du ça*. Trans. L. Jumel. Paris: Gallimard, 1963.

Haase-Dubosc, Danielle, and Nancy Huston. "L'un s'autorise et l'autre pas." Unpublished paper.

Handelman, Susan. *The Slayers of Moses*. Albany: State University of New York Press, 1982.

Harari, Josué. "Critical Factions/Critical Fictions." In *Textual Strategies,* ed. Josué Harari. Ithaca: Cornell University Press, 1979.

Hartman, Geoffrey. *Saving the Text*. Baltimore: Johns Hopkins University Press, 1981.

——. "A Short History of Practical Criticism." in *New Literary History* 10 (1978–79).

Hawkes, John. *The Lime Twig*. New York: New Directions, 1961.

——. *The Passion Artist*. New York: Harper Colophon, 1978.

Heath, Stephen. "Difference." *Screen* 19:3 (Fall 1978).

——. *The Nouveau Roman*. London: Elek, 1972.

——. *The Sexual Fix*. London: Macmillan, 1982.

Hegel, G. W. F. *The Aesthetics*. Trans. T. M. Knox. Oxford: Oxford University Press, 1975.

——. *Phenomenology of Spirit*. Trans. A. V. Miller. Oxford: Clarendon, 1977.

Heidegger, Martin. "Alētheia." In *Early Greek Thinking,* trans. David Farrell Krell and Frank A. Capuzzi. New York: Harper & Row, 1975.

——. *Being and Time*. Trans. John Macquarrie and Edward Robinson. New York: Harper & Row, 1962.

——. "Ce qu'est et comment se détermine la *physis*." In *Questions II*. Paris: Gallimard, 1968.

——. "La doctrine de Platon sur la vérité." In *Questions II*. Paris: Gallimard, 1968.

——. *Hegel's Concept of Experience*. New York: Harper & Row, 1970.

——. "Logos." In *Early Greek Thinking,* trans. David Farrell Krell and Frank A. Capuzzi. New York: Harper & Row, 1975.

——. "On the Essence of Truth." Trans. R. F. C. Hull and A. Crick in *Existence and Being,* ed. Werner Broch. Chicago: Henry Regnery, 1950.

——. *"The Question concerning Technology" and Other Essays*. Trans. William Lovitt. New York: Garland, 1977.

Herrmann, Claudine. *Les voleuses de langue*. Paris: des Femmes, 1976.

Hicks, Eric. *Le débat sur Le roman de la rose*. Paris: Champion, 1977.

L'histoire sans qualités. Paris: Galilée, 1979.

Hyppolite, Jean. "Commentaire parlé sur la 'Verneinung' de Freud." In Jacques Lacan, *Ecrits*. Paris: Editions du Seuil, 1966.

Irigaray, Luce. *Amante marine*. Paris: Editions de Minuit, 1980.

——. *Ce sexe qui n'en est pas un*. Paris: Editions de Minuit, 1977. Translation: *This Sex Which Is Not One*. Ithaca: Cornell University Press, 1985.

——. *Speculum de l'autre femme*. Paris: Editions de Minuit, 1974. Translation: *Speculum of the Other Woman*. Ithaca: Cornell University Press, 1985.

Jabès, Edmond. *The Book of Questions: Yaël, Elya, Aely*. Trans. Rosemarie Waldrop. Middletown, Conn.: Wesleyan University Press, 1983. *Le livre des questions*. Paris: Gallimard, 1963. *Aely*. Paris: Gallimard, 1972. *Elya*. Paris: Gallimard, 1969. *Yaël*. Paris: Gallimard, 1967.

——. *The Book of Yukel, Return to the Book*. Trans. Rosemarie Waldrop. Middletown, Conn.: Wesleyan University Press, 1977. *Le livre de Yukel*. Paris: Gallimard, 1964. *Le retour au livre*. Paris: Gallimard, 1965.

——. *El, ou le dernier livre*. Paris: Gallimard, 1973.

Jacobus, Mary, ed. *Women Writing and Writing about Women*. London: Croom Helm, 1979.

Jakobson, Roman. "Two Types of Language and Two Types of Aphasic Disturbances." In *Fundamentals of Language,* ed. Roman Jakobson and Morris Halle. The Hague: Mouton, 1956.

Jameson, Fredric. "Imaginary and Symbolic in Lacan: Marxism, Psychoanalytic Criticism and the Problem of the Subject." *Yale French Studies* 55/56 (1977).

———. *The Prison-House of Language.* Princeton: Princeton University Press, 1972.

Janet, Pierre. *L'évolution de la mémoire et la notion du temps.* Paris: F. Alcan, 1928.

Johnson, Barbara. "The Frame of Reference: Poe, Lacan, Derrida." *Yale French Studies* 55/56 (1977). Reprinted in *The Critical Difference.* Baltimore: Johns Hopkins University Press, 1980.

Kaufmann McCall, Dorothy. "Simone de Beauvoir, *The Second Sex,* and Jean-Paul Sartre." *Signs* 5:2 (Winter 1979).

Kavanagh, James H. "Marxism's Althusser: Toward a Politics of Literary Theory." *Diacritics* 12 (Spring 1982).

Keller, Evelyn Fox. "Feminism and Science." *Signs* 7 (Spring 1982).

Kelly, Joan. "Early Feminist Theory and the Querelle des Femmes, 1400–1789." *Signs* 8:1 (Autumn 1982).

Kelly-Gadol, Joan. "Did Women Have a Renaissance?" In *Becoming Visible: Women in European History,* ed. Renate Bridenthal and Claudia Koonz. Boston: Houghton Mifflin, 1977.

Kermode, Frank. *The Sense of an Ending: Studies in the Theory of Fiction.* New York: Oxford University Press, 1967.

Key, Mary Ritchie. *Male/Female Language.* New Jersey: Scarecrow, 1975.

Klein, Melanie. *The Writings of Melanie Klein.* London: Hogarth, 1975–80.

Klinkowitz, Jerome. *Literary Disruptions: The Making of a Post-Contemporary American Fiction.* Champaign, Ill.: University of Illinois Press, 1982.

Klossowski, Pièrre. *Les lois de l'hospitalité.* Paris: Gallimard, 1965.

Kofman, Sarah. *Aberrations: Le devenir femme d'Auguste Comte.* Paris: Flammarion, 1978.

———. "Ça cloche." In *Les fins de l'homme,* ed. Philippe Lacoue-Labarthe and Jean-Luc Nancy. Paris: Galilée, 1981.

———. *Caméra obscura, de l'idéologie.* Paris: Galilée, 1973.

———. *L'énigme de la femme dans les textes de Freud.* Paris: Galilée, 1980.

———. "Judith, ou la mise en scène du tabou de la virginité." *Littérature,* no. 3 (October 1971).

———. *Nietzsche et la scène philosophique.* Paris: 10/18, 1979.

———. *Quatre romans analytiques.* Paris: Galilée, 1974.

Kojève, Alexandre. *Introduction to the Reading of Hegel.* Trans. James H. Nichols, Jr. New York: Basic Books, 1969. *Introduction à la lecture de Hegel.* Paris: Gallimard, 1947.

Kolodny, Annette. "The Feminist as Literary Critic." *Critical Inquiry* 2:4 (Summer 1976).

———. "A Map for Rereading; or, Gender and the Interpretation of Literary Texts." *New Literary History* 9 (1980).

———. "Not-So-Gentle Persuasion: A Theoretical Imperative of Feminist Literary

Criticism." Conference on Feminist Literary Criticism, National Humanities Center, Research Triangle Park, North Carolina, 27 March 1981. P. 7.

——. "Some Notes on Defining a 'Feminist Literary Criticism.'" *Critical Inquiry* 2:1 (Fall 1975).

Kristeva, Julia. "L'antisémitisme aujourd'hui." *Art presse* (January 1979).

——. *Desire in Language: A Semiotic Approach to Literature and Art.* Ed. Leon S. Roudiez. Trans. Thomas Gora, Alice Jardine, and Leon S. Roudiez. New York: Columbia University Press, 1980.

——. *Folle vérité.* Paris: Editions du Seuil, 1979.

——. "Héréthique de l'amour." *Tel quel* 74 (Winter 1977).

——. "Un nouveau type d'intellectuel." *Tel quel* 74 (Winter 1977).

——. *Polylogue.* Paris: Editions du Seuil, 1977.

——. *Powers of Horror: An Essay on Abjection.* Trans. Leon S. Roudiez. New York City: Columbia University Press, 1982. *Pouvoirs de l'horreur.* Paris: Editions du Seuil, 1980.

——. *Recherches pour une sémanalyse.* Paris: Editions du Seuil, 1969.

——. *La révolution du langage poétique.* Paris: Editions du Seuil, 1974. Forthcoming in translation from Columbia University Press.

——. "The Subject in Signifying Practice." *Semiotext(e)* 1:3 (1975).

——. *Le texte du roman.* The Hague: Mouton, 1970.

——. "Women's Time." Trans. Alice Jardine and Harry Blake, in *Signs* 7:1 (Autumn 1981). "Le temps des femmes." *34/44: Cahiers de recherche de sciences des textes et documents,* no. 5 (Winter 1979).

Lacan, Jacques. *Ecrits: A Selection.* Trans. Alan Sheridan. New York: W. W. Norton, 1977. *Ecrits.* Paris: Editions du Seuil, 1966.

——. "Entretien avec des étudiants." Yale University, November 24, 1975, published in *Scilicet,* no. 6/7 (1975).

——. *Ethique de la psychanalyse.* Paris: pirate edition, n.d.

——. "Hommage à Marguerite Duras." In *Marguerite Duras.* Paris: Albatros, 1979.

——. "Litturaterre." *Littérature,* no. 3 (1971).

——. "Radiophonie." In *Scilicet* 2/3. Paris: Seuil, n.d.

——. "Séminaire." *Ornicar?* 12/13 (November 16, 1976).

——. *Le Séminaire Livre XX: Encore.* Paris: Editions du Seuil, 1975.

——. "Sosie." In *Séminaire II.* Paris: Editions du Seuil, 1978.

——. *Télévision.* Paris: Editions du Seuil, 1973.

Lacoue-Labarthe, Philippe. "L'imprésentable." *Poétique* 21 (1975).

Lakoff, Robin. *Language and Women's Place.* New York: Harper Colophon, 1975.

Laporte, Roger. "Nulle part séjournant." In *Les fins de l'homme,* ed. Philippe Lacoue-Labarthe and Jean-Luc Nancy. Paris: Galilée, 1981.

Lasch, Christopher. *The Culture of Narcissism: American Life in an Age of Diminishing Expectations.* New York: Warner, 1980.

Le Doeuff, Michelle. *L'imaginaire philosophique.* Paris: Payot, 1980.

Le Guern, Michel. *Sémantique de la métaphore et de la métonymie.* Paris: Larousse, 1973.

Leiris, Michel. *L'âge d'homme.* Paris: Gallimard (Folio), 1939.

Lemoine-Luccioni, Eugénie. *Partage des femmes*. Paris: Editions du Seuil, 1976.
_____. *Le rêve du cosmonaute*. Paris: Editions du Seuil, 1980.
Lévi-Strauss, Claude. *The Savage Mind*. London: Weidenfeld & Nicolson, 1972. *La pensée sauvage*. Paris: Plon, 1962.
_____. *Structural Anthropology*. Trans. Claire Jacobson and Brooke Grundgest Schoepf. London: Basic Books, 1963. *Anthropologie structurale*. Paris: Plon, 1958.
Lewis, Philip. "The Post-structuralist Condition." *Diacritics* 12 (Spring 1982).
Lispector, Clarice. *La passion de G.H.* Paris: des Femmes, 1978.
Lukàcs, Georg. *The Theory of the Novel*. Cambridge, Mass.: MIT Press, 1971.
Lyotard, Jean-François. *La condition postmoderne*. Paris: Editions de Minuit, 1979.
_____. *Dérive à partir de Marx et Freud*. Paris: Editions de Minuit, 1973.
_____. *Economie libidinale*. Paris: Minuit, 1974.
_____. "Energumen Capitalism." *Semiotext(e)* 2:3 (1977).
_____. "For a Pseudo-Theory." *Yale French Studies* 52 (1975).
_____. "One of the Things at Stake in Women's Struggles." *Substance* 20 (1978).
Macherey, Pierre. *A Theory of Literary Production*. London: Routledge & Kegan Paul, 1978.
Macksey, Richard, and Eugenio Donato, eds. *The Structuralist Controversy*. Baltimore: Johns Hopkins University Press, 1972.
MacLean, Ian. *Woman Triumphant: Feminism in French Literature, 1610–1652*. Oxford: Clarendon Press, 1977.
Makward, Christiane. "La critique féministe." *Revue des sciences humaines* 168 (1977).
_____. "Structures du silence/du délire: Marguerite Duras/Hélène Cixous," *Poétique* 35(1978):317.
_____. "To Be or Not to Be . . . a Feminist Speaker." In *The Future of Difference*, ed. Hester Eisenstein and Alice Jardine. Boston: G. K. Hall, 1980.
Marini, Marcelle. *Territoires du féminin avec Marguerite Duras*. Paris: Editions de Minuit, 1977.
Marks, Elaine. "Women and Literature in France." In *Signs* 3:4 (Summer 1978).
Marx, Karl. *Capital*. Trans. E. Paul and C. Paul. London: J. M. Dent & Sons, 1930.
McConnell-Ginet, Sally, Ruth Borker, and Nelly Furman. *Women and Language in Literature and Society*. New York: Praeger, 1980.
Mehlman, Jeffrey. *Revolution and Repetition*. Berkeley: Quantum, 1977.
Merleau-Ponty, Maurice. *In Praise of Philosophy*. Trans. John Wild and James M. Edie. Evanston, Ill.: Northwestern University Press, 1963. *Eloge de la philosophie*. Paris: Gallimard, 1953.
_____. *Sense and Non-Sense*. Trans. Hubert L. Dreyfus and Patricia Allen Dreyfus. Evanston, Ill.: Northwestern University Press, 1964. *Sens et non-sens*. Paris: Nagel, 1948.
Miller, Henry. *Tropic of Capricorn*. New York: Grove Press, 1961.
Miller, Nancy. *The Heroine's Text*. New York: Columbia University Press, 1980.
Mitscherlich, Alexander. *Society without the Father: A Contribution to Social Psychology*. Trans. Eric Mosbacher. London: Tavistock, 1969.
Moers, Ellen. *Literary Women*. London: Women's Press, 1963.

Montrelay, Michèle. *L'ombre et le nom*. Paris: Editions de Minuit, 1977.

——. "Toward the Other Body." Unpublished paper.

Morris, Meaghan. "French Feminist Criticism." *Hecate* 5:2 (1979).

Mulvey, Laura. "Visual Pleasure and Narrative Cinema." *Screen* 16:3 (Fall 1975).

Nancy, Jean-Luc. "La voix libre de l'homme." In *Les fins de l'homme*, ed. Philippe Lacoue-Labarthe and Jean-Luc Nancy. Paris: Galilée, 1981.

Natanson, Maurice. "Phenomenology, Anonymity, and Alienation." *New Literary History* 10:3 (Spring 1979).

Nietzsche aujourd'hui? Paris: 10/18, 1973.

Nietzsche, Friedrich. *The Anti-Christ*. Trans. H. L. Mencken. New York: Alfred A. Knopf, 1918.

——. *Beyond Good and Evil*. Trans. Helen Zimmern. New York: Macmillan, 1924.

——. *The Dawn of Day*. In *The Complete Works*, ed. Oscar Levy, vol. 9. New York: Gordon, 1974.

——. *The Gay Science*. Trans. Walter Kaufmann. New York: Random House, 1974.

——. *The Portable Nietzsche*. Trans. Walter Kaufmann. New York: Viking, 1968.

——. "Twilight of the Idols." In *The Portable Nietzsche*, trans. Walter Kaufmann. New York: Viking, 1968.

Pajaczkowska, Claire. "Imagistic Representation and the Status of the Image in Pornography." Unpublished paper presented at the International Film Conference, University of Wisconsin, March 1980.

Pernoud, Régine. *La femme au temps des cathédrales*. Paris: Stock, 1980.

Petitot, Françoise. "Inter-dire." in *Les cahiers du GRIF* 26 (March 1983).

Pisan, Christine de. *The Book of the City of Ladies*. Trans. Earl Jeffrey Richards. New York: Persea, 1982.

Pleynet, Marcelin. "La levée de l'interprétation des signes." In *Art et littérature*. Paris: Seuil, 1977.

Poe, Edgar Allan. "The Philosophy of Composition." In *The Complete Stories of Edgar Allan Poe, With Selections from His Critical Writings*, ed. A. H. Quinn. New York: Knopf, 1951.

Poggioli, Renato. *Theory of the Avant-Garde*. Cambridge, Mass.: Belknap, 1968.

Poirion, Daniel. *Le moyen âge*. Paris: Arthaud, 1971.

Pynchon, Thomas. *V*. New York: Bantam, 1961.

Rabant, Christiane. "La bête chanteuse." In "Jacques Lacan," *L'arc* 58 (1974).

"Résurgences et dérivées de la mystique." Issue of *Nouvelle revue de la psychanalyse* 22 (Fall 1980).

Ribettes, Jean-Michel. "Le phalsus (Vrai/semblant/vraisemblance du texte obsessionnel)." In *Folle vérité*, ed. Julia Kristeva. Paris: Editions du Seuil, 1979.

Rich, Adrienne. "Diving into the Wreck." In *Diving into the Wreck, Poems 1971–1972*. New York: W. W. Norton, 1973.

Rogers, Catherine M. *The Troublesome Helpmate: A History of Misogyny in Literature*. Seattle: University of Washington Press, 1966.

Roudiez, Leon S. "Twelve Points from Tel Quel." *L'esprit créateur* 14:4 (Winter 1974).

Sade, Marquis de. "Philosophy in the Bedroom." Trans. Richard Seaver and Austryn Wainhouse. New York: Grove, 1965.

Safouan, Moustapha. *La sexualité féminine*. Paris: Editions du Seuil, 1976.

Said, Edward. *Orientalism*. New York: Pantheon, 1978.

_____. "The Problem of Textuality: Two Exemplary Positions." *Critical Inquiry* 4:4 (Summer 1978). Reprinted in *The World, the Text, and the Critic*. Cambridge, Mass.: Harvard University Press, 1983.

Sartre, Jean-Paul. *Being and Nothingness*. Trans. Hazel E. Barnes. New York: Philosophical Library, 1956. *L'être et le néant*. Paris: Gallimard, 1943.

Saussure, Ferdinand de. *Course in General Linguistics*. Trans. Wade Baskin. New York: McGraw Hill, 1966.

Schor, Naomi. "Le détail chez Freud." *Littérature*, no. 37 (February 1980).

_____. "Female Paranoia: The Case for Psychoanalytic Feminist Criticism." *Yale French Studies* 62 (Fall 1981).

Scouras, Danielle. "Toward a 'New Culture': *Il Politecnico, Tel Quel*, and Cultural Renewal." Dissertation, Columbia University, 1981.

Searle, John R. "Reiterating the Differences: A Reply to Derrida." *Glyph I* (1977).

Serres, Michel. "Interview." *Marie-Claire* (May 1981).

Shahar, Shulamith. *The Fourth Estate: A History of Women in the Middle Ages*. London: Methuen, 1984.

Shelley, Percy B. "The Triumph of Life." In *The Poetical Works*. London: Fredrick Warne, 1928.

Showalter, Elaine. *A Literature of Their Own*. Princeton: Princeton University Press, 1977.

_____. "Towards a Feminist Poetics." In *Women Writing and Writing about Women*, ed. Mary Jacobus. London: Croom Helm, 1979.

Snitow, Ann, Christine Stansell, and Sharon Thompson, eds. *Powers of Desire: The Politics of Sexuality*. New York: Monthly Review Press, 1983.

Sollers, Philippe. *Une curieuse solitude*. Paris: Editions du Seuil, 1958.

_____. "Détruire, dit-elle." in *Revue Ça/cinéma*, no. 1.

_____. *Drame*. Paris: Editions du Seuil, 1965.

_____. *Femmes*. Paris: Gallimard, 1983.

_____. "Freud's Hand." *Yale French Studies* 55/56 (1977).

_____. *Logiques*. Paris: Editions du Seuil, 1968.

_____. *Paradis*. Paris: Editions du Seuil, 1981.

_____. *Le parc*. Paris: Editions du Seuil, 1961.

_____. *Sur le matérialisme*. Paris: Editions du Seuil, 1974.

_____. *Vision à New York*. Paris: Grasset, 1981.

Spacks, Patricia M. *The Female Imagination*. New York: Avon, 1972.

Spitz, René. *De la naissance à la parole*. Paris: PUF, 1968.

Spivak, Gayatri. "Displacement and the Discourse of Woman." In *Displacement: Derrida and After*, ed. Mark Krupnick. Bloomington: Indiana University Press, 1983.

_____. "French Feminism in an International Frame." *Yale French Studies* 62 (1981).

_____. "Glas-Piece: A Compte Rendu." *Diacritics* 7:3 (Fall 1977).

Steiner, George. *On Difficulty*. Oxford: Oxford University Press, 1978.

Suleiman, Susan. "Reading Robbe-Grillet: Sadism and Text in *Projet pour une révolution à New York*." *Romanic Review* 68:1 (January 1977).

Tanner, Tony. *City of Words*. London: Jonathan Cape, 1971.

_____. *The Reign of Wonder*. Cambridge: Cambridge University Press, 1965.

Todorov, Tzvetan. "Reflections on Literature in Contemporary France." *New Literary History* 10:3 (Spring 1979).

Tournier, Michel. *Vendredi ou les limbes du Pacifique*. Paris: Gallimard, 1972.

Verdon, René. "La femme dans la société aux Xᶜ et XIᶜ siècles." Dissertation, University of Paris X, 1974.

Vernant, Jean-Pierre. *Myth and Society in Ancient Greece*. Trans. Janet Lloyd. Atlantic Highlands, N.J.: Humanities Press, 1980. *Mythe et société en Grèce ancienne*. Paris: Maspéro, 1974.

_____. *Origins of Greek Thought*. Ithaca: Cornell University Press, 1982. *Les origines de la pensée Grecque*. Paris: PUF, 1981.

Ward, Charles F. *The Epistles on the Romance of the Rose and Other Documents in the Debate*. Chicago: University of Chicago Press, 1911.

Wilden, Anthony. "The Critique of Phallocentrism." In *System and Structure*. London: Tavistock, 1972.

_____. *The Language of the Self*. New York: Delta, 1968.

Wohlfarth, Irving. "Walter Benjamin's Image of Interpretation." *New German Critique* 17 (Spring 1979).

Wolfson, Louis. *Le schizo et les langues*. Paris: Gallimard, 1970.

INDEX

Library of Congress Cataloging in Publication Data

Jardine, Alice.
    Gynesis: configurations of woman and modernity.

    Bibliography: p.
    Includes index.
    1. Femininity (Philosophy)   2. Women in literature.   3. Feminism and
literature.   4. Sex (Psychology)   5. Women—Psychology.   I. Title.
HQ1206.J37   1985   305.4   84-45806
ISBN 0–8014–1768–6 (alk. paper)

55 ª

91   cf note on Jefferson.